MW01193413

THEY WERE
HEROES

THIS PHOTO IS OF MY FATHER, PFC EDWARD F. DEVANEY,
ESCORTING A GERMAN PRISONER HE HAD JUST
SAVED FROM AN ANGRY FRENCH MOB.
DEVANEY FAMILY ARCHIVE

THEY WERE HEROES

A Sergeant Major's Tribute to the Combat
Marines of Iraq and Afghanistan

SgtMaj DAVID K. DEVANEY, USMC (Ret.)

NAVAL INSTITUTE PRESS
ANNAPOLIS, MARYLAND

Naval Institute Press
291 Wood Road
Annapolis, MD 21402

Library of Congress Cataloging-in-Publication Data
Devaney, David K.
  They were heroes : a sergeant major's tribute to the combat marines
of Iraq and Afghanistan / SgtMaj David K. Devaney, USMC (Ret.).
    pages cm
   ISBN 978-1-61251-789-6 (hardcover : alk. paper) — ISBN 978-1-
61251-900-5 (ebook) 1. Iraq War, 2003–2011—Biography. 2. Afghan
War, 2001– —Biography. 3. Marines—United States—Biography. 4.
United States. Marine Corps—Biography. I. Title.
  DS79.766.A1D48 2014
  956.7044'345092273—dc23

                                                        2014042911

♾ Print editions meet the requirements of ANSI/NISO z39.48-1992
(Permanence of Paper).
Printed in the United States of America.

23 22 21 20 19 18 17 16 15   9 8 7 6 5 4 3 2 1
First printing

CONTENTS

CASUALTY ASSISTANCE CALLS OFFICERS

AFGHANISTAN

PREFACE

Although the following story is not the reason I wrote the book, it was the beginning. I wrote this wounded-warrior story because I wanted to remember these warriors. This led to me telling their stories over and over. I continued to write because I enjoy it and enjoy telling the stories of heroes. There is honor in their deeds, but only if we remember those deeds. We cannot forget these amazing warriors, heroes and Americans.

On 15 September 2005 my long-time friend 1st Sgt Carl Gantt and I went to the former Bethesda National Naval Medical Center in Maryland to visit some of our combat-wounded warriors. I was very apprehensive about the visit because I was not sure how the warriors, family members, or hospital staff would react to our presence. I expected some of the warriors to be proud, some to be mad, and some to be frustrated. I had heard stories of wounded warriors becoming upset with random visitors because, as Sgt James Gill once told me, "they felt like they were a part of a petting zoo." In general, the wounded warriors do not want pity; they want understanding and compassion. There is no way to empathize with an amputee unless you are also an amputee. They do not want sympathy. I have been to many facilities to visit with wounded warriors over the years. Usually I just get them talking. Once I have gained their trust and respect with my own experiences, I always ask them what happened. The best psychological therapy for warriors, not just wounded warriors, is to talk. Some will talk openly only with those whom they believe can understand their time in combat.

The first Marine we visited that September day was a thirty-two-year-old corporal (amphibious assault vehicle crewman) with a traumatic brain injury due to an improvised explosive device (IED) blast (approximately 30 percent of his skull was missing). He was unable to speak but could squeeze his mother's hand in response to questions. I was unable to ascertain exactly what happened. The family (mother and wife) had an amazingly positive attitude. I was astounded at the support this Marine was getting.

The second Marine was an eighteen-year-old private first class (infantryman) who was a turret machine gunner on an up-armored highly mobile multiwheeled vehicle (HMMWV). He was injured when his vehicle rolled over him during an accident. He had a broken collarbone, broken left leg, and broken pelvis (in five places). The doctors had to remove his liver, gallbladder, and spleen. The Marine told me that he was not upset; he just wanted to recover and get back to Iraq and his unit. His mother, father, and sister were present and seemed to be in good spirits. They supported him in everything he said. His parents said he was expected to make a full recovery. He stated he plans to stay in the Marine Corps and return to his unit. Although the Marine and his family had a very positive attitude, I do not believe he will recover for a very long time.

The third Marine was a nineteen-year-old lance corporal (infantryman) who was injured by an IED while conducting a foot patrol. He was missing his right leg below the knee and had a hole through his left hand. He complained that doctors wanted to remove the fingers from his left hand, but that he finally convinced them to try to save his fingers. He also complained about severe phantom pain where his leg was missing. He stated that he would be moving to the Walter Reed Army Medical Center (now merged with the Bethesda National Naval Medical Center) in two weeks to receive a prosthetic leg and begin therapy. He also stated that he planned to be running and swimming within the next year. He wanted to return to his unit but knew it would not happen. He stated that he felt guilty that he was in the United States while his friends were still in combat. His lovely young wife was very shy, but she did answer my questions. This young man plans to remain a Marine but will more than likely need to change his military occupational specialty. With his attitude, I believed he would be able to remain in the Marine Corps and do well.

The fourth Marine was a twenty-one-year-old corporal (infantryman) who was injured by an IED while conducting a foot patrol (the same patrol and IED that injured the third Marine). He was missing his right leg below the knee and his entire right arm, all the way into his torso. He stated that he would be moving to the Walter Reed Army Medical Center in two weeks to receive a prosthetic leg and prosthetic arm, and he was looking forward to beginning his therapy. He wanted to remain in the Marine Corps and go to units to give speeches about combat. He expressed his feeling that he felt guilty that he might have been responsible for the injuries to the third Marine because he was the fire team leader. He stated that if he had only done things differently, it wouldn't have happened. After hearing the story, I told him that he had done nothing wrong. He also expressed he felt guilt that he was in the United States while his friends were still in combat. His wife, also a Marine, was absolutely wonderful; she supported him 100 percent.

The fifth and final patient we visited was a twenty-year-old Navy hospital corpsman (attached to a Marine explosive ordnance disposal [EOD] team) who had been shot in the left leg by an insurgent sniper. The bullet went cleanly though his bone, leaving a hole but luckily not breaking the bone. The exit wound was massive and needed a skin graft. He was shot while providing medical support to a wounded Marine from his EOD unit. He had a 99.9 percent chance of a full recovery and said he wanted to return to his unit as soon as possible. His step-father was with him and also had a wonderful attitude about the situation. The corpsman stated that he felt guilty that he was in the United States while his friends were still in combat. I felt he would be able to return to his unit and do well.

After speaking with the patients and the Marine liaisons, I knew the Navy doctors, nurses, other staff members, and the Marine liaisons had much to do with the positive attitudes of the families and wounded warriors. Before we left, we shook all of their hands and thanked them.

The Marine liaisons were outstanding (mostly Reserve Marines pulled from the Individual Ready Reserve, or IRR). One corporal even spent his days off with the Marines and their families. I heard a story about the corporal on his knees praying with the mother of one of our Marines.

Most of the severe injuries were from IED blasts. The overall positive attitudes of these courageous warriors were amazing. I feel blessed to have met each of these young men. They will always be in my prayers. All of the family members had positive attitudes, even in the cases that didn't appear to be going well. The men all stated they wanted to get back to their units and that they felt guilty they were in the United States eating good food and seeing their families. I believe most will have tough but good futures due to their positive attitudes and the support from their families and military medical staffs.

While still conducting my CACO (casualty assistance calls officer) assignment for SSgt Joel P. Dameron, I was given my final assignment by my arts professor at Saint Leo University (at Savannah Center): I had to sing a song, perform a dance, or write a poem. Since I cannot sing or dance, I was left with writing a poem. I had never written one in my life; I did not even like poetry. The next morning I went to my office and looked at my wall, which was covered with photos of my fallen friends. It struck me right then: I would write a poem about all of them. It took me about ten minutes to write it and two weeks to edit it. When I read the poem to my class, I was unable to keep my composure, and tears filled my eyes. I had written the poem, edited it, and practiced it many times, but this was my first time reading it with no thoughts of editing in my mind.

I was inspired to write about warriors right around 15 September 2005, when my good friend and I visited those combat-wounded Marines and Navy corpsmen in Bethesda. I began writing these stories as a way to deal with my own demons—it helped my own psychological well-being. I was encouraged to write *They Were Heroes* by Navy, Marine, and Coast Guard leaders who were members of the U.S. Naval Institute's editorial board for *Proceedings* magazine, of which I was also a member for two years. Many times before our bimonthly meeting or during breaks I would tell a story or two of heroes I had known or had heard about from friends. One day someone suggested that I write this book to honor these heroes. In 2010, after a few months of this encouragement, I began the research needed, and after six months of research and another six months of writing and revising, I felt I had a pretty good handle on the book. As I told stories about these warriors, my friends began telling stories of their Marines, and my list of names grew. I then took the information from my friends and did my own research through the Internet and the USMC awards system (IAPS, or improved awards processing system). My biggest hurdle was trimming the manuscript down to a manageable size; I had way too much information and knew I had to start prioritizing the stories. I would like to remind anyone who reads this book that there are many more stories out there and that this book only scratches the surface. Thank you for helping me honor these warriors. Semper Fidelis.

THEY WERE
HEROES

PFC EDWARD F. DEVANEY

3RD BATTALION, 143RD INFANTRY REGIMENT,
36TH INFANTRY DIVISION

BORN: GENEVA, NEW YORK

AWARDED THE BRONZE STAR MEDAL
FOR HEROIC ACTION 3 SEPTEMBER 1944, FRANCE

I will show you only a small glimpse of the many American warriors that most Americans will never hear about. This book of heroes is dedicated to my hero, my father, Edward F. Devaney. My hero died on 19 February 2011, and my mother asked me to give his eulogy. I have given speeches to thousands of people all over the world, and I am very comfortable speaking to large crowds. But this was not an ordinary speech; it was my father's eulogy, and it was the hardest address I have ever given.

EULOGY FOR MY FATHER, EDWARD FRANCIS DEVANEY

Good morning everyone, and thank you for coming to honor my father.

Warriors weep at funerals; therefore I do not apologize for any tears I may shed during this eulogy.

Mom, I want to thank you for the honor and privilege of allowing me to give this eulogy for Dad. I have given many speeches to thousands of people around the world, to include Foreign Service members, members of each of the American military services, veterans, police officers, and even the members of the Canadian Parliament, but this is different because this speech or eulogy is for my own father.

Losing a loved one is one of the most difficult things we can go through; so much more if it is a parent. No words can express what I am feeling right now, and I am sure only time can help me accept the fact that this great man has passed.

How do I speak of such a great man in about five minutes? As you know, it is impossible. Therefore I will speak very briefly about my HERO: my father, Edward Francis Devaney.

My father was one of those hardworking men of the post–World War II era. He was a proud soldier who fought during World War II and was awarded our nation's fourth-highest medal for valorous actions against the enemy. Once, in France, he actually jumped into the middle of an angry crowd to save the life of a German who was being beaten to death—WHY? Because it was the right thing to do. He refused to watch another human being be treated inhumanly, even if he was the enemy. As a matter of fact, even though Dad was unable to remember many things in his final days, he was able to recite his military service number like it was yesterday. After my father left the Army, he worked part time at a movie theater and again jumped into a crowd, this time to stop a fight—WHY? Because it was the right thing to do. He even spent a while as a reserve police officer here in Geneva—and we all know police officers are real heroes. This sums my father's ideology: he was a man who has risked his life for others and would do anything for anyone in need. I have been called a hero by many people, both civilian and military, but this is untrue. I am no hero, but our father was in so many ways. He was a hero to the U.S. Army, our great nation, our family, and to everyone who ever truly knew him. Our father was without a doubt the most patriotic American I have ever known. Anyone who ever entered the Devaney residence knows this. The Devaney house is absolutely filled with the items of a patriot: flags, decorations, and any item you can image that can adorn the colors Red, White, and Blue.

My dad had a bit of ambiguity about him. He was a combat warrior, but also had a gentle side. He had a bicycle shop in his shed and would fix any of the neighborhood children's bikes at the drop of a hat. He loved to hold his grandchildren and great-grandchildren when they were babies. In fact, he never went to sleep without holding my mother and thanking her for taking care of him, ending with an affectionate "I love you."

My father dedicated his adult life to his family, rearing my eight siblings and me. He worked two jobs during most of our childhoods to ensure we had clothes on our backs, food on our table, and a roof over our heads. He had a work ethic like no other person I have even known. He was a wonderful father, grandfather, great-grandfather, husband, soldier, and man.

For all of you who truly knew my father, you know that he was a quiet man who chose his words very carefully. Plato once said, "Wise men speak because they have something to say; fools because they have to say something." As a child I was the proverbial fool. It took me many years to understand that you learn more by listening than talking. I was an unruly adolescent, but my father never gave up on me. On 10 December of 1980 I was arrested for driving while intoxicated, after which my father handed me a note that stated words to this effect: "I gave you your name and it was clean; do not tarnish it." That note hit me hard. Because of that note I have dedicated my life to serving my country and loving my family. Dad, I always hoped you one day would be proud of me. You were a great example and role model. I am who I am because of you. I have met and interacted with thousands of people throughout America and in more than forty countries around the world, and I have never met a wiser man than my father.

Until recently, Dad rarely showed his feelings, but the first time he told me that he loved me, I felt as if I had finally accomplished my life's mission of making him proud.

Although this funeral is a sad time for us all, I believe we should celebrate his life, rather than mourn his death.

Dad, I know you are in a better place now; you were in much pain for a long time and, although I am very sad, I am also relieved that your pain has ended. Dad, you will always have a place in my heart; therefore you will live forever.

Semper Fidelis, Dad; I LOVE YOU!!

U.S. Army Bronze Star Medal Citation (1945)

Edward F. Devaney, Private First Class, Headquarters Company, 3d Battalion, 143d Infantry Regiment, 36th Infantry Division, for heroic conduct on 3 September 1944 in France. Private First Class Devaney had driven a truck-load of soldiers into a recently liberated French city and was waiting with his vehicle when he saw an angry mob of civilians beating an unarmed German. They were striking him with clubs; and the German whose wounds were bleeding profusely, was in danger of being killed. Private First Class Devaney approached the crowd with his sub-machine gun and, although he narrowly escaped being clubbed, bravely forced his way through the mob until he reached the German. By his bold action he dispersed the crowd, and he remained to guard his prisoner until the proper French military authorities arrived. Entered the service from Geneva, New York.

IRAQ

CPL JARRED L. ADAMS

Scout Sniper Platoon, 1st Battalion
7th Marines, 1st Marine Division

born: Palmer, Alaska

Awarded the Silver Star Medal for heroic actions
6 January 2004, Husaybah, Iraq

On 6 January 2005, at approximately 0230, Scout Sniper Teams 1 and 2 were tasked with establishing an observation post in the vicinity of the intersection of Market and East End Road in the city if Husaybah, Iraq. At approximately 0250, shortly after departing friendly lines, their four-vehicle patrol came under intense and accurate enemy fire from a combination of heavy machine guns, rocket-propelled grenades (RPGs), and small arms. During the initial portion of the engagement, the lead vehicle, trying to exit the engagement area, took a corner too fast and struck a wall, causing the vehicle to become lodged in the wall. As soon as the vehicle came to a halt, Cpl Jarred Adams, without hesitation or reserve, exited the vehicle, exposing himself to heavy enemy fire, took up a security position around the downed vehicle, and returned fire as fellow Marines attempted to dislodge the vehicle from the wall.

While they worked feverishly to dislodge the vehicle, Adams continuously disregarded his own personal safety, moving about various positions around the downed vehicle to return fire and provide security for his fellow Marines. Once the vehicle was free, the Marines quickly remounted the vehicle as the patrol moved again back toward friendly lines. At this time they realized that one of the vehicles that had been providing security had fallen behind and became separated from the patrol, forcing the three remaining vehicles to return to the engagement area in search of the missing vehicle. As the patrol reentered the kill zone for the second time, Adams' vehicle suffered a direct hit from an RPG, causing the interior of the vehicle to erupt into flames. As a result of the fire, the driver lost control of the vehicle and crashed into the adjacent wall. The turret gunner was killed instantly, and all occupants, including Adams, suffered multiple shrapnel wounds, burns, and broken bones. Adams, the team radio operator, immediately exited the vehicle and returned fire on enemy positions. After suppressing the enemy, Adams went back to the vehicle to retrieve his rucksack containing the radio in an attempt to establish communication and notify the command post of the situation. Seconds later the vehicle was engulfed in flames.

Suffering from multiple shrapnel wounds and burns to his neck and arms, Adams returned fire on enemy positions while trying to communicate with the company command post. After these attempts, Adams realized that the body of LCpl Julio Cisneros, the turret gunner, was still inside the burning vehicle. Without regard for his personal safety, Adams jumped back inside the burning wreckage, subjecting himself to the imminent threat of exploding friendly munitions from within the vehicle, in order to retrieve Cisneros. Isolated and alone, with the remaining occupants having established security positions across an intersection one block east of his position, Adams had to stop on several occasions and return fire on the enemy, who had encircled his position from elevated areas. While receiving heavy enemy fire, Adams continued his attempt to free Cisneros' body from the burning vehicle while simultaneously engaging the enemy with accurate fire.

Unselfishly subjecting himself to enemy fire and further harm, Adams refused to depart the area before retrieving the body of Cisneros. Approximately seven to eight minutes after he began his efforts, a fellow team member, Cpl Joseph R. Avila, ran back across the intersection in search of a missing weapon for an injured Marine. Upon his arrival, Avila noticed Adams trying to free Cisneros from the burning wreckage. With the vehicle engulfed in flames, together they attempted to free Cisneros' body while returning fire on the approaching enemy threat. Finally freeing Cisneros from the gunner's turret and after suffering from multiple wounds, Adams and Avila carried Cisneros across the intersection under heavy enemy fire while the remaining Marines provided suppressive fire on the enemy threat.

After reaching the third and fourth vehicles, Adams' team leader noticed that he was bleeding from the neck and arm. When asked if he was okay, he replied that he was "good to go" and took up a security position around the casualties and returned fire while the casualties received medical attention and were loaded into the remaining vehicles. Once the casualties had been loaded, Adams was the last Marine to climb inside the vehicle, which began to push back to base. Not until the patrol was inside the perimeter and clear of enemy fire did Adams receive medical attention. Adams was not directed to accomplish all that he did; he acted on his own initiative and did what an outstanding leader of Marines would do.

While under intense small-arms fire, machine-gun fire, and RPGs from a superior number of enemy insurgents, Adams refused to leave behind the body of a fallen Marine. Suffering from multiple shrapnel wounds and burns, Adams disregarded his own personal safety and exhibited heroic and extraordinary battlefield courage and valor in retrieving the body of Cisneros from the burning vehicle, leaving no man behind.

The following statements were given by Sgt Robert Green, the section leader for the vehicles, and Sgt Lance May, the scout sniper platoon's chief scout (they differ somewhat from the description of the action given earlier in this chapter and from each other). According to Greene,

> On the morning of January 6, 2005, CAAT Red Alpha was tasked to insert the Scout Sniper Platoon near check-point 81 in Husaybah, IZ. Because we were inserting all eight members of Teams One and Two, eight Marines total, we were departing friendly lines with a skeleton crew in four vehicles so as to make room for the Scout Sniper teams. Each vehicle consisted of a driver, vehicle commander, gunner, and two Scout Sniper Marines.

> As we departed friendly lines and headed to the insert point we soon came under heavy enemy fire in what appeared to be a layered ambush. Once the engagement started Red 1 became separated from the rest of the CAAT Team convoy. During our attempt to link back up with Red 1, Red 2 took a direct hit with an RPG

to the gunner's turret. Red 3&4 pushed one block east of the down vehicle to provide security for the Marines attempting to exit from the burning vehicle. Cpl Adams suffering from multiple shrapnel wounds and burns escaped the vehicle and then pulled the body of LCpl Cisneros who had been manning the gun turret from the burning vehicle to safety of a nearby wall. Cpl Adams then ran across the intersection to where the remaining Marines from Red 2 and where Red 3&4 were providing security and returning enemy fire at roof tops and court-yards. After linking up with the Marines from Red 3&4 and getting accountability Cpl Avila and Cpl Adams ran back across the intersection under heavy enemy small arms and RPG fire to retrieve the body of LCpl Cisneros and bring him back to the area near Red 3&4. Both Cpl Avila and Cpl Adams grabbed LCpl Cisneros, dragged his body across the intersection, again under heavy enemy fire, and linked up with the Marines to mount the remaining vehicles and return to base.

Though LCpl Cisneros had been killed from the initial blast of the RPG, Cpl Adams and Cpl Avila refused to leave the body of a fellow Marine. Due to their heroic and unselfish display of unusual courage on the battle-field they were able to recover the body of a fallen com-rade and bring him home.

May stated:

On the morning of 6 January 2005 Caat Red Alpha was routinely inserting Scout Sniper Teams, Raven 1 and 2. Prior to insert Caat Red Alpha was ambushed. While turning around vehicle 4 became stuck in a wall. All Caat vehicles stopped to provide security. Sniper Teams including Cpl. Adams dismounted under heavy fire to return fire at enemy positions. The vehicle was retrieved. At that point vehicle 4 unknowingly went back to base. Due to no communication with vehicle 4, vehicles 1, 2, and 3 turned around and went back through the kill zone thinking vehicle 4 was down. At which point vehicle 2 was struck with a direct hit on the top of the vehicle with an RPG. The vehicle became immobilized and burst into flames. Cpl. Adams exited the vehicle after being wounded by shrapnel. Once he exited the vehicle he returned to grab his rifle and radio and the rifle of another wounded Marine. At which point he tried to establish communication to request a medevac. At this point he was under heavy enemy fire. He then linked up with Cpl. Avila and moved across the intersection where they received heavy enemy fire and rocket fire. Once across Cpl. Adams turned around and noticed that there was a wounded Marine still in the burning vehicle. He then made the decision to go back across the intersection while still receiving heavy enemy fire, along with Cpl. Avila. At this point he reached in the burning vehicle grabbing and pulling the Marine out. He was then assisted by Cpl. Avila in dragging the Marine casualty back across the intersection where they received heavy enemy fire once again. Cpl. Adams and Cpl. Avila then placed the casualty in vehicle 1. Due to his heroic and unselfish display on the battlefield Cpl. Adams was able to recover Lcpl. Cisneros, a fallen comrade.

I know Corporal Adams well. After leaving the III MEF (Marine Expeditionary Force) Special Operations Training Group (SOTG) I was assigned to Company A 1/7. As a sniper instructor I spent much of my time with the 1/7 scout sniper platoon, training them for various missions. Adams was a standout Marine even in a platoon of handpicked warriors. I am extremely proud, but not surprised, by Adams and his heroic actions. He told me, "I don't think I did anything any other Marine wouldn't do; I would do it again if it came down to it." Surprise, surprise—isn't that what all heroes say?

SILVER STAR MEDAL CITATION

The President of the United States of America takes pleasure in presenting the Silver Star to CORPORAL JARRED L. ADAMS, United States Marine Corps, for conspicuous gallantry and intrepidity in action against the enemy while serving as Assistant Team Leader, Scout Sniper Platoon, First Battalion, Seventh Marine Regiment, Regimental Combat Team 7, First Marine Division, I Marine Expeditionary Force, U.S. Marine Corps Forces, Central, in support of Operation Iraqi Freedom on 6 January 2005. In downtown Husaybah, Iraq, Corporal Adams' patrol came under intense enemy fire causing the lead vehicle to crash. He exited the vehicle and began returning fire as fellow Marines attempted to dislodge the vehicle from the wall. After freeing the vehicle and retrograding back to Camp Gannon, the patrol realized one of the vehicles was separated and needed to be located. Re-entering the kill zone again, his vehicle suffered a direct hit from a rocket-propelled grenade, causing the vehicle to erupt into flames. Corporal Adams exited the vehicle and began to fire on enemy positions. Suffering from multiple shrapnel wounds and burns, he began returning fire on enemy positions while trying to com-municate with the command post. Realizing that the turret gun-ner was still inside the burning vehicle, he jumped back inside the burning wreckage, subjecting himself to the imminent threat of exploding friendly munitions from within the vehicle and enemy fire, refusing to depart the area before retrieving the fallen Marine. Freeing the gunner from the turret, and suffering from multiple wounds, he carried the gunner across the intersection under enemy fire while the remaining Marines provided suppres-sive fire on the enemy threat. By his bold leadership, wise judg-ment, and complete dedication to duty, Corporal Adams reflected great credit upon himself and upheld the highest traditions of the Marine Corps and the United States Naval Service.

Information for this account is drawn from the U.S. Marine Corps "Award Summary of Action" (2004) and the Silver Star Medal Citation for Jarred L. Adams (2005); from personal telephone interviews with Adams at Quantico, VA, 9 November 2007, and Lance May at Quantico, VA , 14 September 2007; and from eyewitness statements from Robert Greene (2005) and Lance May (2005).

GYSGT ROBERT J. BLANTON

Company A, 3rd Reconnaissance Battalion,
I Marine Expeditionary Force

born: Santa Rosa, California

Awarded the Silver Star Medal for heroic actions on 10
August 2008, during Operation Dan, Al Anbar Province, Iraq

During 2008 I was stationed on Al Asad Air Base, Iraq. One of my old friends, MSgt Monroe Stuber, was the operations chief for 3rd Recon Battalion, and he needed assets I was able to provide. My unit assisted multiple recon platoons with their operations prep. GySgt Robert Blanton was one of the platoon sergeants, and we spent one day on the range with him and his platoon. I had a live fire set up for our unit's quick-reaction force, and I asked the Gunny if they wanted to shoot with us. That platoon was highly proficient; it was like a well-oiled machine. Soon after this day on the range, Blanton's platoon left Al Asad for Operation Dan.

On the afternoon of 10 August 2008 Blanton's recon platoon was conducting mounted and dismounted clearing operations in support of Operation Dan. After clearing two houses earlier that afternoon, the platoon was traveling north when its lead vehicle identified buildings to the east and north. Blanton's element was tasked with clearing the northern set of buildings. While en route, the platoon's other element became heavily engaged with enemy small-arms fire from the building it was searching. Without hesitating, Blanton ordered his element to immediately proceed to the other element's position for support.

Immediately upon arrival, Blanton's element was engaged by effective small-arms fire from the enemy and was exposed to several sporadic enemy fragmentation grenades. Blanton dismounted his vehicle, exposing himself to enemy fire; without hesitation, he began effectively engaging insurgents inside the building with his personal M4 rifle. Using initiative and quick thinking, Blanton returned to his vehicle and directed it to ram the building's wall in order to expose the insurgents within. As his vehicle, a seven-ton truck, was backing out of the building, an insurgent wearing a suicide vest ran to his vehicle and tried to open the driver side door. As other Marines engaged the insurgent, he detonated his vest against the vehicle. With his vehicle now disabled, Blanton quickly ensured that his driver and turret gunner were unharmed and then provided effective covering fire to allow them to dismount.

While receiving effective enemy fire, Blanton mustered an element to clear the building. At this time an insurgent made himself visible from the wreckage of the building in order to surrender. Blanton called for an immediate cease-fire in an attempt to recover the insurgent unharmed. After successfully acquiring the insurgent and passing him onto the platoon's embedded human intelligence Marine for tactical questioning, Blanton finished organizing his element and led it around the building in order to clear its rooms. After mustering with the other element on the opposite side of the building and as Marines removed a fellow wounded Marine from inside the building, Blanton continued to engage insurgents as they presented themselves. During one such engagement, after Blanton's M4 malfunctioned, he seamlessly transitioned to his M9 pistol in order to continue engaging insurgents.

Once the wounded Marine had been recovered and the platoon ordered back to a minimum safe distance for close-air support, Blanton took over communication with the incoming medevac helicopters and the F/A-18 elements on station. After he provided the medevac helicopters with a landing zone brief, all three of the platoon's casualties were successfully loaded and extracted from the engagement site. Blanton then coordinated with the F/A-18s to drop a GBU-51 low-collateral-damage bomb on the insurgent stronghold, effectively ending the engagement.

Following the engagement, Blanton returned with a small element from the platoon to conduct a battle damage assessment, during which Blanton identified two possible insurgent explosives under the rubble of the house and directed the embedded explosive ordnance detachment technicians to reduce them in place. On 11 August, the following day, a sensitive site exploitation (SSE) team confirmed the bodies of twelve enemy combatants. Along with the enemy bodies, the SSE team discovered a plethora of weapons, ammunition, suicide vests, medical gear, computers, cell phones, a digital video camera, external hard drives, assorted propaganda, and identification badges. As a result of the SSE of the building and the information extracted from the detainee, vital information was obtained for future operations. Blanton's lack of hesitation and resolute leadership, combined with his warrior mindset, are undoubtedly the reason for the platoon's success during the hour-long-plus engagement.

SILVER STAR MEDAL CITATION

The President of the United States of America takes pleasure in presenting the Silver Star to GUNNERY SERGEANT ROBERT J. BLANTON, United States Marine Corps, for conspicuous gallantry and intrepidity in action against the enemy while serving as Platoon Sergeant, First Platoon, Company A, Third Reconnaissance Battalion, I Marine Expeditionary Force (Forward), on 10 August 2008, in support of Operations Iraqi Freedom FY-08. As an element of Gunnery Sergeant Blanton's platoon began clearing what appeared to be an abandoned house, it became heavily engaged with enemy small arms fire from a strong point located inside the building. Gunnery Sergeant Blanton immediately repositioned his element's vehicles to support the engaged element. Bravely exposing himself to enemy fire, he dismounted his vehicle and began engaging insurgents as they presented themselves. Using initiative and quick thinking, Gunnery Sergeant Blanton returned to his vehicle and directed it to ram the building's outer wall in order to expose additional insurgents within the building. He then led a small group of Marines to clear the building and recover a wounded Marine trapped inside. During the recovery, Gunnery Sergeant Blanton courageously transitioned from his rifle to his pistol and began engaging insurgents located in close proximity to his position. Once the recovery was complete, Gunnery Sergeant Blanton coordinated with supporting aircraft on station to deliver precision guided munitions directly on the insurgent stronghold, effectively ending the engagement. By his bold leadership, wise judgment, and complete dedication to duty, Gunnery Sergeant Blanton reflected great credit upon himself and upheld the highest traditions of the Marine Corps and the United States Naval Service.

Information for this account is drawn from the U.S. Marine Corps "Award Summary of Action" (2008) and the Silver Star Medal Citation for Robert J. Blanton (2009), and from personal telephone interviews with Blanton at Quantico, VA, 10 September 2011 and Monroe Stuber at Quantico, VA, 12 May 2011.

GYSGT JEFFREY E. BOHR JR.

COMPANY A, 1ST BATTALION, 5TH MARINES,
1ST MARINE DIVISION

BORN: OSSIAN, IOWA

AWARDED THE SILVER STAR MEDAL, POSTHUMOUSLY,
FOR HEROIC ACTIONS ON 10 APRIL 2003, BAGHDAD, IRAQ

On 10 April 2003 Alpha Company, 1st Battalion, 5th Marines (1/5), was part of the mission to attack along Route 2 and into the heart of downtown Baghdad to seize one of Saddam's presidential palace complexes, which was suspected of being defended by an enemy infantry battalion. Before the commencement of the attack, the company was staged in a tactical assembly area inside an adjacent battalion's defensive perimeter.

Approximately an hour before crossing the line of departure, the battalion commander directed that all noncritical vehicles and soft-skin vehicles be moved to the logistics trains to link up with the battalion later. The precedent during the operation to date was that it could be up to several days before they could link up with the company logistical train. The unit commander discussed this issue with Gunnery Sergeant Bohr via radio and stated that going on the mission would be on a voluntary basis. The company's water and ammunition supply could become critical if cut off from their logistics trains for any extended period of time. Bohr responded that he would be moving with the mechanized column in his two high-back highly mobile multi-wheeled vehicles. During the movement, the company logistics vehicles were following in trace of the company and in front of a section of their countermechanized platoon. On Route 2 the battalion was attacked from both sides of the roads at all intersections and overpasses. Bohr personally supplied suppressive fire against the dismounted enemy with his assault rifle. He was personally responsible for at least two killed enemy combatants during the initial contact. They were receiving heavy

17

small-arms and machine-gun fire as well as numerous rocket-propelled grenade (RPG) shots.

After his unit was about two-thirds of the way to the battalion objective, the company commander's tracked vehicle was immobilized, and the company had to stop temporarily for repairs. During that time, Bohr moved his two vehicles behind the company commander's track and performed an administrative halt to confirm the vehicle's status and to ensure they were not wounded. During the repairs, the amount of fire received by the company became sporadic, with mortar rounds striking approximately one street over. Under these dangerous conditions Bohr made his way to the company commander's track, climbed up, and got a face to face with the commander for coordination. They discussed the problems with the movement with regard to fratricide due to the battalion having become disorganized. Bohr remained perfectly calm and gave sound advice about future movement plans and the scheme of maneuver.

As the company began moving again, another company was already securing the presidential palace from the battalion. While moving to the palace, the company passed through a "killsack" (similar to a kill zone) from an enemy-reinforced company. Alpha Company passed through the position to a dead end (a bridge that led into U.S. Army's 3rd Infantry Division's zone), which left the logistical vehicles exposed in the killsack as the company finally began to turn around. At this time Bohr had the company's logistical vehicles continue moving into the middle of the column, bypassing amphibious assault vehicles for protection from the intense RPG and small-arms fire. Bohr continued to deliver accurate rifle fire at the numerous enemy combatants in his vicinity. When he was informed by squad radio that one of the headquarters' Marines was wounded with a bullet through the wrist, he quickly called in a medevac while still providing cover fire from his vehicle. During his attempted medevac of the injured Marine, Bohr was killed instantly by small-arms fire.

During this battle Bohr killed an unknown number of enemy combatants while providing suppression and protection to his driver and the company's logistics train. The company vehicles were riddled with small-arms fire during the action, and at least two RPGs passed through the canvas of the company gunnery sergeant's vehicle. The logistical supplies provided by the two vehicles and the resulting sacrifice of Bohr proved critical as the battalion's logistical trains did not arrive at the presidential palace until two days later. Bohr's moral and physical courage were inspirational to his Marines in the logistics train and the men of the company. His volunteering to go on the mission was above and beyond the call of duty. His sound decision making under the most extreme fighting conditions kept his subordinates alive and achieved mission accomplishment of combat resupply for the company.

SILVER STAR MEDAL CITATION

The President of the United States of America takes pride in presenting the Silver Star (posthumously) to GUNNERY SERGEANT JEFFREY E. BOHR, JR., United States Marine Corps, for conspicuous gallantry and intrepidity in action against the enemy while serving as Company Gunnery Sergeant, Company A, First Battalion, Fifth Marine Regiment, Regimental Combat Team 5, First Marine Division, I Marine Expeditionary Force in support of Operation Iraqi Freedom on 10 April 2003. With his company assigned the dangerous mission of seizing a presidential palace in Baghdad and concerned that logistical resupply might be slow in reaching his comrades once they reached the objective, Gunnery Sergeant Bohr selflessly volunteered to move in his two soft-skinned vehicles with the company's main armored convoy. While moving through narrow streets toward the objective, the convoy took intense small arms and rocket propelled grenade fire. Throughout this movement, Gunnery Sergeant Bohr delivered accurate, effective fires on the enemy while encouraging his Marines and supplying critical information to his company commander. When the lead vehicles of the convoy reached a dead end and were subjected to enemy fire, Gunnery Sergeant Bohr continued to boldly engage the enemy while calmly maneuvering his Marines to safety. Upon learning of a wounded Marine in a forward vehicle, Gunnery Sergeant Bohr immediately coordinated medical treatment and evacuation. Moving to the position of the injured Marine, Gunnery Sergeant Bohr continued to lay down a high volume of suppressive fire, while simultaneously guiding the medical evacuation vehicle, until he was mortally wounded by enemy fire. By his bold leadership, wise judgment, and complete dedication to duty, Gunnery Sergeant Bohr reflected great credit upon himself and upheld the highest traditions of the Marine Corps and the United States Naval Service.

Information for this account is drawn from the U.S. Marine Corps "Award Summary of Action" (2003) and the Silver Star Medal Citation for Jeffrey E. Bohr Jr. (2004).

SGTMAJ JAMES E. BOOKER

2ND BATTALION, 4TH MARINES, 1ST MARINE DIVISION

HOME OF RECORD: FORT WAYNE, INDIANA

AWARDED THE SILVER STAR MEDAL FOR HEROIC ACTIONS
FROM FEBRUARY TO SEPTEMBER 2004, RAMADI, IRAQ

During February 2004 SgtMaj James E. Booker deployed with his battalion, 2nd Battalion, 4th Marines (2/4), to the city of Ramadi, Iraq, for a turnover with an Army infantry battalion. On the night of 31 March the battalion command element attended a combined planning session with the commissioner of the Al Anbar Province police to conduct a series of raids on high-value targets within the city of Ramadi; because the Iraqi police were unable to provide positive location for the targets, time sensitivity necessitated a Marine accompany a senior undercover police officer in performing this task. Booker unhesitatingly accepted the challenge due to the potential impact on the success of this mission. He donned the typical clothing of an Iraqi and, armed with only a pistol and hand grenade, drove through the back streets of the city to identify the target houses. After passing through several armed checkpoints manned by insurgents and tribal security, he located the house for further exploitation. He never considered his own safety or the intentions of his Iraqi guide. He conducted further reconnaissance with this police officer and subsequently returned to refine the mission planning. Unknown at the time, the undercover police officer would pass along to an insurgent cell leader that the Marines were planning a raid later that night.

At about midnight Booker accompanied the command element to stage for the raid. As they traveled along the main supply route, now devoid of traffic and streetlights, the convoy came under intense machine-gun and rocket-propelled grenade (RPG) fire. Two RPGs hit in front of and behind the vehicle in which he was traveling, wounding one Marine in the forward vehicle. As the convoy halted to assess the situation, he immediately and without concern for his own safety dashed up to the corner from which the enemy had attacked, at which time another burst of green tracers cut across the street in front of him. Taking up a firing position in the dim glow of a single streetlight, he suppressed the enemy attackers with his weapon, forcing them to flee. Without concern for his own safety, he raced down the street after the enemy. As the battalion commander and operations officer attempted to follow, Booker caught sight of another RPG gunner taking aim at these officers. He instinctively fired an initial shot that alerted the enemy gunner, who turned and now took aim at Booker from fifty meters. He then fired another shot, this time striking his target, which forced the enemy to drop his weapon and flee into the darkness, once again pursued by Booker. He would pursue the enemy for several hundred meters and down unlit city blocks before returning to the original site of the attack. He followed a blood trail that led to an adjoining house, forced entry into the compound, and discovered that his assailant was dead from a gunshot wound to the throat. Upon a subsequent search, a PKM machine gun was uncovered, along with belts of ammunition, the discarded RPG, and evidence leading to the arrest of the eight men inside the dwelling. It was found that this same cell was responsible for the earlier death of a Marine by RPG fire in the same spot. Later, upon careful interrogation, it was discovered that one of the detainees was the brother of the undercover police officer who had accompanied Booker on the earlier reconnaissance, and it was determined that this police officer had been attempting to lead Booker into a trap, which was modified and turned into an ambush. The undercover police officer was later killed under unknown circumstances. Booker's immediate actions and quick shooting saved the lives of several Marines, including that of the battalion commander, and led to a decrease in enemy activity in western Ramadi.

According to 2/4's operations officer, Maj J. D. Harrill:

> On 1 April 2004, the battalion's Forward Command
> Post was ambushed by enemy rocket, small arms and
> machinegun fire. Without regard to his safety and
> through a hail of gunfire and rockets, Sergeant Major

> Booker immediately dismounted his vehicle and maneuvered on the enemy. Isolated in an alley with only two other Marines, Sergeant Major Booker engaged a numerically superior enemy force killing one insurgent as he was aiming an RPG and capturing 7 others. This action resulted in the destruction and detainment of an RPG cell that had previously attacked the battalion on three separate occasions.

On 6 April Booker accompanied the battalion's forward command element, this time in response to a distress call from two squads that were surrounded and in heavy contact within the city. As the four lightly armed command vehicles approached from the south, they came under small-arms fire that forced them to dismount. Booker calmly walked among the drivers and led them along the abandoned streets for two miles. Gunfire was directed at the convoy all along the street, but this did not keep the Marines from being led forward. As the command element approached the scene of battle, Booker moved to establish contact with the Golf Company commander who was now on the scene; two Marines were killed at this site. Heavy gunfire and house-to-house fighting absorbed the entirety of this rifle company, now reinforced by Weapons Company. In spite of this intense gunfire within one hundred meters of his position, Booker calmly and carefully gathered the remains of the fallen Marines and placed them in his vehicle. He then reentered the fight by clearing several buildings adjacent to the fighting, with only one other Marine as cover, in order to gain a vantage point over the city. Once atop this three-story structure, he was able to direct forces and point out enemy fighters attempting to stop Golf Company's advance. He engaged several enemy personnel with his sniper rifle, forcing them to flee. Booker would establish this pattern of building clearing and acquiring vantage points for the remaining hours of this fight and many times thereafter during other operations. Although more than two hundred enemy fighters were counted dead following this and the next morning's battles, he would process the remains of twelve Marines and a Navy corpsman killed in action; Booker took this heavy responsibility upon himself so as to spare the battalion's subordinate units from the horror of seeing their lifeless comrades—this too would become his trademark for every one of the thirty-four Marines who would fall in his battalion.

Major J. D. Harrill stated:

> On 6 April of 2004, the enemy launched an offensive throughout the city of Ar Ramadi. During this time, the battalion engaged in two days of close quarters urban combat. Sergeant Major Booker continually moved to the point of friction and led squads forward into the fight. On 10 April, during Operation BUGHUNT, Sergeant Major Booker again moved to the front and personally assaulted fortified enemy positions. On one occasion, he and another Marine cleared multiple houses and killed numerous insurgents to allow the rest of the company to maneuver. At the end of the 2 days of fighting and Operation BUGHUNT, the battalion accounted for an estimated 250 enemy killed in action and 90 detainees. His actions and bravery during this period disrupted large-scale enemy offensive actions for the foreseeable future

On 10 April 2/4 participated in Operation Bug Hunt, which was a seven-company cordon and search of eastern Ramadi. Following the initial raids across the area of operations, E 2/4 became heavily engaged during three separate fights. Once again the forward command element jumped into the fray and moved to the sound of the guns. As the convoy approached the firefight, it was attacked by two large improvised explosive devices (IED). When the Marines dismounted, they quickly came under small-arms fire. Booker calmly walked the route for more than a mile, encouraging Marines to move forward and take the fight to the enemy. While the lead elements were halted due to intense RPG and machine-gun fire, he approached their position from the rear, already looking for his first vantage point. The enemy threw hand grenades and fired automatic weapons from as close as ten feet away, which forced the Marines to bunch up and crouch behind the cover of the outer walls; following Booker's lead, they counterattacked the enemy through fire and maneuver. At this point Booker ordered one of the E Company Marines to join him, and together they commenced clearing buildings and rooftops for the next several hours.

Then Booker, now joined by a handful of Marines, fought alongside this ad hoc fire team as they killed and wounded several enemy combatants, all the while mindful of protecting the terrorized civilians. As they continued deeper off the main road, the remainder of his fire team, now overextended, departed, leaving him alone with a single cover man. Undeterred by their numbers, Booker and his fellow warrior pursued combatants across several houses and courtyards when, from the roof of a cleared building, they encountered a platoon from E Company attempting to enter a house. Booker provided covering fire, killing one insurgent from his overwatching rooftop and warning the Marines below of the enemy's presence. As they entered the house, a booby trap located inside severely wounded one of the Marines. Without hesitation, Booker organized a house-clearing team and personally led them as the point man inside and went upstairs toward the enemy. He cleared the top room, suspected of harboring fighters, with a hand grenade and followed the blast through the door; the enemy fighters were found dead or dying inside the room and on the roof. His actions saved other Marines whose attention was centered on the medevac of the injured. Had Booker not maintained the presence of mind and careful observation, several more Marines surely would have suffered from the enemy attacks. All told, nearly one hundred insurgents were killed and hundreds more wounded during this engagement. Several tons of equipment and weapons were also confiscated and destroyed as a result. Booker's actions in leading and inspiring the Marines during these battles would earn him a place of honor among the Marines and sailors of 2/4.

According to 1st Lt Juan Valdez of E 2/4:

> On 10 April 2004, First Platoon came under heavy enemy attack during one of the battalion's operations, Operation Bug Hunt. It was during this operation that the platoon made contact with enemy forces along Route Apple. This resulted in a firefight that lasted approximately 3 hours. I was with second squad of the platoon and we had taken fire from a two-story house

to the east. We turned our firepower to this house and had one team lay a base of fire down while other Marines went around the flank to gain entrance on the house. After we had initially gained a foothold on the bottom deck of the house we stormed the roof only to get hit by an IED that was planted in the doorway of the rooftop. We had one Marine, Private First Class Texidor, who needed immediate medevac and just at that time when we were administering to him and regrouping to take the rooftop Sergeant Major Booker walked in with Lance Corporal Contreras. We realized that there were at least three insurgents in the second story of the house we were occupying. SgtMaj Booker then threw two grenades up the stairwell in order to eliminate the enemy threat. Once the grenades exploded, SgtMaj Booker stormed up the stairwell and dispatched the insurgents that had not been killed by the hand grenades. He did this without regard for his safety. I then saw SgtMaj Booker move down the street in order to clear several other houses, along with Lance Corporal Contreras. I know for a fact that he cleared at least two other houses with Lance Corporal Contreras. Each contained enemy insurgents. I cannot say how many were in each. I estimate between 10 and fifteen enemy were killed in all. Lance Corporal Contreras would have known; however, he was killed later during our deployment. I can say that SgtMaj Booker's actions took place under heavy enemy fire.

During the next several weeks, 2/4 conducted six battalion-level operations and more than one hundred company-size raids and searches that kept the enemy off balance and never able to regain the initiative. The insurgents remained hidden during this period, with only sporadic attacks, mostly from IEDs. Booker took it upon himself to organize a team of Marines to operate as a clandestine reconnaissance element in order to ferret out the enemy. Selecting members either for their Arabic-language skills or for their resemblance to the Iraqi population, he procured clothing and vehicles to cover their missions. Operating under the name Team Bearded

Guys, this six-man cell would perform daylight and nighttime surveillance of the city of Ramadi. Insurgents became aware of their presence after the first two weeks, but the team remained determined to provide an irreplaceable asset to the battalion. Booker's experience from previous billets and his natural instincts would serve as the impulse behind these operations. Team Bearded Guys provided valuable insight as to the daily routine within the city when the population was free from scrutiny by multinational forces. Only with the acquisition of a platoon of Iraqi Specialized Special Forces, which were more equipped to reduce the risk involved, would Booker's team cease operating. The leadership he exhibited and the example of commitment to winning was the lasting contribution of his project.

The impact of Booker's leadership to this battalion cannot be measured. His aggressive lead-from-the-front gallantry served as an inspiration to hundreds of Marines and sailors otherwise consumed by the terror of combat. His personal bravery on a number of high-risk, clandestine reconnaissance missions provided a positive example of a "man of action" stepping in to create an opportunity on the battlefield. His regular disregard for his own safety in order to direct and participate in the fight within Ramadi went above and beyond the normal expectation of a battalion sergeant major.

SILVER STAR MEDAL CITATION

The President of the United States of America takes pleasure in presenting the Silver Star to SERGEANT MAJOR JAMES E. BOOKER, United States Marine Corps, for conspicuous gallantry and intrepidity in action against the enemy while serving as Sergeant Major, Second Battalion, Fourth Marine Regiment, First Marine Division, I Marine Expeditionary Force, U.S. Marine Corps Forces, Central Command, in support of Operation Iraqi Freedom from February to September 2004. Sergeant Major Booker courageously exposed himself to enemy fire while leading Marines and eliminating enemy forces in several battalion engagements. On 31 March 2004 the forward command element came under intense machine gun and rocket-propelled grenade fire. With utter disregard for his own safety, Sergeant Major Booker dismounted the vehicle, engaged the enemy and forced their withdrawal. He pursued his attackers down several darkened city streets and mortally wounded a rocket-propelled grenade gunner who was engaging the command group. Sergeant Major Booker subsequently led a search that resulted in the arrest and capture of an eight-man cell and several weapons. On 10 April 2004, the forward command element came under fire from insurgents during cordon and search operations. He calmly led a team of Marines in a counterattack, personally clearing several buildings, eliminating one insurgent fighter, and facilitating the evacuation of a severely wounded Marine. Sergeant Major Booker's efforts enabled the forward command element to regain freedom of maneuver and inspired Marines to fearlessly engage the enemy. By his bold leadership, wise judgment, and loyal dedication to duty, Sergeant Major Booker reflected great credit upon himself and upheld the highest traditions of the Marine Corps and the United States Naval Service.

Information for this account is drawn from the U.S. Marine Corps "Award Summary of Action" (2004) and the Silver Star Medal Citation for James E. Booker (2005), and from witness statements from J. D. Harrill and Juan Valdez.

LCPL MOSES CARDENAS

1ST LIGHT ARMORED RECONNAISSANCE BATTALION,
REGIMENTAL COMBAT TEAM 2, II MARINE EXPEDITIONARY FORCE

HOME OF RECORD: FULLERTON, CALIFORNIA

AWARDED THE SILVER STAR MEDAL, FOR HEROIC ACTIONS ON
2 AUGUST 2007, OPERATION MAWTINI,
AL ANBAR PROVINCE, IRAQ

At 0630 on 2 August 2007, LCpl Moses Cardenas and the quick-reaction force (QRF) platoon to which he was assigned were tasked with conducting a zone recon-naissance and interdictions operation within the regimental security area south. The QRF platoon was task organized with two light armored vehicle 25s (LAV-25), one LAV logistical variant (LAV-L), and one LAV command and control variant (LAV-C2). These four vehicles were further task organized into an Alpha Section consisting of one LAV-25 and the LAV-C2, and a Bravo Section consisting of one LAV-25 and the LAV-L. Cardenas was carrying an M249 squad automatic weapon (SAW) and was mounted aboard the LAV-25 in Alpha Section.

The platoon was assigned a specific sector within the regimental security area to conduct its mission, and it began its operation from its company assembly area at 0630. While moving to its sector, the platoon identified two medium-size tanker trucks departing a nomadic camp at a high rate of speed heading east along an unimproved surface road. Although the trucks and camp were identified outside of their assigned sector, the platoon commander decided to stop the trucks to investigate. As the platoon closed with the first truck, the second truck continued at a high rate of speed away from the chasing LAVs. The platoon then split into two sections, with Alpha Section trailing one truck and Bravo Section trailing the other.

When the truck being trailed by Alpha Section finally stopped, the LAV-25 also stopped approximately one hundred meters from and perpendicular to the driver's side of the truck.

The other LAV within the section stopped to the right of the first and parallel to the truck facing its rear end approximately 150 meters away. The scouts in the back of the LAV-25 dismounted. Concurrently, Bravo Section vehicles radioed that the vehicle they were chasing had a male atop the truck tossing weapons and explosives over the side as they continued the chase. As the Alpha Section scouts closed within 50 meters of the truck, the man in the cab of the truck dismounted on the passenger side and moved to the front of the truck. Cardenas spoke to the man in Arabic, telling him to place his hands on his head. The man raised his hands in an "I don't know" manner and then quickly ducked behind the passenger side of the cab, reemerging with an AK-47 rifle aimed at the scouts. The scout team leader (TL) shouted at him to drop the weapon. After determining hostile intent, the TL opened fire with his M4 rifle, and the remaining scouts also opened fire. Almost immediately, 3 insurgents appeared atop the truck, from a slightly covered position, and fired with AK-47s in full automatic mode. As the firefight ensued, the scouts fell back to the cover of the LAV-25, which was now approximately 50 meters behind them. As the 4 scouts bounded back to the LAV, the TL was shot and collapsed on the deck.

Once behind the LAV-25, Cardenas and one of his fellow scouts realized that their TL was wounded, and both Marines immediately decided to go back and help him back to the cover of the LAV. Because the TL was directly in front of the LAV-25, it was unable to provide any suppressive fire for the scouts' movement toward him. The other LAV was likewise unable to support with automatic fire due to a weapons malfunction. Cardenas and his fellow scout fought their way back, approximately fifty meters over flat open desert terrain toward the TL, with only their individual weapons. While they were approaching their TL's position, the insurgents tossed grenades at the Marines. As soon as the Marines reached the TL, Cardenas received a gunshot wound in the neck, which exited his upper back and caused him to fall onto his back.

Cardenas' fellow scout continued to return fire at the insurgents as fast as he could. Moments later, Cardenas regained his bearings, got back up, began firing his SAW again, and fought his way a few more meters toward his TL and fellow scout. During these final few meters, Cardenas realized that he had expended all rounds in his two-hundred-round ammunition drum. Prior to reloading, he shouted, "Reloading," which allowed his fellow scout to pick up his rate of fire and continue to suppress the insurgents and protect his TL's position. Cardenas was able to reload his SAW in less than ten seconds and then began to pick up suppression of the insurgents with his SAW. Once he was at his TL's position, Cardenas placed his SAW in a chicken wing manner (the underarm assault position—butt stock under one arm between torso and upper arm) and used his free hand to grasp his TL's aid strap on the back of his body armor. Cardenas then alternated between pulling the TL backward toward the LAV and firing five- to ten-round bursts of automatic fire from his SAW with one arm. He continued this action for a total of seventy-five meters.

At one point, Cardenas' SAW malfunctioned while he was pulling his TL; without hesitation and under complete control, he stopped pulling his TL and took a knee in a completely uncovered position to perform immediate action on his weapon. While this was occurring, a minimum of four insurgents were still firing back at him and his team members with a high rate of automatic small-arms fire and rocket-propelled grenades. Enemy rounds continued to impact all around Cardenas' position, from no more than seventy-five meters from the enemy's covered positions to the front and rear of the stopped truck, but Cardenas calmly cleared his weapons malfunction. Once again Cardenas continued his rescue mission by alternating between firing five- to ten-round bursts at the insurgents and pulling his TL to safety.

While Cardenas continued to pull his TL, the LAVs had repositioned and were now able to engage the insurgents located behind the truck's passenger side, which had left the scouts completely exposed. Cardenas continued to pull the TL for at least another twenty meters away from the close-quarters firefight and continued to provide accurate fires with only one arm on his weapon. By now, blood had begun to cover Cardenas' flight suit; his gunshot wound was so severe that blood had soaked his entire back. However, disregarding his wounds and with bold action, he continued selflessly to bring his TL to safety. Once Cardenas had brought his TL far enough away from the insurgent vehicle, a LAV-25 began to open fire with the 25-mm main gun system to dispose of the remaining enemy. Cardenas kept up his suppressive fire and concurrently rendered aid to the wounded Marine. When the enemy weapons were finally silenced, other Marines were able to rush to the aid of the TL and another Marine, who was ultimately mortally wounded during the fight. It was not until the corpsman arrived and instructed Cardenas to relax and receive needed care that he stopped providing first aid to his TL.

Through his actions, Cardenas showed his unselfish dedication to his comrades, as well as his tactical and technical skill and proficiency. In order to save the life of a fellow Marine, he had selflessly exposed himself to five enemy combatants with automatic weapons and explosive ordnance at close range (no more than fifty meters). He maintained his bearing and composure while facing a numerically superior ground force. Even after he was severely wounded, he remained focused, did not panic, and summoned the strength to pull a helpless Marine to safety. Throughout the firefight, Cardenas exemplified the warrior ethos and Marine courage. His extreme fighting spirit and commitment to his comrades saved the life of his team leader.

SILVER STAR MEDAL CITATION

The President of the United States of America takes pleasure in presenting the Silver Star to LANCE CORPORAL MOSES
CARDENAS, United States Marine Corps, for conspicuous gallantry and intrepidity in action against the enemy while serving as Scout, Headquarters and Service Company, 1st Light
Armored Reconnaissance Battalion, Regimental Combat Team
2, II Marine Expeditionary Force (Forward) on 2 August 2007 in
support of Operation Iraqi Freedom 06–08. While conducting a
combat patrol, Lance Corporal Cardenas' platoon was attacked
by heavy automatic fire, a suicide bomber, and rocket propelled
grenades after stopping two suspicious trucks. During the initial
stage of the fight, a Marine fell wounded in the open between the
opposing forces. Realizing that the bulk of friendly weapons were
masked, Lance Corporal Cardenas left his safe position behind a
vehicle and fought his way across 50 meters of fire-swept, open
desert against five armed insurgents to rescue the fallen Marine.
After sustaining a gunshot wound to the neck that knocked him
to the ground, Lance Corporal Cardenas tenaciously rose to his
feet, calmly reloaded his squad automatic weapon, and continued
his assault until he reached the wounded Marine. With rounds
impacting around him, Lance Corporal Cardenas alternated
between pulling the wounded Marine and shooting bursts of controlled automatic fire at the enemy. After pulling the wounded
Marine 100 meters, he continued suppressive fire while rendering
first aid until medical personnel arrived to tend to both Marines'
wounds. Throughout this close and fierce fight, he ignored his
own severe wounds, remained fixed on his task, and saved the life
of a fellow Marine. By his bold leadership, wise judgment, and
complete dedication to duty, Lance Corporal Cardenas reflected
great credit upon himself and upheld the highest traditions of the
Marine Corps and the United States Naval Service.

*Information for this account is drawn from the U.S. Marine Corps "Award Summary
of Action" (2007) and the Silver Star Medal Citation for Moses Cardenas (2008).*

HM3 JOSHUA T. CHIARINI

BATTERY G, 1ST BATTALION, 2ND MARINES,
22ND MARINE EXPEDITIONARY UNIT,
SPECIAL OPERATIONS CAPABLE (MEU-SOC)

BORN: COVENTRY, RHODE ISLAND

AWARDED THE SILVER STAR MEDAL FOR HEROIC ACTIONS ON
10 FEBRUARY 2006, AL ANBAR PROVINCE, IRAQ

On 10 February 2006 HM3 Joshua T. Chiarini was on patrol, traveling south on main supply route Bronze when his patrol was attacked by a remote-detonated improvised explosive device (IED). The IED detonated beside the lead vehicle in the convoy. Chiarini was riding in the fourth vehicle and upon seeing the blast ordered the driver of his vehicle to pull forward so he could check for casualties. As his vehicle was pulling forward, he got on the radio, informed the battery headquarters that the patrol had been attacked by an IED, and requested the quick-reaction force (QRF) and told them that casualties were likely.

Meanwhile, the Marines from the first two vehicles had pulled forward, attempting to get out of the kill zone and dismount to cordon off the area and search for the triggerman. As soon as the Marines dismounted the vehicles, a second IED detonated right beside the dismounted Marines, throwing them to the ground and injuring four Marines and an interpreter. Simultaneous with the second IED attack, insurgents began firing a heavy and consistent volume of small-arms fire from covered positions in buildings on the east side of the road. With the road now blocked by disabled vehicles, and realizing the potential for other IEDs next to the road, Chiarini ordered his driver to stop his vehicle. Seeing the explosion and hearing the incoming enemy fire, and in disregard for his own safety, he quickly got out of his vehicle and ran across one hundred meters of open terrain, completely exposing himself to the continuous enemy fire in order to reach the wounded Marines.

En route to the lead vehicle, he encountered a Marine who had received numerous shrapnel wounds. After quickly assessing the identifiable injuries and realizing that the Marine was in shock, he had another Marine help him place the casualty into the passenger side of the second vehicle.

Chiarini then continued forward through the hail of enemy fire to the lead vehicle and discovered that there were more casualties. He immediately triaged the casualties and identified that the interpreter had the most serious injuries, with massive shrapnel wounds to his right arm. The joint from his right shoulder was completely missing, and his collarbone and other bones in his arm were exposed. Chiarini then grabbed the interpreter, using his own body to shield him from the enemy fire that was still impacting around him, and moved him behind the vehicle to begin immediate life-saving measures by applying a dressing and pressure to slow the massive bleeding. He knew that it was impossible to bring any other vehicles forward to evacuate the casualties since all of the Marines who were not wounded were fighting and the two lead vehicles were disabled from the blast. Therefore, once the interpreter was stable enough to move, Chiarini picked him up with one arm, holding his rifle in the other. Placing himself between the interpreter and the enemy, he began to escort him back across the fire-swept terrain, almost one hundred meters, to place him in the closest vehicle capable of being used for medevac. The enemy quickly noticed Chiarini moving across the open terrain with the casualty and began to concentrate the majority of their fires on his position. Realizing that the intensity of the enemy fire had increased significantly in his direction, he immediately returned fire with his free hand, providing suppressive fire toward the enemy, and he continued forward until reaching the vehicle. Once there, Chiarini quickly opened the armored back door of the vehicle, placed the casualty inside, and, using the door as a shield, continued to return fire in an attempt to reduce the pressure of the attack on his position. Once the enemy's focus shifted from his position, he gave the interpreter a shot of morphine and closed the door of the vehicle.

Realizing that more casualties awaited, Chiarini once again crossed through withering fire until he reached the remaining casualties. As he approached another wounded Marine leaning up against a vehicle returning fire, he noticed that the Marine's trouser leg was soaked with blood. Kneeling down behind the cover of the vehicle, Chiarini drew his bayonet; instructing the wounded Marine to continue firing, Chiarini cut open the Marine's trousers to assess his wounds. Disregarding the rounds impacting near him, he dressed the wounds. Once he completed the dressing, and realizing that the wound would require further attention from the medical officer, he decided to place the Marine on the medevac vehicle. Chiarini moved the casualty using the same technique as before; he assisted the casualty with one hand while firing his rifle with his other in an attempt to suppress the enemy. Once back at the medevac vehicle, he placed the casualty in the back and checked the status of the interpreter to ensure he was stable. He then called for a Marine to come back to the medevac vehicle in order to monitor the casualties and provide cover for them.

Chiarini then made his fifth trip across the dangerous terrain and through intense fire to help the other casualties. It was at this time that the QRF arrived with the ambulance, medical officer, and additional corpsmen. Chiarini had made it to the second vehicle and was cutting off the first casualty's boot and sock when the additional corpsmen came to the scene. He informed them of the situation and sent some of them forward to check for more casualties while he continued working on the casualty's foot. Once he had finished applying bandages to the casualty's wounds, he escorted him to the medevac vehicle while again delivering suppressive fire toward the enemy. The QRF then moved into position, engaged the enemy, and silenced the enemy fire that had been impacting around them. Upon getting the casualty safely into the vehicle, Chiarini gave him a shot of morphine, checked on the interpreter and other casualty, and moved back to the front to assist with the other casualties. As the medevac vehicle departed, Chiarini returned to the lead vehicle and discovered that another casualty had also received multiple shrapnel wounds. He immediately ran to stop the medevac vehicle and then returned, treated, and assisted the casualty to the evacuation vehicle. Once the Marines and the interpreter were evacuated, Chiarini continued with the remainder of his squad and the QRF in the search for insurgents.

Chiarini's actions on this day were nothing short of heroic. He crossed terrain that exposed him to enemy fire six times in order to treat and evacuate five casualties. On three occasions he selflessly shielded the casualties with his body and used one arm to support the casualty while moving to the casualty collection point and used his free hand to fire his weapon to suppress the enemy until he was able to place them into an armored vehicle. His quick decision making, calm under pressure, professional skill, and courage under fire saved the lives of four Marines and an interpreter.

SILVER STAR MEDAL CITATION

The President of the United States of America takes pleasure in presenting the Silver Star to HOSPITAL CORPSMAN THIRD CLASS JOSHUA T. CHIARINI, United States Navy, for conspicuous gallantry and intrepidity in action against the enemy as Platoon Corpsman, 1st Platoon, Battery G, Battalion Landing Team 1/2, Twenty-Second Marine Expeditionary Force (Forward) in support of Operation Iraqi Freedom 04–06, in Al Anbar Province, Iraq, on 10 February 2006. While conducting a combat patrol, 3d Squad was attacked by two improvised explosive devices followed by heavy small arms and machinegun fire that wounded five Marines and one interpreter. Witnessing the initial attack and seeing that the road ahead was blocked by disabled vehicles, Petty Officer Chiarini immediately left the relative safety of his vehicle and fought his way across one hundred meters of fire-swept terrain to reach the casualties. He then used his own body to shield the wounded from the increasingly high volume of incoming rounds as he moved them to cover. Realizing that most of the wounded needed to be evacuated, without hesitation, he placed himself between the casualty and the enemy fire, assisting the casualty with one arm while providing suppressive fire on the enemy with his rifle in the other. He then fought his way back across the one hundred meters of fire-swept terrain to the casualty collection point. He repeated this action three times until each casualty was stabilized and safely loaded for evacuation. Despite the insurgents concentrating their fire on him, he remained focused on saving the lives of his wounded comrades. By his zealous initiative, courageous actions, and exceptional dedication to duty, Petty Officer Chiarini reflected great credit upon himself and upheld the highest traditions of the United States Naval Service.

Information for this account is drawn from the U.S. Marine Corps "Award Summary of Action" (2006) and the Silver Star Medal Citation for Joshua T. Chiarini (2006).

SSGT DANIEL J. CLAY

Scout Sniper Platoon, 2nd Battalion, 7th Marines,
1st Marine Division

home of record: Pensacola, Florida

Awarded the Purple Heart Medal after being killed in action
on 1 December 2005, Fallujah, Iraq

Imet SSgt Daniel Clay in 2002 when I was the guest speaker for a gathering of scout snipers from the 7th Marine Regiment. He struck me as a gentle man, which, believe it or not, is very common within the scout sniper community.

Clay, a twenty-seven-year-old Pensacola native, was one of ten U.S. Marines killed by an IED in an abandoned flour factory near Fallujah on Thursday, 1 December 2005. Clay was one of five children in a very strong Christian family. A sister, Jennifer, had died suddenly of an aneurysm a year earlier, shortly after the birth of her fourth child. She's mentioned in this letter. Just before he began his second tour of Iraq, Clay gave the following letter to his father to read in the event that he was killed:

MOM, DAD, KRISTIE, JODIE, KIMBERLY, ROBERT, KATY, RICHARD, AND MY LISA: Boy do I love each and every one of you. This letter being read means that I have been deemed worthy of being with Christ. With MaMa Jo, MaMa Clay, Jennifer . . . . all those we have been without for our time during the race. This is not a bad thing. It is what we hope for. The secret is out. He lives and His promises are real! It is not faith that supports this. . . . But fact and I now am a part of the promise. Here is notice! Wake up! All that we hope for is Real. Not a hope. But Real.

But here is something tangible. What we have done in Iraq is worth any sacrifice. Why? Because it was our duty. That sounds simple. But all of us have a duty. Duty is defined as a God given task. Without duty life is worthless. It holds no type of fulfillment. The simple fact that our bodies are built for work has to lead us to the conclusion that God (who made us) put us together to do His work. His work is different for each of us. Mom, yours was to be the glue of our family, to be a pillar for those women (all women around you), Dad, yours was to train and build us (like a Platoon Sgt) to better serve Him. Kristie, Kim, Katy you are the five team leaders who support your Squad ldrs, Jodie, Robert and Richard. Lisa you too. You are my XO and you did a hell of a job. You all have your duties. Be thankful that God in His wisdom gives us work. Mine was to ensure that you did not have to experience what it takes to protect what we have as a family. This I am so thankful for. I know what honor is. It is not a word to be thrown around. It has been an Honor to protect and serve all of you. I faced death with the secure knowledge that you would not have to. This is as close to Christ-like I can be. That emulation is where all honor lies. I thank you for making it worthwhile.

As a Marine this is not the last Chapter. I have the privilege of being one who has finished the race. I have been in the company of heroes. I now am counted among them. Never falter! Don't hesitate to honor and support those of us who have the honor of protecting that which is worth protecting.

Now here are my final wishes. Do not cry! To do so is to not realize what we have placed all our hope and faith in. We should not fear. We should not be sad. Be thankful. Be so thankful. All we hoped for is true. Celebrate! My race is over, my time in war zone is over. My trials are done. A short time separates all of us from His reality. So laugh. Enjoy the moments and your duty. God is wonderful.

I love each and every one of you.

Spread the word. . . . Christ lives and He is Real.

Semper Fidelis,
Daniel.

The following is a letter written by his father, Bud Clay, and given to Florida congressman Jeff Miller to give to President Bush along with the letter Daniel wrote to his family.

Pensacola, FL,
December 7, 2005.
President George Bush,
The White House, Washington, D.C.

DEAR PRESIDENT BUSH: My name is Bud Clay. My son, SSgt Daniel Clay—USMC was killed last week, 12/01/05, in Iraq. He was one of the ten Marines killed by the IED in Fallujah.

Dan was a Christian—he knew Jesus as Lord and Savior—so we know where he is. In his final letter (one left with me for the family—to be read in case of his death) he says "if you are reading this, it means my race is over." He's home now—his and our real home.

I am writing to you—to tell you how proud and thankful we (his parents and family) are of you and what you are trying to do to protect us all. This was Dan's second tour in Iraq—he knew and said that his being there was to protect us.

I want to encourage you. I hear in your speeches about "staying the course." I also know that many are against you in this "war on Terror" and that you must get weary in the fight to do what is right. We and many others are praying for you to see this through—as Lincoln said, "that these might not have died in vain."

You have a heavy load—we are praying for you.

God bless you,
Bud Clay.

I am grateful to the Clay family for granting me permission to include their letters here.

SSGT JASON S. DEMPSEY

Explosive Ordnance Disposal Team,
15th Marine Expeditionary Unit

HOME OF RECORD: INTENTIONALLY WITHHELD

Awarded the Bronze Star Medal with Combat Distinguishing
Device "V" for heroic actions from 26 November 2006
through 20 March 2007, Al Anbar Province, Iraq

S
Sgt Jason S. Dempsey was awarded the Bronze Star Medal
with Combat Distinguishing Device "V" for heroic achieve-
ment while serving as the explosive ordnance disposal
(EOD) team leader, 15th Marine Expeditionary Unit (MEU)
(Task Force Bullrush), II Marine Expeditionary Force (Forward)
during combat operations in area of operations Mobile, western
Al Anbar Province, Iraq, in support of Operation Iraqi Freedom
05–07 and 06–08 from November 2006 to March 2007. During
four months of combat operations, including direct-action
(DA) raids to capture Jaysh al Islami and Jama'at al-Tawhid
Wa'al-Jihad insurgent cell leaders on the task force Bullrush
high-value individual list, three separate phases of Operation
Gateway clearing operations in Ar Rutbah, and three months of
counterinsurgency and security operations, Dempsey demonstrated the highest level of professionalism and bravery in
actions against the enemy. Through his leadership and individual actions, Dempsey executed 144 total missions, including
the rendering safe of 19 improvised explosive devices (IEDs),
29 weapons caches consisting of 4,268 pieces of ordnance, 249
pounds of bulk explosives, 27 unexploded ordnance items, and
61 weapons; conducting 8 postblast assessments, 13 DA raids,
and more than 100 day and night foot patrols; and clearing more
than 150 buildings.

As the EOD team leader, Dempsey demonstrated exceptional tactical employment of his EOD team. He conducted all
EOD-specific missions and reinforced maneuver elements from
light armored reconnaissance (LAR), force reconnaissance,

and battalion reconnaissance units contributing to the capabilities and combat power within the 15th MEU. A natural leader, Dempsey's mentoring and expertise developed additional skills and enhanced performance within his EOD team. Dempsey also spearheaded the cross-training of LAR scouts in demolitions, including urban breaching techniques; weapons reduction; and the construction, operation and emplacement of IEDs. As the 15th MEU's duty expert on IEDs, Dempsey was relied upon to provide tactical direction to all units within the area of operations to counter IED threats. Frequently, the MEU commander would personally seek Dempsey's recommendations and insight in enemy tactics, techniques, and procedures.

Dempsey exhibited fearlessness and the utmost level of competence in reducing and rendering safe complex and highly lethal IEDs on virtually a daily basis. For instance, on 23 January 2007 Dempsey responded to an EOD request in the center of Ar Rutbah. Upon arrival, Dempsey exposed himself to the direct observation of the enemy to render safe a remote-controlled IED (RCIED) that consisted of two 122-mm projectiles. Since the device was located a few meters from the entrance to a school, he limited collateral damage at the risk of himself and his teammates to transport the IED to another location and destroy the remaining components.

On 24 January 2007, while supporting maneuver elements in offensive operations in Ar Rutbah, Dempsey located an IED less than five meters from a group of dismounted Marines. As the dismounted infantrymen pushed back behind cover, Dempsey, with no electronic countermeasure protection and with complete disregard for his own safety, swiftly moved to the IED with another EOD team member. His calm and steady actions rendered the IED safe. The RCIED consisted of two 160-mm high-explosive mortars set to be initiated by a live remote-control device.

On 28 January 2007 multiple IEDs were discovered on main supply route Mobile by a combat logistics battalion convoy. As Dempsey conducted procedures to render the first IED safe, the EOD team's Talon Robot became inoperable. Unhesitatingly, Dempsey made the decision to manually approach and disarm the live IED and recover the disabled robot. During Dempsey's approach, he discovered a remote-detonated antiremoval secondary device. Due to his wide range of IED knowledge, he was able to quickly rig the power source on the secondary device for remote removal and moved to the safe area with the disabled robot. After making a quick repair of the Talon Robot, Dempsey then rendered safe the second IED, allowing for the safe passage of more than fifty Marines in the combat logistics battalion convoy and reopening the only main supply route leading to Camp Korean Village.

On 30 January 2007 Dempsey displayed tremendous courage and disregard for his own life when an IED consisting of a live remote-control initiator and more than one hundred pounds of high explosives in an acetylene tank was discovered just five meters away from ten Marines of 2nd Platoon, Echo Company, Battalion Landing Team 2/4 inside Ar Rutbah. Dempsey, within ten meters of the IED, immediately directed all the dismounted Marines to cover. He then gave tactical direction to his EOD team to get behind the armor of their vehicle, and he rapidly deployed the Talon Robot. His individual actions enabled the IED to be rendered safe prior to certain detonation. The next day he led his EOD team to conduct a dismounted IED sweep through the center of Ar Rutbah. Dempsey's team was the first unit to move dismounted from the eastern traffic-control point to the western traffic-control point in Ar Rutbah since 15th MEU forces entered the city.

To direct his efforts on specific locations in uncovering IEDs, Dempsey used sensitive source reporting that indicated a number of IEDs along the route. His team operated fully exposed, in the open, along alternate supply route Michigan, and amid numerous sniper and small-arms engagements with adjacent units. Dempsey expertly employed his team to locate and render safe an IED located in the concrete consisting of one 100-kg aerial bomb and two 122-mm projectiles. Dempsey and his team also located three more 100-kg aerial bombs prepared to become another RCIED. While responding to an immediate EOD request on 2 March 2007, Dempsey interrogated an IED with the Talon Robot. Suddenly the IED detonated, destroying the robot. Without knowing whether there was another IED, Dempsey approached downrange to recover the robot and conduct a postblast analysis. The analysis provided the evidence of an antitampering device directed at first responders such as Dempsey and his EOD team.

On 24 January 2007 Dempsey led his team in dismounted clearing operations in Ar Rutbah with 15th MEU's LAR detachment. He provided the capability of explosive breaching to gain entry into five structures. He and his team personally cleared more than twenty-five structures in a single day. His proficiency with infantry tactics resulted in uncovering several weapons caches, including twenty-five assault rifles, four machine guns, eight RPGs, four rockets, five insurgent uniforms, and anticoalition forces' material.

From 16 to 20 February 2007 Dempsey provided additional combat power during counterinsurgency operations. Dempsey and his team conducted dismounted satellite patrols in the urban sprawl of Ar Rutbah for the security of screening potential Iraqi police recruits. For five continuous days and for over ten hours a day he planned routes, coordinated boundaries with adjacent units, and led his EOD team as well as LAR scouts on patrols. His aggressive and offensive small-unit leadership deterred enemy action against the lucrative target of potential Ar Rutbah police recruits.

On 2 March 2007, during DA raids with the Maritime Special Purpose Force (MSPF), 15th MEU, in Ar Rutbah, Dempsey employed his team to isolate the objective area as the cordon force in support of the LAR detachment. As the assault force breached the objective, the cordon force observed several individuals fleeing the area. Dempsey and his team immediately responded and pursued the individuals. With a combined EOD team and LAR scout team, they prevented the individuals from escaping by deploying an inner cordon and rapidly clearing three structures. Dempsey located those attempting to escape coalition forces and detained them on scene. Through further exploitation by counterintelligence, one of the individuals provided actionable intelligence on a location of a nearby buried weapons cache. Dempsey immediately shifted his efforts to locating and then excavating a large weapons cache consisting of three sniper rifles, two machine guns, eight assault rifles, explosives and ordnance, and sufficient material to produce in excess of twenty IEDs.

Another example of Dempsey conducting missions beyond the normal capabilities of an EOD team includes the events on 7 March 2007. During DA raids in Ar Rutbah with the MSPF, Dempsey and a LAR detachment were directed to a possible weapons cache based on actionable intelligence provided by a human intelligent source. After clearing four multiple-story structures in the area, he uncovered a weapons cache concealed in a garage. This large weapons cache consisted of 3 high-powered rifles, 3 pistols, 1 assault rifle, 450 assorted weapons magazines, and more than 5,000 rounds of ammunition.

Dempsey continuously employed his EOD team in a capacity far surpassing expectations. Regardless of the situation, Dempsey volunteered his team and its capabilities. He performed his duties under the constant threat of enemy fire and explosive devices. His unsurpassed technical skill, proficiency in all infantry and reconnaissance operations, and dedication to participate in all missions were an inspiration to every Marine and sailor. Dempsey's intrepidity in the presence of certain danger prevented the possible loss of life of fellow Marines and Iraqi civilians.

BRONZE STAR MEDAL WITH COMBAT DISTINGUISHING DEVICE "V" CITATION

For heroic achievement in connection with combat operations involving conflict with an opposing force while serving as a Explosive Ordnance Technician Team Leader, 15th Marine Expeditionary Unit, II Marine Expeditionary Force (Forward) from November 2006 to March 2007 in support of Operation Iraqi Freedom 05–07 and 06–08. While conducting route clearance in Ar Rutbah, STAFF SERGEANT DEMPSEY received accurate small arms and machine gun fire from an elevated position. Leading the counterattack, he directed the fires of his team to suppress the enemy positions. Without hesitation, he rapidly cleared the occupied positions, forcing the enemy personnel to egress and expose themselves to light armored vehicles and sniper fires, which resulted in five enemy killed in action. On 28 January, while rendering two improvised explosive devices safe, his team's robot became inoperable. Unhesitatingly, he approached and disarmed the live improvised explosive device. Unexpectedly, he discovered a remote detonated, anti-tampering secondary device within three feet of his position. Directing the Marines to take cover and with disregard for his own safety, he manually disabled the anti-tampering device. He contributed to the success of operations through 144 total missions, including the rendering safe of 19 improvised explosive devices, 8 post-blast assessments, 13 direct action raids, and the reduction of 29 weapons caches consisting of 4,268 pieces of ordnance, 249 pounds of bulk explosives, 27 unexploded ordnance items, and 61 weapons. By his zealous initiative, courageous actions, and exceptional dedication to duty, Staff Sergeant Dempsey reflected great credit upon himself and upheld the highest traditions of the Marine Corps and the United States Naval Service.

Information for this account is drawn from the U.S. Marine Corps "Award Summary of Action" (2007) and the Bronze Star Medal Citation for Jason S. Dempsey (2007).

LCPL IAN DOLLARD

2ND BATTALION, 7TH MARINES, II MARINE EXPEDITIONARY FORCE

HOME OF RECORD: PLEASANTON, CALIFORNIA

AWARDED THE SILVER STAR MEDAL FOR HEROIC ACTIONS ON
24 JUNE 2007, SAQLAWIYAH, IRAQ

On 24 June 2007 LCpl Ian Dollard was a member of 2nd Squad, 2nd Platoon, Company F, 2/7. His unit was conducting a mounted security patrol in the Shu'hada 2 area, 3.5 km east of Saqlawiyah. This patrol consisted of thirteen Marines, one corpsman, and one interpreter mounted in three M1114 UAH high-mobility multiwheeled vehicles (HMMWVs) and 1 M1123 high-back HMMWV. At approximately 1130 the patrol was moving in a southern direction when it observed a suspicious dump truck with wires protruding from the front grill. Initial visual inspection also identified a new battery box and battery; therefore, the squad leader and platoon commander made the decision to search the vehicle. The platoon commander, three Marines, and the interpreter dismounted to investigate the vehicle while the other Marines provided observation and cover from the vehicles. The Marines initially checked the cab of the vehicle with nothing significant to report. Observing a pile of fabric in the back, one Marine climbed into the bed of the truck while Dollard moved into position to provide security on the northern side of the vehicle, and another Marine moved to the south side of the vehicle.

As a fellow Marine climbed into the bed, he was immediately hit by a round of 7.62-mm fire from the east. As the Marine collapsed into the bed of the truck, Dollard quickly gained positive identification of the enemy firing position, a shooter in the rear of a taxi approximately 350 meters east of their position. He immediately engaged with his M16A4 assault rifle while directing the remainder of the squad to the enemy position. Sustained semiautomatic rifle fire began impacting around the rear of the truck at a rate of one round every two to three seconds. Another

Marine, upon hearing Dollard's direction and the thud of a Marine falling, immediately rushed to the truck and climbed the north side near Dollard, vaulting into the bed to reach the wounded Marine. The on-scene corpsman, dismounting when he was alerted to the casualty, ran past the platoon commander and climbed over the tailgate into the bed as the lieutenant attempted to drop the tailgate to get the wounded Marine out of the line of fire. As a Marine and the corpsman assessed and treated the wounded Marine under fire, another Marine drove vehicle 4 up to Dollard's position so the turret gunner could observe and engage the enemy. Dollard continued to stand exposed in the midst of the enemy fire, suppressing the fire coming from the taxi, to allow them to assist the casualty. The platoon commander directed the Marines and called in a contact report when he was struck and fell to the ground near the rear left tire of the truck.

Seeing his platoon commander fall amid enemy fire, Dollard ran around the cover to the western side of the truck and then rushed directly into the enemy fire to reach his platoon commander. As rounds continued to impact around the rear of the truck and the lieutenant, Dollard briefly knelt to assess the platoon commander's wound and provide immediate first aid when he was struck twice in the front small-arms protective plate by the enemy fire. At this point, vehicle 1 drove around the truck to block enemy fire and shield the casualties. As vehicle 1 pulled into position, and despite his platoon commander outweighing him by nearly one hundred pounds, Dollard, while under fire, grabbed him by his gear and dragged him for approximately twenty-five meters, at which point the lieutenant was wounded a second time. Once he had pulled the lieutenant to relative safety near vehicle 1, Dollard cut away the lieutenant's flight suit to apply a pressure bandage to his wounds. As the suppression from vehicles 1 and 4 intensified on the insurgent vehicle, it ceased fire and fled to the south. Immediately, heavy automatic weapons fire from a second position to the southeast impacted around the Marines. Despite the rounds impacting and skipping near him, Dollard remained at his platoon commander's side to provide aid and protect him from the incoming fire.

As the turret gunner in vehicle 2 returned fire against the second enemy position, vehicle 3 drove through the fires to form a protective barrier around the wounded Marines. As vehicle 3 moved into position, rounds continued to skip under the vehicle and impact around Dollard and his wounded lieutenant. At this point Dollard was shot a third time, with this round hitting him in the leg. Seeing that a protective cordon was established, and sensing his inability to positively assist in his current state, Dollard limped back to vehicle 4 to gain additional assistance. Upon reaching vehicle 4, he refused medical attention and ordered other members of his fire team to assist the lieutenant and the other wounded Marine. At this time the lieutenant was able to get up and get into vehicle 3 under his own power. As the lieutenant got up, he was shot a third and fourth time with two rounds impacting the front of his Kevlar vest. He continued to the back of vehicle 3 as Marines from Dollard's fire team arrived to help. They saw the lieutenant safely into the medevac vehicle, and they swept the area for serialized gear and provided assistance as the corpsman and another Marine lifted the initial casualty out of the dump truck and moved him to vehicle 3.

Once all casualties were loaded, the squad leader verified accountability of all personnel and equipment and the unit departed the scene under sporadic fire from the southeast as additional units arrived on the scene. Upon return to Firm Base Riviera, Dollard immediately dismounted and began assisting the aid and litter teams in carrying the casualties. Only after both casualties were turned over to the care of the forward battalion aid station and stabilized did Dollard seek out the first sergeant and report his wounds. An on-site corpsman provided medical attention, and Dollard continued to assist in the treatment of the casualties until the medevac helicopter touched down.

SILVER STAR MEDAL CITATION

The President of the United States of America takes pleasure in presenting the Silver Star to LANCE CORPORAL IAN DOLLARD, United States Marine Corps, for conspicuous gallantry and intrepidity in action against the enemy while serving as Fire Team Leader, Company F, 2d Battalion, 7th Marines, Regimental Combat Team 6, II Marine Expeditionary Force (Forward) in support of Operation Iraqi Freedom 06–08. On 24 June 2007, while investigating a vehicle near Saqlawiyah, Lance Corporal Dollard's squad was ambushed by precision small arms and machine-gun fire. He immediately returned suppressive fire, allowing the other squad members to move to the aid of a Marine wounded in the attack. As the enemy withdrew from its position, the squad came under an attack by automatic weapons fire from a second position, inflicting two gunshot wounds on his platoon commander. Without regard for his own safety and still under enemy fire, he maneuvered across open ground to his lieutenant's aid. Within seconds of reaching him, he shielded his lieutenant's body from direct exposure and was struck twice in his upper torso body armor. Though dazed, he initiated medical care for his commander. As rounds continued to impact around him, he dragged his platoon commander 25 meters to cover to continue first aid. Seconds later, Lance Corporal Dollard was struck in the leg by small arms fire. Refusing medical care, he directed his team's efforts towards stabilizing the platoon commander. As support arrived, he climbed into a vehicle whereupon his squad moved to the forward aid station. Upon arrival, he assisted the aid and litter teams with the other casualties before being treated for his own wounds. By his bold leadership, courage under fire, and complete dedication to duty, Lance Corporal Dollard reflected great credit upon himself and upheld the highest traditions of the Marine Corps and the United States Naval Service.

Information for this account is drawn from the U.S. Marine Corps "Award Summary of Action" (2007) and the Silver Star Medal Citation for Ian Dollard (2008).

HM2 ALLAN M. CUNDANGA ESPIRITU

Explosive Ordnance Disposal Team,
7th Engineer Support Battalion, 2nd Force Service Support
Group, II Marine Expeditionary Force

home of record: Oxnard, California

Awarded the Purple Heart Medal after being
killed in action on 1 November 2005, Ramadi, Iraq

———————————————— ✦ ————————————————

I met HM2 Allan M. Cundanga Espiritu in late 2002. He was the corpsman ("Doc") for the 1st Battalion 7th Marine's (1/7) Scout Sniper Platoon. Being the corpsman for a battalion's scout sniper platoon is arguably the most dangerous job a corpsman can have in an infantry battalion; Doc Espiritu volunteered for this duty. Doc was well known and well liked because he was physically fit, mentally fit, and a true warrior. Doc was with our battalion (1/7) for the invasion of Iraq and during stabilization operations in An Najaf. Espiritu was one of very few Navy corpsmen (other than SEALs) who had ever graduated from Marine Corps scout sniper school, gaining the military occupational specialty 8541. This is an example of how Espiritu was always striving to be better and going the extra mile in everything he did.

After serving in combat with 1/7, Doc was assigned to shore duty at Naval Base Ventura County Medical Clinic, Port Hueneme, near his home in Oxnard. While working at the Port Hueneme clinic, Espiritu met Erika, a Navy hospital corpsman, whom he later married. He treated Erika's daughter, Alexy, like his own (Tinio-Lopez 2005).

In July of 2005 Espiritu volunteered for a second combat tour with the Marines in Iraq. Due to a shortage of corpsmen in many Marine Corps combat units, the Navy went looking for volunteers for shore posts, such as Port Hueneme. Although Espiritu could have served within a medical support unit, he volunteered to serve with the explosive ordnance disposal (EOD)

52

platoon of the 7th Engineer Support Battalion. There are two corpsman billets in the EOD platoon. They must be volunteers and must have had prior special operations background experience. EOD Marines are required to have great patience and cool nerves, especially under fire, to work with explosive devices that have to be neutralized. The EOD platoon's primary duty was to seek out and destroy the improvised explosive devices (IED) that it encountered on a daily basis. Its area of operation was the city of Ramadi. The platoon was on call twenty-four hours a day, seven days a week.

Espiritu's four-man team rode in a highly mobile multi-wheeled vehicle (HMMWV); he was the corpsman in case anything happened. In October of 2005 an EOD team was moving on a foot patrol when one of the EOD technicians was hit by enemy fire, collapsing his right lung and immobilizing his right arm. Doc Espiritu treated the EOD tech on the spot and got him evacuated. According to Tinio-Lopez (2005), "ten days later, while responding to a call-out, Doc's team parked their [HMMWV] to approach an IED that had been discovered. As two of the Marine EOD techs stepped out the back doors of the [HMMWV], a second hidden IED under where they had parked was detonated. It blew the [HMMWV] in the air, killing the driver and Allan who had been seated in the front passenger seat."

Doc Espiritu was laid to rest with full military honors at the Ivy Lawn Cemetery in Ventura on 10 November, the Marine Corps' birthday—how fitting. Many Marines were present, both officers and enlisted, and included a squad's worth of EOD techs wearing their EOD "Crabs" (a badge worn by EOD techs). "We go into harm's way that our children will sleep safely tonight."

Allan did not receive a medal for valor, therefore someone may ask why he is recognized in this book as a hero. The answer is simple for me: he was a Filipino immigrant who volunteered to serve in the U.S. Armed Forces, was one of only a few corpsmen ever to graduate from Marine Corps Scout Sniper School, and volunteered to serve as a corpsman for Scout Sniper Platoon 1/7 and an EOD platoon at a time when EOD techs and Scout Snipers were being killed disproportionately in Iraq and Afghanistan. Yet, Doc volunteered time and again for dangerous duty.

As the third verse of the Marines' Hymn tells us, "If the Army and the Navy ever look on Heaven's scenes, they will find the streets are guarded by United States Marines." But I know Doc Espiritu is right behind them, just in case they need assistance. He dedicated his adult life to protecting Marines, and I am sure he continues this dedication today, in Heaven. Semper Fi, Doc.

Tinio-Lopez, Franz. 2005. "Inside Story on Oxnard Sailor Who Gave the Ultimate Sacrifice in Service of His Country." Oxnard Journal, November, http://www.oxnard-journal.com/espiritu.htm.

CPL MARK A. EVNIN

Scout Sniper Platoon, 3rd Battalion,
4th Marines, 1st Marine Division

born: Burlington, Vermont

Awarded the Purple Heart after being killed in action
on 3 April 2003, Al Kut, Iraq

Cpl Mark A. Evnin was the first Jewish casualty in the Iraq War, the grandson of a rabbi, remembered as being macho yet soft-hearted. Evnin was a scout sniper who was in one of the lead vehicles going into Al Kut on 3 April 2003. Iraqi fighters were waiting in ambush and fired the first shots; one of them killed Evnin. He died in the helicopter that was evacuating him. He was the first 3/4 Marine to die during the invasion of Iraq. Evnin had two roles in the war: he drove the battalion sergeant major, David Howe, and he was a scout sniper.

On the day of the attack into Al Kut, tanks led the large procession that crossed over the Tigris River followed by armored personnel carriers and then the Humvees. While the light vehicles were ambushed, Evnin got out of his vehicle to act as the spotter for his fellow scout sniper. When Howe got out he noticed bunkers that were fortified with sandbags; this was where a lot of the fire was coming from. Howe told Evnin to get off the Humvee and fire one of the grenades at the bunker. He carried one of the grenade launchers, an M203, with him. Howe grabbed it and fired a couple of rounds so Evnin could spot impacts. Because Evnin could not see the bunker at first, he went over to a small clump of dirt to fire. He then moved behind the amphibious vehicle to reload. Evnin was partly behind the armored vehicle and stepped out and fired again when he was hit and mortally wounded.

Information for this account is drawn from a personal interview with David Howe, Quantico, VA, 12 April 2010.

HA LUIS E. FONSECA

COMPANY C, 1ST BATTALION, 2ND MARINES,
TASK FORCE TARAWA

BORN: FRANKFURT, GERMANY

AWARDED THE NAVY CROSS FOR HEROIC ACTIONS ON
23 MARCH 2003, AN NASIRIYAH, IRAQ

During the assault on An Nasiriyah, 23 March 2003, HA Luis E. Fonseca was attached to the amphibious assault vehicle (AAV) platoon, Company C, 1st Battalion, 2nd Marines. During the company's assault of the north bridge spanning the Saddam Canal, Fonseca was traveling in the platoon's medevac AAV with the platoon sergeant and company first sergeant. His AAV was the last vehicle in the platoon's convoy through the city; when it arrived on the north side of the bridge, another AAV was hit by a rocket-propelled grenade (RPG) and burned in the road. Fonseca heroically left the relative safety of his vehicle, exposing himself to small-arms fire, and rushed to the aid of the vehicle's crew and the Marines caught inside. After helping to evacuate the burning AAV, Fonseca began treating the wounded Marines. Two of the wounded had suffered total or partial loss of their legs as a result of the blast; three others were also injured. Under fire, Fonseca dragged the Marines away from the burning AAV, which had begun to cook off its cargo and ammunition. He then established a casualty collection point (CCP) for the wounded Marines.

When it became evident that enemy fire was too intense to call in a medevac helicopter, Fonseca ordered his AAV cleared, had litter kits set up, and instructed his Marines on how to drag the wounded while staying out of the hail of enemy rounds. After loading the five Marines onto his AAV, he administered morphine to the two Marines who had suffered partial or total loss of their legs, tied one tourniquet, rinsed the eyes of a flashburn victim, and continued to give aid to the other Marines.

Soon after, the Marines came under intense indirect fire. The first mortar rounds resulted in additional casualties. While Fonseca was treating his wounded Marines, a call for a corpsman came from another AAV. Fonseca again left his vehicle and ran alone down the line of AAVs amid falling mortars and artillery to find the other wounded Marines.

When he returned to his AAV, the vehicle began taking heavy indirect fire, and it became apparent that the vehicle was being bracketed and therefore had to be moved immediately. Soon after, the AAV took two direct hits from enemy mortars and an RPG round that severed the transmission gears. Fonseca orchestrated the evacuation of the wounded Marines from the now disabled vehicle and established another CCP in a creek to the west of the road. He triaged the Marines and called another AAV to his position to load up his two urgent casualties. After the Marines were safely inside the AAV, Fonseca was ordered to take them out and reestablish his CCP for additional wounded. As ordered, he emptied out the AAV and dragged the Marines back to the creek.

Under heavy indirect fire, small-arms fire, and machine-gun fire, and with RPGs landing around him, Fonseca rushed to another AAV to render aid to more wounded Marines. Knowing that two of his Marines had serious leg wounds and needed additional care, he "ordered" another AAV over to his position to load the wounded. From his CCP, he dragged the two most seriously wounded Marines to the AAV, loaded them inside, and climbed in himself in order to provide continuous care as the vehicle was driven south back into An Nasiriyah and through the city. Once south of the city and after his medevac AAV vehicle had crossed both bridges, Fonseca made liaison with 2nd Battalion, 8th Marines (2/8) Battalion Aid Station (BAS); at this point in the fight he was running critically low on medical supplies. At 2/8's BAS he received additional resources and administered another IV bag to each of the seriously wounded. He then coordinated with the BAS personnel as to the status and details of each patient. After the 2/8 Marines had taken custody of his wounded Marines, he returned to his AAV and traveled back north through the city.

Once north of the bridge and reunited with his company, Fonseca immediately assisted the company first sergeant in treating, prioritizing, and providing care to the wounded. He administered continuous care to the Marines until four medevac helicopters landed an hour later. Fonseca's quick actions, medical expertise, and willingness to sacrifice for his wounded saved the lives of four Marines and helped several more.

According to one eyewitness, SSgt Jacques Lefebure,

> I came around the plt SGT's vehicle 212, and saw HA Fonseca approx 20 yds beyond C212 in slight depression, sheltering a wounded Marine from indirect fire. . . . After the two casualties were loaded, my vehicle headed south HA Fonseca continued to give medical aid, using the vehicle first aid kit. As we re-entered friendly lines, I could not find a casualty collection point, so I continued south until I found a 2/8 ambulance. HA Fonseca took the lead in directing the 2/8 corpsman on the casualties' status and what needed to happen. . . . I was impressed by HA Fonseca's devotion to duty, bravery, and disregard for his own safety.

GySgt David Meyer stated, "He alone was responsible for saving at least 5 lives." Another eyewitness, Sgt William Beavers, stated, "During this time, HA Fonseca showed no fear or hesitation when he moved from the medevac vehicle to the wounded Marines, made sure myself and my crew were not injured, and then proceeded to evaluate the wounded who were laying on the side of the road near the burning vehicle. HA Fonseca then instructed the Marines around him on how to move the wounded to the medevac vehicle and then helped move the wounded himself."

NAVY CROSS CITATION

The President of the United States of America takes pleasure in presenting the Navy Cross to HOSPITALMAN APPRENTICE LUIS E. FONSECA, United States Navy, for conspicuous gallantry and intrepidity in action against the enemy while serving as Corpsman, Amphibious Assault Vehicle Platoon, Company C, First Battalion, Second Marines, Regimental Combat Team Two, Task Force Tarawa, First Marine Expeditionary Force, in support of Operation Iraqi Freedom on 23 March 2003. During Company C's assault and seizure of the Saddam Canal Bridge, an amphibious assault vehicle was struck by a rocket-propelled grenade inflicting five casualties. Without concern for his own safety, Hospitalman Apprentice Fonseca braved small arms, machine gun, and intense rocket propelled grenade fire to evacuate the wounded Marines from the burning amphibious assault vehicle and tend to their wounds. He established a casualty collection point inside the unit's medical evacuation amphibious assault vehicle, calmly and methodically stabilizing two casualties with lower limb amputations by applying tourniquets and administering morphine. He continued to treat and care for the wounded awaiting evacuation until his vehicle was rendered immobile by enemy direct and indirect fire. Under a wall of enemy machine gun fire, he directed the movement of four casualties from the damaged vehicle by organizing litter teams from available Marines. He personally carried one critically wounded Marine over open ground to another vehicle. Following a deadly artillery barrage, Hospitalman Apprentice Fonseca again exposed himself to enemy fire to treat Marines wounded along the perimeter. Returning to the casualty evacuation amphibious assault vehicle, he accompanied his casualties south through the city to a battalion aid station. After briefing medical personnel on the status of his patients, Hospitalman Apprentice Fonseca returned north through the city to Company C's lines and to his fellow Marines that had been wounded in his absence. His timely and effective care undoubtedly saved the lives of numerous casualties. Hospitalman Apprentice Fonseca's actions reflected great credit upon himself and upheld the highest traditions to the Marine Corps and the United States Naval Service.

Information for this account is drawn from the U.S. Marine Corps "Award Summary of Action" (2003) and the Navy Cross Medal Citation for Luis E. Fonseca (2005), and from the eyewitness statements of Jacques Lefebure (2003), David Meyer (2003), and William Beavers (2003).

LCPL MARTIN GRAHAM

COMPANY B, 1ST BATTALION, 6TH MARINES,
I MARINE EXPEDITIONARY FORCE

BORN: WINCHESTER, VIRGINIA

AWARDED THE NAVY AND MARINE CORPS ACHIEVEMENT MEDAL
FOR ACTIONS ON 15 DECEMBER 2006, RAMADI, IRAQ

O n 15 December, at 1355, Observation Post (OP) Horea came under a complex attack of an estimated forty-five anti-Iraqi elements. Following a suicide-vehicle-borne improvised explosive device (SVBIED) attack on OP Horea, all posts began receiving indirect and direct fire. During the opening moments of the attack, two rocket-propelled grenades were fired at post 2 from the southeast, followed by an SVBIED and accurate indirect fire.

At this time a lance corporal became an urgent casualty. LCpl Martin Graham had just awakened and was posted to cover the front door. A corporal conducted triage of the casualty and was ordered to prepare to manifest two vehicles for the medevac. Graham volunteered to drive. The OP was under intense enemy small-arms and indirect fire from no less than five target reference points and an estimated fifteen to twenty anti-Iraqi elements. Through this fire Graham assisted in carrying the casualty from the casualty collection point to the medevac vehicle and in providing security.

Graham, on his own initiative, conducted the medevac to Charlie Medical at Camp Ramadi. However, due to the damage sustained by the SVBIED, the M-113 armored vehicle used as a gate was destroyed and not mobile. Graham then, with no thought for his own safety and not knowing how accessible the gap created by the SVBIED was, drove his vehicle through the gap, which was completely engulfed in flames at the time. His initiative undoubtedly helped save the lives of his fellow Marines.

In a personal interview, Graham stated the following:

It was pretty quiet in Ramadi that day when a dump truck–size VBIED came driving down an alley and straight at our FOB [forward operating base]. Our FOB was about 60 meters away from the road and it was [a] three-story building. When the truck exploded it left one-half where it blew up and the other portion on the three-story building. Being on radio watch, I called up to the post to try to figure out was going on. My platoon commander grabbed my radio microphone and told me to go and gear up so I could go up on the roof to engage the enemy. As I was leaving the Command Operations Center [COC] we had about six to eight mortars hitting our FOB. One of the mortars severely injured a Marine who was just outside the COC.

When I saw the Marine go down I was trying to help him, but I could not due [to] the severity of the wounds so I called the doc over to assist. I was covering him just in case there was a cave-in. The doc looked at me and said we have to get him out of here fast or he could die. I knew I had to get to my truck to get the Marine out of the FOB. As I was moving to my truck I was taking fire so I was engaging those targets so that we could get the casualty into the vehicle. My platoon commander called in the QRF [quick-reaction force] to link us up and lead me to Camp Ramadi.

I noticed that at the gate, the route to Camp Ramadi, was blocked by [a] huge tank-looking thing and there was no way I could get out by going that way. But I could wait no longer so I, without permission and not knowing what was behind that wall of flames, gunned my engine and headed right for the flames, not thinking about anything except for saving [the] Marine's life. As I went through the gate I realized that half of the dump truck was still there. So I sped up and went through the flames and I hit it. When I hit it with the speed I was going, I moved the dump truck out of the way. When we got through the gate the QRF was en route to the gate and I almost hit their lead vehicle.

> When we got to the main road I slowed down to try to
> allow the QRF to lead, so we could follow them. When I
> did this they did not get in front of me; they were wait-
> ing behind me, so I decided the longer we wait the less
> time the Marine had to live. So I led the way to Camp
> Ramadi. Just two humvees rolling down the most dan-
> gerous road in Ramadi—pretty shady. It usually takes
> eight to ten minutes to Camp Ramadi; we made it in
> four minutes. When we got to Camp Ramadi, the doc-
> tors grabbed the casualty and took him in to medical.
> A nurse told me that if we had been a minute later, he
> would have died.

For these actions, he received a Navy and Marine Corps
Achievement Medal, without combat distinguishing device.
This is an egregious error in justice. Graham should have
been awarded a much higher award for his actions, such as a
Bronze Star Medal with Combat Distinguishing Device, aka
the Combat V. I asked a former commander from this battle
who stated, "Sergeant Major, you are right, we made an egregious error on this award, but we had Marines making heroic
actions such as this on a daily basis in Ramadi back then."

Graham was one of my Marines at Weapons Training
Battalion, Quantico, Virginia. He is a combat marksmanship
trainer for our unit. Within eighteen months after this event
in Iraq, Graham would commit another heroic act, this time in
Afghanistan.

NAVY AND MARINE CORPS ACHIEVEMENT MEDAL CITATION

Meritorious achievement as Rifleman, 1st Platoon, Bravo Company, 1st Battalion, 6th Marines, 1-Brigade Combat Team, I Marine Expeditionary Force (Forward) in Support of Operation Iraqi Freedom 05–07. On 15 December 2006, 1st Platoon was conducting security and observation operations at Observation Post Horea, when the position came under a large scale attack initiated by a suicide vehicle-borne improvised explosive device. When the platoon suffered an urgent casualty LANCE CORPORAL GRAHAM volunteered in conducting the medevac of that Marine to Charlie Medical. Lance Corporal Graham, exposing himself under heavy enemy small arms, indirect fire and rocket propelled grenades, moved the casualty into pre-staged vehicles. Lance Corporal Graham was forced to drive though a wall of flames created by a vehicle borne improvised explosive device due to damage to the parameter entrance. Lance Corporal Graham's initiative, perseverance and devotion to duty reflected credit upon him and were in keeping with the highest traditions of the Marine Corps and the United States Naval Service.

Information for this account is drawn from the U.S. Marine Corps "Award Summary of Action" (2006) and the Navy and Marine Corps Achievement Medal Citation for Martin Graham (2007), and from multiple personal interviews with Graham at Quantico, VA, 2010.

HM3 JESSE P. HICKEY

Company F, 2nd Battalion, 1st Marines, 2nd Marine Division,
II Marine Expeditionary Force

home of record: Farmington, New Mexico

Awarded the Silver Star Medal for heroic actions on
16 November 2005, Operation Steel Curtain,
Al Anbar Province, Iraq

O n 16 November 2005 at 0640 Company F commenced a sweep-and-clear mission in Al Anbar Province, Iraq, during Operation Steel Curtain. Thirty-three structures were cleared that morning without incident. While attacking to clear its assigned sector, HM3 Jesse P. Hickey's unit encountered twenty-one enemy personnel who engaged them from four well-fortified, mutually supported positions. Upon entry to the enemy stronghold, Company F received heavy enemy gunfire followed by multiple grenades from six insurgents inside and around the immediate perimeter of the building, wounding two Marines inside the front room and two Marines just outside the front door. The insurgents within the building fought from behind the cover provided by the interior walls of the structure, using recessed firing ports and grenade chutes within these walls and furniture in the central hallway to induce casualties with grazing fire throughout the house. Twelve more enemy in other buildings delivered heavy fire upon the unit's right flank and to the company's frontage. As a platoon commander called a tank section in direct support of the unit forward, the squad was relieved of its tank security tasking and received heavy enemy fire, with impacts landing five meters to its right flank.

Along with his squad, Hickey was exposed to frontal and flanking fires in a seventy-five-meter rush through the enemy's kill zones to provide medical assistance to the casualties of another squad. After taking cover within a building, Hickey heard a request for medical assistance at the enemy stronghold of another building and rushed through twenty-five more meters of open terrain within the enemy's kill zones to the next structure. As Hickey arrived at the near wall of the building, he saw the rifleman of the first fire team immobilized with shrapnel wounds to his lower legs. Hickey assisted with recovering the wounded rifleman and transporting him to the platoon casualty collection point (CCP). At the platoon CCP he bandaged and used tourniquets on the wounded Marine's legs with the assistance of the other platoon corpsman. Additionally, he assisted the Marines who were performing buddy aid within the platoon CCP to a gunshot wound to the leg of an engineer attached to the platoon. As Hickey diverted his attention to the priority of treating the rifleman, who was going into shock, he heard another request for medical assistance at a different building.

Hickey and the other platoon corpsman ran through the enemy kill zones and grenades to the enemy stronghold, where several wounded Marines were lying outside the near wall of the building. As Hickey and the other platoon corpsman treated a team leader, enemy grenades exploded around them and caused the wounded team leader's leg to burst into flames from an incendiary grenade in the cargo pocket of his trousers. The enemy grenades seriously wounded six Marines, Hickey, and the other platoon corpsman. Refusing treatment for his shrapnel wounds, Hickey disposed of the incendiary grenade from the team leader's pocket and extinguished the flames on the team leader's leg. While the enemy was engaging the platoon from several directions, Hickey alerted all Marines present that he had additional tourniquets. With the assistance of a Marine, Hickey bandaged the other corpsman's worst shrapnel wounds first. He moved next to a Marine who had lost his leg when a grenade detonated and applied a tourniquet to the leg that had arterial bleeding. He then moved to the front door of the enemy's stronghold, where he saw more wounded Marines just outside the front doorway. He rapidly removed their gear to conduct vital-sign checks, repeated the process for assurance, and declared a machine-gunner, a team leader, and his platoon commander as fatalities and designated them for evacuation.

Continuing to search for urgent casualties, Hickey moved closer to the front door and quickly recovered the wounded Marines' weapons and gear that were just within the doorway to prevent the enemy from utilizing these resources against the Marines. He pulled a Marine, lying just inside the building, from the doorway and confirmed that the Marine was still breathing. The Marines covering Hickey told him to carry the casualty back to the platoon CCP. With the assistance of a combat aidsman, Hickey transported the wounded Marine and began treating the wounded Marine's gunshot and fragmentation wounds. In extreme pain from his own wounds, Hickey was able to use only his right arm in providing treatment to the wounded Marines in the platoon CCP. He applied a pressure bandage to the wounded Marine's shoulder and then directed the combat aidsman in wrapping plastic around the wounded Marine's abdomen to treat an abdominal evisceration. With the assistance of the aidsman, he created a nasal airway for the wounded Marine and handed him to the litter bearers for further evacuation to the company CCP. During the treatment of this wounded Marine, a grenadier bandaged Hickey as he gave orders to the combat aidsman. Hickey had to be ordered to vacate the platoon CCP and board the medevac aircraft. Prior to departing the platoon CCP, he insisted that the other company corpsman receive his gear to provide further treatment to wounded Marines. During his evacuation from the company CCP to the aircraft, he refused painkiller narcotics, stating that there were wounded Marines who needed it more than he did.

His courageous and bold initiative, determination in the recovery of wounded Marines, and vital medical expertise were instrumental in saving at least four lives and resulted in the company gaining a foothold against a well-entrenched enemy. Five Marines from his platoon were fatally wounded by heavy automatic gunfire and grenades from enemy personnel inside and around the immediate perimeter of the fortified enemy position. Ten more Marines and sailors from his platoon were wounded in multiple enemy buildings during the recovery efforts to evacuate the wounded to the platoon CCP. Hickey's decision to cross the enemy kill zones more than four times, his prompt treatment of casualties within enemy kill zones, and his selfless refusal to receive treatment or to evacuate proved vital in the recovery efforts of the wounded Marines. Hickey's leadership, bravery, and loyalty to his fellow Marines and sailors were heroic under heavy enemy fire during an intense battle that resulted in the destruction of eighteen insurgents.

SILVER STAR MEDAL CITATION

The President of the United States of America takes pleasure in presenting the Silver Star to HOSPITAL CORPSMAN THIRD CLASS JESSE P. HICKEY, United States Navy, for conspicuous gallantry and intrepidity in action against the enemy while serving as Platoon Corpsman, Second Platoon, Company F, Battalion Landing Team 2/1, Thirteenth Marine Expeditionary Unit (Special Operations Capable), Regimental Combat Team Two, Second Marine Division, II Marine Expeditionary Force (Forward), in support of Operation Iraqi Freedom in New Ubaydi, Iraq, on 16 November 2005. During Operation Steel Curtain, 21 enemy personnel engaged Petty Officer Hickey's platoon with frontal and flanking automatic fire from four well-fortified, mutually supporting positions. Petty Officer Hickey exposed himself to automatic gunfire while rushing 75 meters through an enemy kill zone to assist and evacuate wounded Marines. After saving a wounded Marine's life in an immediate evacuation, he treated another Marine within the casualty collection point. As the enemy employed multiple grenades in a nearby exchange of fire, Petty Officer Hickey ran into the heart of the fierce melee to provide first aid to a severely wounded Marine who lay immobilized in the kill zone. Enemy grenade explosions wounded Petty Officer Hickey with shrapnel to his entire body. Undeterred by his wounds, he continued treating casualties and evacuated a gravely wounded Marine to the casualty collection point. With one of his arms incapacitated by his wounds, Petty Officer Hickey refused treatment for himself while he directed Marines to conduct the proper medical procedures required to stabilize the wounded within the casualty collection point. Petty Officer Hickey's valiant efforts were instrumental in saving numerous lives. By his bold leadership, wise judgment, and complete dedication to duty, Petty Officer Hickey reflected great credit upon himself and upheld the highest traditions of the United States Naval Service.

Information for this account is drawn from the U.S. Marine Corps "Award Summary of Action" (2005) and the Silver Star Medal Citation for Jesse P. Hickey (2006).

1ST SGT BRADLEY A. KASAL

Weapons Company, 3rd Battalion, 1st Marines,
1st Marine Division

home of record: Afton, Iowa

Awarded the Navy Cross for heroic actions on
13 November 2004 during Operation Al Fajr,
Fallujah, Iraq

On 13 November 2004 1st Sgt Bradley A. Kasal was assisting Combined Anti-Armor Team (CAAT) 1, which was providing a traveling overwatch for a platoon from Company K, which had cleared a zone from a phase line toward their forward operating base. As the CAAT section moved north, an adjacent element encountered a large weapons cache that required destruction. One two-vehicle squad of the four-vehicle CAAT section provided overwatch for an infantry squad, and the second CAAT squad, with Kasal, provided overwatch for another squad. The third squad of that platoon was ordered to move ahead to the next block, begin clearing houses, and continue moving north.

When the second and third CAAT squads reached the next block, they heard a large volume of fire erupt and then observed wounded members of another platoon rapidly exiting a structure to their immediate front. They were informed that Marines were pinned down within the house by an unknown number of enemy personnel. Noticing the element was short of personnel to make an entry and clear the structure, the third squad leader asked the second CAAT squad leader if it could assist with clearing the building. Without hesitation, Kasal volunteered. The squad, with Kasal leading the way, swiftly and confidently entered the structure, suppressing and killing the enemy personnel, who were fighting from hardened positions within the house. After the first room was cleared, Kasal and two other Marines continued to clear the other rooms when they observed a wounded Marine two rooms away from their position. They moved to clear the first of the two rooms; upon entry, Kasal immediately confronted, engaged, and killed an insurgent. Continuing toward the wounded Marine, they received heavy enemy fire as soon as they entered the second room. Kasal and another Marine were both struck in the legs by enemy fire, and both became urgent casualties. Rapidly assessing that the fire was coming from an elevated position, Kasal began searching for an object to provide protection for the other wounded Marine and himself. The enemy fighters, upon observing the wounded Marines pinned down below them, incorporated grenades into their fire. With great presence of mind, Kasal attempted to drag the corpse of an insurgent into a position that would protect them. Realizing that he lacked the strength to move the corpse due to his wounds, he rolled on top of the other wounded Marine in order to shield him from any further wounds. When an attempt was made to extract them, limited manpower allowed for only one Marine to be extracted. After reinforcements arrived, Kasal refused medical attention or extraction until the other Marines were treated or removed. A total of seven wounded men were ultimately evacuated from this enemy strongpoint before Kasal would allow them to extract him. During the extract operations, Kasal continued to provide support, both verbally and with his weapon. Once he was finally extracted from the house, it was later confirmed that Kasal had seven gunshot wounds, and his body had been penetrated by five pieces of shrapnel.

According to Cpl John Mitchell:

> As we entered the house 1st Sgt Kasal shot a guy that was in the room we were headed to. There was no outside suppression of the house at the time and I know that 1st Sgt and another Marine were taking heavy fire and grenades from insurgents located on the second floor. When I heard that 1st Sgt Kasal and the other Marine had been hit, I immediately made my way over to the room they were in. 1st Sgt Kasal had put himself between the other Marine and the doorway in order to protect him. He was providing security with his handgun trained on the door. He then calmly explained the situation even though he had sustained serious bullet and shrapnel

wounds. He then instructed me to administer first aid to the other Marine first. Despite his injuries he was in complete control of himself. We then proceeded to evacuate them from the house, first the other Marine and then the 1st Sgt, as he had ordered us to do.

Cpl Alex Nicoll was the wounded Marine Kasal had protected. Here is the account from his perspective:

On 13 November 2004, during Operation AL FAJR, my platoon was tasked with clearing west between routes Heather, Henry, Isaac and Isabelle. As we pushed west, we came upon a house where a number of Marines had been trapped by a small group of insurgents holed up in fortified positions inside of the house. As we entered the house, I ran into the room, where another Marine, Lance Corporal Carlisle, was hit. There were approximately seven other Marines in the house at the time. I remember hearing First Sergeant Kasal ask if the rest of the house had been cleared at that point. Someone stated that it hadn't. First Sergeant Kasal then organized a small group of Marines to clear the rest of the house. He stacked himself at the front of the door. I immediately ran up behind him. We then went through the doorway at the end of the room and turned left into the living room of the house. There was another room to our left, the Marines inside yelled that it had not been cleared, so we proceeded to clear it. First Sergeant Kasal was still in the lead. He popped through the doorway, stuck his weapon around the corner, and shot off about 5–10 rounds from his M16A4. He then looked back at me and said, "that was a close one Nicoll." At that moment, insurgents from the second floor began firing at us from up a flight of stairs. I don't recall very much of what happened next, however I do recall trying to get back to the door that led outside, however my legs would not work because I had been shot. First Sergeant Kasal then started pulling me into the room where he had just shot and killed the insurgent. I crawled as far into the corner of that room as possible, but we were still exposed to the insurgents' line of fire. Soon after, Corporal Mitchell ran into the room and was able to drag me even further into the room. The insurgents then threw two grenades near the room entrance. First Sergeant Kasal saw them and immediately threw himself on top of me to shield me from the blast, absorbing most of the shrapnel with his body. First Sergeant then instructed Corporal Mitchell to take care of me. He stated that he had been hit badly, but that Corporal Mitchell should take care of me first. The entire time he was holding security at the door with his 9mm pistol. To tell you the truth I don't know how he acted as level headed as he did but I guess that's why he's the First Sergeant.

NAVY CROSS CITATION

The President of the United States of America takes pleasure in presenting the Navy Cross to FIRST SERGEANT BRADLEY A. KASAL, United States Marine Corps, for extraordinary heroism while serving as First Sergeant, Weapons Company, Third Battalion, First Marine Regiment, Regimental Combat Team 1, First Marine Division, I Marine Expeditionary Force, U.S. Marine Corps Forces Central Command in support of Operation Iraqi Freedom on 13 November 2004. First Sergeant Kasal was assisting 1st Section, Combined Anti-Armor Platoon as they provided a traveling over watch for 3d Platoon when he heard a large volume of fire erupt to his immediate front, shortly followed by Marines rapidly exiting a structure. When First Sergeant Kasal learned that Marines were pinned down inside the house by an unknown number of enemy personnel, he joined a squad making entry to clear the structure and rescue the Marines inside. He made entry into the first room, immediately encountering and eliminating an enemy insurgent, as he spotted a wounded Marine in the next room. While moving towards the wounded Marine, First Sergeant Kasal and another Marine came under heavy rifle fire from an elevated enemy firing position and were both severely wounded in the legs, immobilizing them. When insurgents threw grenades in an attempt to eliminate the wounded Marines, he rolled on top of his fellow Marine and absorbed the shrapnel with his own body. When First Sergeant Kasal was offered medical attention and extraction, he refused until the other Marines were given medical attention. Although severely wounded himself, he shouted encouragement to his fellow Marines as they continued to clear the structure. By his bold leadership, wise judgment, and complete dedication to duty, First Sergeant Kasal reflected great credit upon himself and upheld the highest traditions of the Marine Corps and the United States Naval Service.

Information for this account is drawn from the U.S. Marine Corps "Award Summary of Action" (2004) and the Navy Cross Medal Citation for Bradley A. Kasal (2006), and from witness statements from John S. Mitchell (2004) and Alex Nicoll (2004).

SGT LANCE D. MAY

Scout Sniper Platoon, 1st Battalion,
7th Marines, 1st Marine Division

born: Jonesboro, Louisiana

Awarded the Bronze Star Medal with Combat Distinguishing
Device for heroic actions from September 2004
through March 2005, Husaybah and Karabilah, Iraq

On 6 January 2005 Scout Sniper Teams 1 and 2 were tasked with establishing an observation post in the vicinity of the intersection of Market and East End Roads in the city of Husaybah, Iraq. At approximately 0250, shortly after departing friendly lines and in the vicinity of checkpoint 81, the four-vehicle patrol came under intense and accurate heavy enemy fire with a combination of heavy machine guns, rocket-propelled grenades (RPGs), and small arms. During the initial portion of the engagement the lead Combined Anti-Armor Team (CAAT) Red vehicle, trying to exit the engagement area, struck a wall, causing the vehicle to become immobilized. The patrol immediately came to a halt, and without hesitation, Sgt Lance D. May exited his vehicle and was able to orient his team members in the direction of the enemy and quickly cordon off the area to provide security for the downed vehicle. While the CAAT feverishly worked to free the vehicle from the wall, May continued to control the situation while simultaneously provided suppressive fire on the approaching enemy threat.

Once the vehicle was free from the wall, the Marines quickly remounted the vehicle and the patrol moved again back toward friendly lines. At this time May realized that one of the vehicles that had been providing security had fallen behind and was separated from the patrol. He then made the decision to return the patrol back to the engagement area in search of the missing vehicle. As the patrol reentered the kill zone, the lead vehicle suffered a direct hit from an RPG, killing one Marine, wounding several others, and causing the interior of the vehicle to burst into flames. The crippled vehicle crashed into an adjacent wall. Observing the situation unfold from his vehicle, May ordered the second and third vehicles to quickly maneuver around the burning vehicle and stop approximately one block east to provide security and blocking positions.

May immediately and unhesitatingly dismounted his vehicle under enemy fire and began issuing orders to his remaining team members to take up security positions around the downed vehicle while returning fire on the enemy. As May oriented himself to his surroundings, he calmly guided his Marines as they evacuated the casualties and secured the vehicle. As insurgents emerged from hiding positions to engage the Marines, May coolly directed his Marines to return fire. After setting his team into positions, May exposed himself to enemy fire on numerous occasions and ran across open terrain in order to set up a secure casualty collection point for the wounded Marines. Not having a corpsman on scene to provide medical aid to the casualties, May administered first aid to the wounded himself while he engaged approaching enemy fighters. With the enemy advancing toward their position, and with small-arms fire and RPGs impacting around him, he continually exposed himself to danger and courageously directed precision fire upon the enemy threat while applying pressure dressings to the badly wounded casualties. Understanding the need for immediate medical care, he initiated an air medevac. After loading the casualties into the vehicles, May quickly moved to each of the individual security positions while under heavy hostile fire, ensuring that all Marines were accounted for, and directed their fire toward enemy positions. After establishing accountability of all Marines, including a Marine who had been killed as a result of the RPG attack, he began retrograding his team members back to the vehicles in order to extract the patrol from the kill zone.

Arriving at the emergency landing zone, May ordered his team to secure the area in order to allow the inbound medevac helicopter to safely land and extract the wounded Marines to the forward resuscitative surgical suite in Al Qa'im. Once the medevacs were complete, May voluntarily proceeded back into the city for the third time to aid the reaction forces in securing the site where the RPG had destroyed the vehicle. Upon arriving at the downed vehicle, May and two team members established an overwatch position from the top of a nearby house, where they remained for the duration of the operation while Marines extinguished the fire on the burning vehicle and prepared it for tow back to friendly lines. From this vantage point May was able to decisively command the situation.

On 14 January 2005 at approximately 0030, May departed friendly lines as the team leader of three five-man teams tasked with establishing an observation position in the town of Karabilah. That morning May successfully led his teams on a dismounted movement through extremely hostile territory and into their observation positions. The first day into the operation, at approximately 1400, two Iraqi men walked into one of his team's positions, compromising its location. May made the decision to hold his position but to reorganize his forces by splitting one of his five-man teams and consolidating his men into two separate locations with observation on both major supply routes leading into Husaybah. It would be this sound judgment and solid combat decision making that would ultimately shape the battlefield in the day to come and would lead to the success of their mission.

On 15 January 2005 at approximately 1745, May's second team, located approximately eight hundred meters west of his position, came under intense attack by surprisingly accurate RPGs and small-arms and machine-gun fire from enemy insurgents who had encircled their position. May, knowing that he could not effectively engage insurgents without the risk of fratricide, immediately contacted the company command post and requested air support and reaction forces. Throughout the fight May calmly maintained his situational awareness and control of the battle, even while communicating to team members under intense hostile fire and relaying information to the company command post. In doing so, he was able to describe an extremely accurate picture of the events that were unfolding, allowing the company commander to best employ fire and forces in support of the ongoing fight.

Soon after Marines from team 2 began returning fire at enemy personnel, insurgents dispersed and retreated along the route that was covered by May's first team. As the insurgents moved into his view, May identified a white pickup truck with a heavy machine gun mounted in the back and with seven insurgents inside the vehicle, followed by a second car with an additional three enemy insurgents inside. May immediately recognized the opportunity to catch these enemy fighters in a deadly ambush, so he ordered his team members to hold their fire until he gave the order. As the last of the insurgents entered the kill zone, and on May's direct order, the team members violently executed the ambush, catching the vehicles and enemy personnel by surprise. Within seconds May and his team had effectively disabled the vehicles and killed all ten enemy insurgents. The devastating ambush initiated by May and his team immediately alerted other insurgents in the area to their location. Shortly afterward, May's position was again attacked by heavy volumes of small-arms and machine-gun fire, and more insurgents could be seen advancing toward their building. While continuously checking his Marines' security positions within their observation post, communicating with higher headquarters, gaining accountability and injury reports from his second team, and returning fire at a growing number of enemy personnel, May continued to exemplify the coolheadedness and calmness under fire of a proven combat leader.

As the second attack on his position continued to grow in ferocity and the volume of incoming fire increased, May expertly communicated with air assets now on station and provided detailed information to request a repeat mission for call for fire from 81-mm mortars on enemy personnel less than two hundred meters from their position. May successfully led his team through their second intense hostile engagement against a superior number of enemy personnel, estimated at three times their own strength. Casualties sustained for friendly units were minimal, while casualties inflicted on enemy personnel were devastating. Through sound judgment, quick decision making, and uncommon courage on the battlefield, May successfully led his teams through multiple enemy engagements against a superior number of enemy personnel. His dedication, unselfish disregard for personal safety, and calm under heavy enemy fire is a testament to his combat leadership. May proved that he is a strong noncommissioned officer who always sets an outstanding example for his peers and subordinates alike. He is a quick decision maker and takes care of his Marines by ensuring they have the necessary tools to succeed during missions.

May stated in a personal interview, "It was the instant reaction due to my training; my job was pretty easy due to the stellar Marines I had in my platoon. They never hesitated to follow orders. This medal is really a reflection on the entire platoon." LCpl Stacy Alexander, a mortarman, said, "I was in the vehicle hit by the RPG; he [May] was the first man I saw and he immediately started wrapping my leg." Alexander said he had always looked up to May since his arrival to the unit in April 2003: "He's an awesome guy who cares about his troops—he's always teaching his Marines everything he knows." May credits his leadership qualities to his father and the noncommissioned officers and staff noncommissioned officers he has come across.

May's actions do not surprise me at all. I have known him since 1998, when he was a young corporal. At the time he was with the 2/4 Scout Sniper Platoon, 31st Marine Expeditionary Unit. May is one of the many Marines I have known that exited the Marine Corps after their first enlistment and returned to the Corps after the terror attacks on 11 September 2011. During the three years I was in 1/7, I spent much of my time working with and training the 1/7 scout sniper platoon. Just before we invaded Iraq, May arrived in Kuwait; I was happy to see that such an experienced operator was joining the 1/7 scout sniper platoon for the invasion. I am very proud of him; he is an amazing Marine, scout sniper, and human being. Semper Fi, my friend.

BRONZE STAR MEDAL WITH COMBAT DISTINGUISHING DEVICE "V" CITATION

For heroic achievement in connection with combat operations involving conflict with an opposing force while serving as Team Leader, Scout Sniper Platoon, 1st Battalion, 7th Marine Regiment, Regimental Combat Team 7, 1st Marine Division, I Marine Expeditionary Force, U.S. Marine Corps Forces, Central from September 2004 to March 2005, in support of Operation Iraqi Freedom II. During multiple combat engagements against a superior enemy force, SERGEANT MAY consistently disregarded his personal safety while effectively employing the sniper teams. On 6 January, while inserting into an observation post, he successfully led the team through an enemy ambush by a superior number of enemy insurgents. With extraordinary calmness and resolve, he directed the team members during intense and heavy hostile fire while personally administering combat aid to casualties from a vehicle that had been hit with a rocket-propelled grenade. With enemy fire impacting his position, stopping only to engage and eliminate attacking insurgents, he ensured that all of the casualties were treated and accounted for before moving them to the medical evacuation landing zone. On 15 January, as one of the teams was caught in another enemy ambush, he quickly and decisively directed a team in a counter-ambush position. As the attacking insurgents attempted to maneuver around the engaged sniper team, he and the team ambushed them in the open, eliminating 10 and wounding several others, thereby crushing their attack and relieving the beleaguered team. By his zealous initiative, courageous actions and exceptional dedication to duty, Sergeant May reflected great credit upon himself and upheld the highest traditions of the Marine Corps and the United States Naval Service.

Information for this account is drawn from the U.S. Marine Corps "Award Summary of Action" (2005) and the Bronze Star Medal Citation for Lance D. May (2005), and from a personal telephone interview with May at Quantico, VA, 19 December 2007. S. Alexander's witness statement (2005) is available at the Marine Corps Scout Sniper Association website, http://sniper.pmadv.com.

CPL ROBERT J. MITCHELL JR.

COMPANY K, 3RD BATTALION, 1ST MARINES, 1ST MARINE DIVISION

HOME OF RECORD: OAKLAND, IOWA

AWARDED THE NAVY CROSS FOR HEROIC ACTIONS ON
13 NOVEMBER 2004, FALLUJAH, IRAQ

CORPORAL MITCHELL ALSO WAS AWARDED
FOUR PURPLE HEART MEDALS IN FIVE MONTHS

The first time Cpl Robert J. Mitchell Jr. was injured was 7 July near Fallujah, two weeks after his unit had arrived in Iraq. Mortars came over the wall of the compound that he was in. He and several other Marines headed for the wall to return fire. As they did, another mortar round came down almost directly on top of them and blew up. A dime-size piece of shrapnel hit Mitchell on his forehead, directly between his eyes. Fifteen minutes later, Cpl Mitchell was out on patrol with his face sticky with blood from the shrapnel.

On 12 November 2004 Mitchell was wounded for the second time. He and his team encountered an insurgent who was firing through a closed gate. One round went through Mitchell's triceps and another round ricocheted off a wall and struck his leg. When he was shot, he again was determined to finish the job by pushing through the excruciating pain in his injured arm to return fire. Mitchell does not remember when or where he was wounded the third time. However, he has evidence of his third injury: a small piece of shrapnel embedded in his chin.

Mitchell was told by his commanding officer that it would be best if he did not go back out. But he insisted that he was going to remain with his Marines. He was given a choice: go home or remain with his battalion. He felt that he had come to lead a squad and that he needed to finish the job.

For the fourth time in five months, Mitchell would again be injured during the fierce fighting in Fallujah. On 13 November 2004 Mitchell and his Marines sprang into action. Entering the first room of a house, the Marines noticed a dead man on the ground, which suggested the room had been cleared. Two rooms over, Mitchell could see a Marine down who needed to get out. Mitchell and three other Marines, including 1st Sgt Bradley A. Kasal, tried to cross the larger of the two rooms to reach the wounded Marine. As soon as they entered the next room, they received incoming fire from the top of a stairwell to their left. Insurgents were shooting down the staircase and throwing fragmentation grenades. They made it through to the next room; there were other Marines there trying to help the Marine who was down. The insurgents had the Marines trapped in their rooms with their direct line of fire covering the only exit.

Mitchell and his comrades could not move the wounded Marine because he had been shot in the upper thigh and was in a lot of pain and screaming. During their movement, Kasal and another Marines had been hit. Unable to make it to the room with Mitchell, they remained on the ground in a room slightly behind the stairs. Mitchell ran from the room to Kasal and the other injured Marine. Kasal had been shot in the right leg but was still conscious. He told Mitchell that he had taken a few shots in his calf; the blood around the area was evidence enough. Mitchell's other Marine had been shot in the leg as well, but Kasal thought the Marine might have also been shot in the stomach. Mitchell attempted to help Kasal, but Kasal told him to take care of the other Marine first. Mitchell went over to the Marine and started stripping his gear off, looking for wounds. He had not been shot in the stomach, but he had been shot in the left center of his back, and Mitchell thought that maybe he had taken a lung shot.

The Marine that Mitchell was tending to happened to be one of his best friends. Seeing his friend injured hit Mitchell pretty hard, but he set aside his emotions and prepared to do something. He was a combat aidsman and therefore carried a medical kit, which he used to dress the wounds and to place a tourniquet around his friend's leg to stop the bleeding. Although Mitchell did not have enough tourniquets to use on Kasal, he noticed that the wounds were not bleeding too excessively, and he knew the first sergeant was a tough Marine. The Marine he had just treated was still conscious and looking around. He pointed out to Mitchell that his weapon had been damaged. Mitchell looked at it and noticed that a round had hit the bolt. At this point Mitchell started feeling a little bit weak in the leg and looked down and realized his leg was pretty bloody. He thought fragments from the concrete around the wall had hit him.

He continued to monitor the wounded Marines and the radio and to direct traffic until help arrived from a rifle squad, which showed up just in time to help the Marines plan a medevac. The rescue platoon managed to get a squad inside the house to help evacuate the casualties and the other Marines by taking up positions to suppress the fire while they escaped. Once everyone was out of the house and a safe distance away, the Marines planted satchel charges on the house to bring it down on the insurgents inside. Once they had the chance to account for everyone, they determined that Mitchell's squad was down from thirteen to seven capable members. Mitchell also had a chance to look at his own wounds. He found that shrapnel had been lodged in his thigh for some time during the encounter in the building, but could not remember when it had happened.

Navy Cross Citation

The President of the United States of America takes pleasure in presenting the Navy Cross to Corporal Robert J. Mitchell, Jr., United States Marine Corps, for extraordinary heroism while serving as Squad Leader, Company K, Third Battalion, First Marine Regiment, Regimental Combat Team 1, First Marine Division, I Marine Expeditionary Force, U.S. Marine Corps Forces, Central, in support of Operation Iraqi Freedom on 13 November 2004. During a ferocious firefight with six insurgents fighting inside a heavily fortified house, Corporal Mitchell courageously attacked the enemy strongpoint to rescue five wounded Marines trapped inside the house. Locating the enemy positions and completely disregarding his own safety, he gallantly charged through enemy AK-47 fire and hand grenades, in order to assist a critically wounded Marine in an isolated room. Ignoring his own wounds, he began the immediate first aid treatment of the Marine's severely wounded leg. Assessing that the Marine needed immediate intravenous fluids to survive, he suppressed the enemy, enabling a corpsman to cross the impact zone. Once the corpsman arrived, he moved to the next room to assist other casualties. While running across the impact zone a second time, he was hit in the left leg with a ricochet off of his weapon and with grenade shrapnel to the legs and face. While applying first aid, he noticed a wounded insurgent reach for his weapon. With his rifle inoperable, he drew his combat knife, stabbed the insurgent, and eliminated him instantly. Demonstrating great presence of mind, he then coordinated the casualties' evacuation. Limping from his own wounds, Corporal Mitchell assisted in the evacuation of the last casualty through the impact zone under enemy fire, ultimately saving the lives of multiple Marines. By his bold leadership, wise judgment, and complete dedication to duty, Corporal Mitchell reflected great credit upon himself and upheld the highest traditions of the Marine Corps and the United States Naval Service.

Information for this account is drawn from the U.S. Marine Corps "Award Summary of Action" (2004) and the Navy Cross Medal Citation for Robert J. Mitchell Jr. (2005).

GYSGT JAVIER OBLEAS

COMPANY A, 2ND RECONNAISSANCE BATTALION

BORN: FALLS CHURCH, VIRGINIA

AWARDED THE BRONZE STAR MEDAL, POSTHUMOUSLY,
FOR HEROIC ACTIONS FROM SEPTEMBER THROUGH DECEMBER 2004
DURING OPERATION IRAQI FREEDOM

GySgt Javier Obleas died on 1 December 2004 at the Landstuhl Regional Medical Center, Germany, from injuries received 25 November 2004, as result of enemy action in Al Anbar Province, Iraq.

Obleas was a very good friend. When I was the chief reconnaissance and surveillance (R&S) instructor at III Marine Expeditionary Force Special Operations Training Group (SOTG), Obleas was a close-quarters battle instructor, also with SOTG. Obleas also attended the urban sniper course run by the R&S section. Obleas was an incredible shot with handguns, assault rifles, and sniper weapon systems. Obleas was also extremely intelligent and well liked by everyone who encountered him. Of the fifty-seven (and counting) of my friends who have died in the war on terror, Obleas' death hit harder than most. He was a great Marine and a wonderful human being. I am proud to say he was my friend and I am proud of the fact that he went down fighting—a warrior's death.

During Alpha Company's deployment, Obleas demonstrated exceptional bravery and gallant leadership during the conduct of twenty-two combat patrols consisting of cache sweeps, cordon and searches, vehicle checkpoints, R&S, and sniper operations. His tactical acumen in the employment of sniper assets and R&S teams proved invaluable. He was an example of consummate professionalism, courage, and exceptional leadership for all to emulate.

During September and October, Obleas' platoon conducted numerous cache sweeps, vehicle checkpoints, and cordon and knock/search operations within the Ziadon region of central Iraq. During these operations his platoon was responsible for locating and destroying 32 separate cache sites consisting of 400-plus mortars (60 mm, 120 mm, 155 mm), 30-plus AK-series weapons, 21 wire-guided rockets, 6 antipersonnel landmines, 10 improvised explosive devices (IEDs), 20 mortar sites, 9 sniper positions, and more than 10,000 machine-gun and small-arms rounds. As the demolitions expert for the platoon, Obleas developed the demolition plan and spearheaded the detonation of each cache. During the conduct of more than fourteen cordon-and-search operations, Obleas acted as the assault element leader, entering, clearing, and leading the detailed search of each target building.

On the afternoon of 13 November 2004, during Operation Phantom Fury, Obleas continued to be the consummate leader and mentor of the platoon. His decisiveness and courage under fire were a steady example for all to emulate. A patrol was sent from the platoon's patrol base to conduct cache sweeps and establish a presence in the outskirts of Fallujah, Iraq. Upon the patrol's return, one of the engineers discovered an IED approximately fifty meters from the patrol base. Moments after the IED was uncovered, it was command detonated by the enemy. There were seven Marines in the immediate vicinity of the blast. Obleas immediately began medevac procedures, radioing in the current situation and requesting the appropriate assets. He single-handedly managed the platoon, establishing an outer cordon of the area and directing the recovery and evacuation of the casualties. Upon arrival of the quick reaction force, he immediately devised a plan for their tactical employment in support of the cordon and coordinated their efforts in conducting ground medevacs of the seriously wounded Marines. He further coordinated the integration of aviation assets to provide armed reconnaissance of the surrounding area and evacuation route. Obleas' composure and ability to bring order to an extremely dynamic and chaotic situation ensured the security of the remainder of the platoon and saved the life of a Marine who was in the immediate vicinity of the detonation.

On 14 November 2004 the recon platoon was tasked with a sniper operation on the Euphrates River in the vicinity of the Thar Thar and Nu'amiyah regions of Iraq. Contrary to traditional sniper operations, Obleas had the foresight to employ a four-man sniper team equipped with M240G and M249 machine guns. Shortly after the team was set in position, it reported that three suspicious men were traveling rapidly across the river in a pontoon boat. The team was directed to detain the individuals for questioning. Only seconds after a two-man element from the sniper team had exposed them and gave away their position, fifteen to twenty Iraqi men pointed and shouted at the sniper team from across the river. Moments later the sniper team came under heavy direct-fire attack. As a result of their machine-gun assets, the team immediately returned a high volume of suppressive fire. Obleas directed the remainder of the platoon, staged approximately one kilometer away, to conduct an emergency extract of the sniper team. He then dismounted his vehicle and led a four-man element, under fire across an open field, to the sniper team's position. Once in position, he directed suppressive fire against the enemy, enabling the sniper team to bound back to safely withdraw.

On 25 November 2004 the platoon was on patrol in the Zaidon region of Iraq. Its five-vehicle convoy was moving to a patrol base when a command-detonated IED exploded, destroying the vehicle in which Obleas was a passenger. Despite being mortally wounded, his first words, once pulled from the vehicle, were to direct a team leader to set security. He followed that order with sentiments of concern for the other wounded, ordering the platoon corpsman to help the other Marines first and directing him to provide a casualty report to higher head-quarters. It was fitting that some of his last words were of concern for his men, demonstrating his love for the Marines within his unit.

Obleas consistently distinguished himself in battle by maintaining a steadfast, calm demeanor that enabled him to make split-second decisions that have saved numerous lives. His experience, leadership, and confidence in every situation proved to be decisive on numerous occasions. His actions during this time were nothing short of the finest examples of courageous leadership and selfless service.

Bronze Star Medal with Combat Distinguishing Device "V" Citation

For heroic service as Platoon Sergeant, 2d Platoon, Company A, 2d Reconnaissance Battalion, 2d Brigade Combat Team, 1st Marine Division, I Marine Expeditionary Force from September to December 2004 in support of Operation Iraqi Freedom II. During this period Gunnery Sergeant Obleas performed his duties in an exemplary and highly professional manner. Gunnery Sergeant Obleas' gallant leadership was instrumental during the conduct of 22 combat patrols that located and destroyed more than 10,506 pieces of enemy ordnance. On 14 November, an isolated sniper team came under direct fire attack by 15–20 insurgents. Leading a four-man element across 300 meters of exposed terrain, under enemy fire, and in order to recover the team, he established a support-by-fire position and directed hellacious fire on the enemy allowing the team to safely extract. On 25 November, an improvised explosive device destroyed Gunnery Sergeant Obleas' vehicle. Prior to being mortally wounded, he continued to direct Marines to establish security positions and refused medical treatment until all other casualties had received aid. His undaunting leadership and selfless dedication saved lives and directly led to the success of the unit. By his noteworthy accomplishments, perseverance, and devotion to duty, Gunnery Sergeant Obleas gallantly gave his life for his country, and reflected credit upon himself and upheld the highest traditions of the Marine Corps and United States Naval Service.

Information for this account is drawn from the U.S. Marine Corps "Award Summary of Action" (2004) and the Bronze Star Medal Citation for Javier Obleas (2005).

SGT RAFAEL PERALTA

Company A, 1st Battalion, 3rd Marines, 1st Marine Division

born: Mexico City, Mexico

Awarded the Navy Cross, posthumously,
for heroism on 15 November 2004,
during Operation Phantom Fury/Al Fajr, Fallujah, Iraq

O n 15 November 2004 insurgent groups were occupying vacant buildings throughout Fallujah, operating primarily in four- to eight-man cells. Insurgent tactics varied from actively seeking out and engaging coalition forces to remaining dormant inside buildings until coalition forces entered the building. When coalition forces forced contact, insurgents generally fought from fortified positions inside houses, using automatic weapons and grenades, and they attempted to flee after inflicting casualties on the first coalition forces to enter the building. Insurgents were supplied via weapons and food caches prepositioned throughout the city. 1st Battalion 3rd Marines (1/3) was attacking in zone during the initial assault on Fallujah, from 8 through 10 November. Upon reaching its limit of advance, 1/3 established company sectors and conducted search-and-attack operations throughout its tactical area of responsibility. Operating independently, each company of 1/3 came into contact with insurgent forces on a daily basis. They also initiated psychological operations on 11 November 2004 to encourage insurgents to surrender; these operations were conducted in conjunction with humanitarian aid operations at the Mujahareen and Al Haydra mosques. Sgt Rafael Peralta was originally recommended for the Medal of Honor for his conspicuous gallantry and intrepidity at the risk of his life above and beyond the call of duty.

At approximately 0830 on 15 November 2004 Peralta was conducting search-and-attack operations with a squad he was augmenting due to recently sustained casualties. They were clearing their seventh house of the day and Peralta was positioned in the center of the squad between the first and second fire teams as they prepared to enter the house.

The squad met no resistance during initial entry into the house, and they cleared the front rooms without incident; the door to the back rooms of the house was closed. The squad stacked up for entry into the back rooms, with Peralta positioned just behind the point man. As the point man pushed open the door, the squad immediately came under ferocious close-range automatic-weapons fire from multiple insurgents located in the back rooms. The Marines instantaneously returned fire, wounding one of the insurgents. As the Marines sought cover, Peralta was shot in the head as he attempted to maneuver out of the line of fire. He fell to the ground, still attempting to speak, though his words were unintelligible.

After the initial exchange of gunfire, the insurgents broke contact, throwing a fragmentation grenade toward the Marines as the insurgents fled the building. The grenade bounced off the side of a couch and came to rest approximately one foot away from Peralta's head, resting between Peralta and other members of the squad. Though mortally wounded, Peralta, without hesitation, reached out and scooped the grenade under him and used his body to bear the brunt of the explosion, shielding other Marines of the squad who were only feet away. The grenade exploded underneath Peralta, his body absorbing most of the blast; other members of the squad nearby received only minor shrapnel wounds from the explosion. Peralta was immediately evacuated but succumbed to his wounds and was pronounced dead at 0915 on 15 November 2004 while en route to Bravo Surgical Company.

LCpl T. J. Kaemmerer was a combat correspondent attached to Company A 1/3 on 15 November 2004. That day he found himself without his camera, his camera batteries dead; instead, he volunteered to help clear the insurgent-filled buildings that lined streets of Fallujah. As an attachment to the unit, he placed himself within the stack. At one point he found the stacks had gotten out of order, so he fell in behind Peralta. Kaemmerer recalled, "Two Marines stacked to the left of the door as Peralta, rifle in hand, tested the handle. Ready to rush into the rear part of the house, Peralta threw open the door.

'POP! POP! POP!' Multiple bursts of cap-gun-like sounding AK-47 fire rang throughout the house. Three insurgents with AK-47s were waiting for us behind the door."

Several AK-47 rounds hit him in his upper torso and face and struck Peralta. Kaemmerer said,

> I saw four Marines firing from the adjoining room when a yellow, foreign-made, oval-shaped grenade bounced into the room, rolling to a stop close to Peralta's nearly lifeless body. Peralta—in his last fleeting moments of consciousness—reached out and pulled the grenade into his body. . . . Later that night, while I was thinking about the day's somber events, Cpl. Richard A. Mason, an infantryman with Headquarters Platoon, who, in the short time I was with the company became a good friend, told me, "You're still here, don't forget that. Tell your kids, your grandkids, what Sgt. Peralta did for you and the other Marines today."

According to Garry Morrison, the father of a Marine in Peralta's unit—LCpl Adam Morrison—Rafael Peralta "saved the life of my son and every Marine in that room." Peralta enlisted in the Marines when he received his green card and then volunteered for front-line duty in Fallujah; he had one last act of heroism in him—saving the lives of his fellow Marines.

Sgt Peralta was originally put in for the Medal of Honor, but it was downgraded because a neurosurgeon stated, during the investigation, that it was impossible for him to have consciously pulled the grenade into his body after receiving such a fatal wound to his brain. I am not a doctor, but I felt that nothing was for sure. Multiple eyewitnesses stated that he reached out and pulled the grenade into his body. I find it offensive that testimony from a doctor back in the U.S. would, in my opinion, cheat this hero out of his MOH.

NAVY CROSS CITATION

The President of the United States of America takes pride in presenting the Navy Cross (posthumously) to SERGEANT RAFAEL PERALTA, United States Marine Corps, for extraordinary heroism while serving as Platoon Guide with 1st Platoon, Company A, First Battalion, Third Marines, Regimental Combat Team 7, First Marine Division, in action against Anti-Coalition Forces in support of Operation Al Fajar, in Fallujah, Iraq, on 15 November 2004. Clearing scores of houses in the previous three days, Sergeant Peralta asked to join an under-strength squad and volunteered to stand post the night of 14 November, allowing fellow Marines more time to rest. The following morning, during search and attack operations, while clearing the seventh house of the day, the point man opened a door to a back room and immediately came under intense, close-range automatic weapons fire from multiple insurgents. The squad returned fire, wounding one insurgent. While attempting to maneuver out of the line of fire, Sergeant Peralta was shot and fell mortally wounded. After the initial exchange of gunfire, the insurgents broke contact, throwing a fragmentation grenade as they fled the building. The grenade came to rest near Sergeant Peralta's head. Without hesitation and with complete disregard for his own personal safety, Sergeant Peralta reached out and pulled the grenade to his body, absorbing the brunt of the blast and shielding fellow Marines only feet away. Sergeant Peralta succumbed to his wounds. By his undaunted courage, intrepid fighting spirit, and unwavering devotion to duty, Sergeant Peralta reflected great credit upon himself and upheld the highest traditions of the Marine Corps and the United States Naval Service.

Information for this account is drawn from the U.S. Marine Corps "Award Summary of Action" (2004) and the Navy Cross Medal Citation for Rafael Peralta (2008), from the witness statements of T. J. Kaemmerer (2004) and Richard A. Mason (2004), and from Oliver North, "No More Heroes?" Military.com, December 16 2004, http://www.military.com/Opinions/0,,FreedomAlliance_121604,00.html.

CPL JOHN ETHAN PLACE

Scout Sniper Platoon, 2nd Battalion,
1st Marines, 1st Marine Division

Born: St. Louis, Missouri

Awarded the Silver Star Medal for heroic actions from
March through April 2004, Fallujah, Iraq

O n 18 March 2004 Cpl John Ethan Place conducted a key leader ride-along with Bravo Company, 1st Battalion, 505th Brigade, 82nd Airborne Division in order to provide security for the Fallujah Provisional Authority Council meeting. At approximately 1300 five enemy 82-mm mortar rounds impacted within the friendly defensive perimeter. One defensive position took seventeen casualties. Within minutes of the mortar attack, the enemy fired rocket-propelled grenades (RPGs) and small arms from multiple positions in an attempt to kill American soldiers and Marines. Place immediately located an enemy RPG gunner and his assistant gunner from his rooftop sniper position. Taking careful aim, he fired at and killed both insurgents. Place's precision fire helped halt the enemy attack and allowed for the safe evacuation of the wounded soldiers and Marines.

On 26 March 2004 Place's company conducted security patrols into the city of Fallujah, Iraq, in response to enemy attacks on coalition convoys. From approximately 1000 to 2100, Place patrolled deep into the city and was under enemy fire almost the entire time. Dozens of enemy RPGs were fired at his position, as well as many mortar rounds and hundreds of rounds of enemy machine-gun and small-arms fire. Place and his team provided overwatch for the rifle platoons as they patrolled in Fallujah. His steadfast patience and discipline resulted in the elimination of two insurgents armed with AK-47s; he killed them with his M40 sniper rifle. Despite often intense enemy fire and numerous enemy ambushes, Place maintained stalwart determination to his mission; his calm, collected demeanor gave confidence to his Marines in an environment where enemy RPGs often exploded within twenty-five meters of friendly positions while bullets cracked overhead only inches away. His personal example and sturdy leadership steadied his men during enemy contact and allowed them to penetrate deep into enemy-occupied territory.

On 4 April 2004 Company E established a blocking position north of Fallujah. Corporal Place and his team provided detailed observation and conducted reconnaissance of several routes in support of battalion and company missions.

On 7 April 2004 Place and his team joined Echo Company the day after it attacked into Fallujah, patrolling to the company defensive position as heavy enemy fire impacted all around them. Place did not hesitate to deploy his team. Upon linking up with Company E in a seized house in the northwest part of Fallujah, he climbed to the rooftop and immediately killed enemy RPG gunners and AK-47 gunmen. Despite intense fire from multiple coordinated mortar, RPG, and small-arms attacks, he diligently searched for and located the enemy. Within hours Place had personally killed nine armed enemy personnel.

On 8 April 2004 the enemy fired at Place and his team throughout daylight hours and mounted at least three coordinated attacks, firing mortars, RPGs, machine guns, small arms, and BM21 rockets. Place personally killed eight enemy personnel from ranges of 225 meters to 800 meters. Place was so effective at destroying the enemy that the local Arabic radio stations reported insurgent demands for the Marines surrounding Fallujah to withdraw their snipers or the insurgents "would launch an all-out attack." Place's remarkable combat leadership instilled mortal fear within the enemy of the Jolan Heights of Fallujah.

On 9 April 2004 the Marines of Company E could see stray dogs wandering among the corpses of seven dead insurgents whose bodies littered the streets of Fallujah where Corporal Place had dropped them with his sniper rifle. His lethal accuracy intimidated the enemy to the point that the enemy would rarely be seen for more than a few seconds within sight of Place's company's defensive position; enemy small-arms and

RPG accuracy decreased significantly as a result. Because of this, Place single-handedly protected the Marines of Company E from injury or death.

On 10 April 2004 enemy insurgents made the mistake of driving within 250 meters of Place. Three armed insurgents could be seen in the vehicle, and Place and his team engaged them, killing all three. The company commander whom Place supported decided to retrieve the body of one of the insurgents to determine if he was a foreign fighter. While dismounted, a leader's reconnaissance with the tank platoon commander was conducted to pick the best route to the dead insurgents; an RPG gunner ran out and tried to engage Marines within Company E's defensive position. Place immediately acquired the RPG gunner, killed him, and then successfully overwatched the leader's reconnaissance as it returned to friendly lines. One of the enemy combatants whom Place had killed was recovered during a tank-infantry assault, providing valuable information to higher headquarters.

From 11 through 24 April 2004 Place's keen observation skills and unwavering perseverance ensured that Company E maintained a forceful long-range counter to enemy direct-fire attacks. Place maintained sniper coverage during daylight hours for the duration he was attached to Company E, and consequently he was the Marine exposed to enemy fire for the longest duration. Often enemy fire came within inches of him. Place's formidable reputation preceded the arrival of an Army Special Forces unit at his position on 24 April 2004, as the unit commander of the elite special forces organization asked for him by name. Place integrated into joint sniper missions seamlessly and provided invaluable professional recommendations and expertise on sniper employment particular to his area of operations. Senior U.S. Army personnel noted his maturity, and he was personally asked to screen for a position with the elite special forces organization. Place represented the U.S. Marine Corps in the finest manner and further strengthened the phenomenal legacy of Marine Corps scout snipers.

On 26 April 2004 Company E conducted a platoon-size security patrol into Fallujah in support of Operation Vigilant Resolve. At about 1100 a numerically superior enemy force attacked Company E's position from the north, east, and south. Approximately four thousand rounds from enemy machine guns and small arms impacted the platoon position in the first fifteen minutes of the attack, as well as no fewer than thirty RPGs. The enemy assaulted to within twenty meters of friendly positions, threw hand grenades, and sprayed AK-47 fire. During this assault, Place left the cover of his company's defensive position in order to achieve a better angle of fire to engage a group of enemy armed with AK-47s as they attempted to maneuver on the platoon-size security patrol. He killed five of the armed insurgents with his M40.

When Place was finally detached from Company E on 4 May, he had personally accounted for at least thirty-one enemy killed. LCDR Jeff Saville, the battalion chaplain, told Marines and civilians gathered for the award ceremony that although all life is precious, "evil must be restrained sometimes by force" (Perry 2005). In fact, Place and the other snipers were so feared that insurgents pleaded with the United States to withdraw them during the negotiations (ibid.).

> "He didn't kill 32 people. He saved numerous lives by protecting our perimeter," said Sgt. Maj. William Skiles. "That's how the Marines look at it." . . . The sniper school . . . where Place was an honor student, has a motto taken from the Chinese: "Kill one man, terrorize a thousand." That's the role of the sniper: Keep the enemy off-balance, deny him the opportunity to rest and regroup, destroy his morale and will to continue fighting. . . . Place mentioned the names of Marines killed in Al Fallujah and said they were the true heroes. He said he would never forget the faces of the enemy he killed to protect his fellow Marines. "You can make your peace with it," Place said. "But you think about it every day."

SILVER STAR MEDAL CITATION

The President of the United States of America takes pleasure in presenting the Silver Star to CORPORAL JOHN ETHAN PLACE, United States Marine Corps, for conspicuous gallantry and intrepidity in action against the enemy while serving as Team Leader, Scout Sniper Platoon, Second Battalion, First Marines, First Marine Division, I Marine Expeditionary Force, U.S. Marine Corps Forces, Central Command, Iraq, from March to April 2004 in support of Operation Iraqi Freedom II. On 18 March 2004, while conducting a key leader ride-along, Corporal Place's convoy was attacked by two insurgents. He immediately located and destroyed their position, which enabled the convoy to proceed unharmed. On 26 March 2004, while conducting security patrols, Corporal Place encountered two more insurgents and neutralized their position. During these actions, Corporal Place instilled confidence in his Marines with his calm, collected demeanor under intense combat conditions. On 7 April 2004, Corporal Place coordinated with another company and engaged and eliminated enemy forces while under intense enemy fire. From 11 to 24 April 2004, Corporal Place's keen observation skills ensured his supported rifle company maintained a lethal, long-range response to enemy attacks. On 26 April 2004, an enemy force attacked a company patrol 400 meters away from friendly lines. Corporal Place disregarded his own safety and left the cover of his defensive position to close with and destroy the enemy. By his steadfast initiative, courageous actions, and exceptional dedication to duty, Corporal Place reflected great credit upon himself and upheld the highest traditions of the Marine Corps and the United States Naval Service.

Information for this account is drawn from the U.S. Marine Corps "Award Summary of Action" (2004) and the Silver Star Medal Citation for John Ethan Place (2005), from a witness statement from William Skiles (2010), and from Tony Perry, "Marine Sergeant Wins Silver Star for Iraq Combat," Los Angeles Times, 26 June 2005, http://articles.latimes.com/2005/jun/26/local/me-sniper26.

LCPL JASON C. REDIFER

COMPANY A, 1ST BATTALION, 2ND MARINES,
24TH MARINE EXPEDITIONARY UNIT

FROM: STUARTS DRAFT, VIRGINIA

AWARDED THE NAVY AND MARINE CORPS ACHIEVEMENT MEDAL,
POSTHUMOUSLY, FOR ACTIONS 6 JANUARY 2004,
NORTHERN BABIL PROVINCE, IRAQ

The primary mission for 1st Battalion, 2nd Marines (1/2) while deployed to northern Babil Province was to protect the critical infrastructure in the area, including a power plant, power lines, oil pipelines, bridges, a main supply route, and an alternate supply route. Throughout six months of demanding, sustained combat operations, LCpl Jason C. Redifer displayed superb dedication in the execution of his duties and assisted in the overall success of the battalion landing team.

Upon arrival in Iraq, 1/2 was positioned inside a power plant compound at Camp Iskandariyah, Iraq, and was subjected to indirect fire attacks almost daily; in addition, improvised explosive device (IED) attacks were directed at the battalion's patrols on a daily basis and occurred as often as five to six times a day. Redifer's variety of tasks included conducting countermortar, counter-IED, and security patrols, in addition to serving as a member of the battalion's quick-reaction force for almost three months.

During Redifer's time in Iraq, he participated in numerous cordon-and-search operations, vehicle checkpoint operations, and more than 120 combat patrols. Due to the vast area of operations and large number of tasks assigned to the battalion, his patrols sometimes lasted longer than 12 hours. Through his stamina, devotion to duty, and tenacious attitude, Redifer no doubt assisted in ensuring a more stable and secure environment in the area of operations.

Redifer always adapted to any task he faced. Arriving in Iraq, his company was transformed into a motorized rifle company using up-armored highly mobile multiwheeled vehicles (HMMWV). Redifer was chosen as a new HMMWV driver. Because the area was filled with unimproved canal roads, drivers were forced to operate both day and night on unfamiliar, hazardous terrain. Redifer perfected his driving skills more quickly than did his peers. His skillful handling of this difficult vehicle was recognized, and he was assigned the duty of being his platoon commander's driver. The platoon commander had no doubt that Redifer would be able to handle the difficult driving assignment with the ease of a professional.

On 9 August 2004 Redifer's mechanized patrol was attacked by two simultaneous IEDs along the alternate supply route San Juan, just west of the Euphrates River. Immediately following the attack Redifer recognized that several Marines had been wounded in the explosion. He took the initiative and assembled several Marines for security, identified a potential helicopter landing zone, notified his platoon commander, and secured the site. His quick thinking and decisive actions enabled the evacuation of casualties in a timely and efficient manner.

Redifer's duties extended beyond that of the average rifleman. Before deployment he was recognized as an expert marksman, and his shooting abilities earned him the position of the platoon's designated marksman. He perfected these skills and ensured that his weapon was meticulously maintained and ready for action. In addition to his shooting skills, he diligently learned all immediate action drills performed by the platoon in order to best support his fellow Marines under any circumstance. On countless occasions Redifer provided his critical expertise in observation and marksmanship as a guardian angel for the Marines around him. In the dangerous environment he was faced with, he used his scope to provide additional situational awareness to his fellow Marines and give them accurate and timely reporting on their surroundings.

The day after Iraq's successful election on 30 January 2005, Redifer was conducting a patrol to provide security for the battalion's forward operating base and deter enemy mortar attacks against it. The patrol was moving south along a heavily attacked route near the Euphrates River when it was attacked with an IED. The force of the IED destroyed the vehicle Redifer was riding in, wounding two Marines and killing three Marines instantly, including Redifer.

Redifer was dedicated in every aspect of his duties. Serving in a hostile area as an infantryman, he was subjected to almost daily indirect fire, direct fire, and IED attacks. His subordinates, peers, and superiors alike admired his devotion to duty and fearless attitude. Throughout sustained combat operations, Redifer was an inspiration to his platoon. His total dedication to mission accomplishment assisted in creating a safe environment for the Iraqi citizens to vote in their first free election. Redifer was on his final mission when the IED bomb killed him.

NAVY AND MARINE CORPS ACHIEVEMENT MEDAL CITATION

Heroic achievement while serving as Designated Marksman and Rifleman, 2d Platoon, Company A, Battalion Landing Team, 1st Battalion, 2d Marines, 24th Marine Expeditionary Unit in support of Operation Iraqi Freedom II from 23 July 2004 to 31 January 2005. LANCE CORPORAL REDIFER displayed determination and courage in pursuit of mission accomplishment. He conducted cordon and search operations, vehicle checkpoints, and was in over one hundred twenty combat patrols to gain security and prevent indirect fire and improvised explosive device attacks on coalition forces. On 9 August 2004, enemy forces attacked his patrol with two improvised explosive devices causing casualties. Without hesitation, he identified and secured a helicopter landing zone to evacuate wounded Marines. On numerous occasions, he employed skills as a designated marksman and served as guardian angel for his fellow Marines. His efforts assisted in making the area of operations a more stable and secure environment to support the first free elections in Iraq. Lance Corporal Redifer's courage, tenacious attitude, and devotion to duty reflected credit upon himself and were in keeping with the highest traditions of the Marine Corps and the United States Naval Service.

It is my opinion that this award should have been authorized with the Combat Distinguishing Device. I have observed too many heroic awards such as this where the Marine was not deservingly recognized. Below is a letter from Lance Corporal Redifer's mother to President Bush:

February 9, 2005

President George W. Bush
The White House
1600 Pennsylvania Avenue NW
Washington, DC 20500

Dear Mr. President,
I am sending you this letter as a card of thanks. You were my son's Commander In Chief as well as his President. I am the mother of Lance Corporal Jason C. Redifer, USMC, who died on January 31, 2005 in the Babil Province of Iraq as a result of an IED explosion that ripped through the Humvee that he was in.

Jason was scheduled to return from his tour of duty in Iraq just nine days after the accident that claimed his life. He had just departed on his final mission and was killed only two hours after speaking with me on the phone. He was but a new nineteen years old, yet an old soul in many ways.

Like so many of those serving their country, Jason was the embodiment of patriotism and honor. The horrific attack on our country on September 11, 2001 cast his future and he left for Parris Island just three days after graduation from high school at only seventeen years of age. He believed, as you do, that this is a war of necessity and absolutely needs to be addressed on their soil, not ours.

Jason went to Iraq with the ideal of defending our freedoms even though many of his fellow countrymen exercised theirs by condemning what he did. Once there, he immediately grasped the importance of being part of the vast effort to liberate the Iraqi people and bring them a semblance of the democracy we enjoy. This filled him with as much purpose and importance as what he had originally viewed as his mission to keep terrorism from the doorstep of his brothers.

Jason lived only long enough to know that the elections were deemed a success and to feel the relief that the numbers of voters were greater than anticipated and the number of casualties far less. He had many concerns that the battles waged and the lives given may not be enough to insure the liberation that we have all prayed for. He knew that the final verdict of success would rest as a tally in a record of history. He knew for the meantime, however, that to fight the battle against tyranny and to march ahead under the banner of freedom was work that God himself had commissioned.

While I was lost in my grief and struggling to continue forth with the mundane details that these times require of the surviving loved ones, I heard your voice call to me. You had come into my living room and were standing among my family. You were delivering The State of the Union Address, but that was only the venue you used to chat with me. You reminded me of the pride of country and love of life that filled my son. I was able to look into the eyes of the man he so deeply respected and I knew exactly why he was so proud to deploy and fight on your orders. I knew, as he did, that the loss of but one life was too many and that your decision was not one that you made without the heavy weight of human cost.

You steadied my trembling being and cradled my breaking heart delicately in your mighty hands. You lifted my chin and my gaze was held by someone who felt the loss of our troops and the grief of their families. You implored us, even without words, not to break ranks but to continue to hold strong our bond of determination to end terrorism so our children, and their children, may someday sleep in peace throughout the world.

You brought with you friends. I swelled with pride at the young Iraqi woman who was born into a life of oppression as were those born before her. She told me that on Monday, she opened her eyes to see the faint light of hope for the first time in her life. She showed me her fingers that were stained with the blood of my son. That vote reminds us all that my child did not die in vain!

You also introduced me to another family who, like us, had let go of their son's hand to send him away to pay the ultimate price for our beliefs. Their tears mingled with mine and their warmth filled my very soul. Their pride, their anguish, was mine and ultimately, their unwavering support of their President shone like mine all around us.

When that chamber filled with people erupting in applause time and time again, I felt a peace engulf me that has sustained me throughout the days since.

We laid my son, America's son, to rest in Arlington National Cemetery yesterday and committed him to a piece of hallowed ground reserved for the celebration of the values and beliefs that the rest of us could only aspire to hold so dearly. He shared your vision, honored your courage, and proudly fought on your command. He also prayed every night that God would grant you the strength and wisdom to make the decisions that only you can make.

We share your vision, honor your courage and offer the same prayers for you, your family and all those who advise you. You reminded me of all of those things during your visit to my home. It is with that great gift that I humbly say thank you and may God Bless the United States of America.

Sincerely,
Rhonda L. Winfield

Information for this account is drawn from the U.S. Marine Corps "Award Summary of Action" (2004) and the Navy and Marine Corps Achievement Medal Citation for Jason C. Redifer (2004). I am grateful to Rhonda Winfield for granting me permission to include her letter here.

MAJ ALAN ROWE

Weapons Company, 1st Battalion, 7th Marines,
1st Marine Division

home of record: Hagerman, Idaho

Awarded the Purple Heart after being killed in action on
3 September 2004, Al Anbar Province, Iraq

Maj Alan Rowe was my last company commander while I served in 1st Battalion, 7th Marines (1/7). He was a very highly respected leader of Marines. He was an enlisted Marine who served with 1st Force Reconnaissance Company and chose to get out of the Marine Corps and go to college. He then reentered the Marine Corps through the Officer Candidate School. Once he arrived at 1/7, in Iraq, he immediately proved to all, officers and enlisted, that he was a tactical wizard. He first served with the battalion's S-3 as an assistant operations officer and then was moved to Company A, my company, and finally to Weapons Company. I was his company first sergeant, and I enjoyed many conversations about tactically employing the Marines, and about our families and our mutual friends.

On 3 September 2004 Rowe was killed by a triple-stacked improvised explosive device (IED). He was conducting a leader's recon and turnover with Marines from 3/7. At the time of the incident they were conducting a bridge engineering inspection of a military ribbon bridge across the Euphrates. As they were preparing to remount their vehicles, an IED that was buried under a rapidly deployable earth-filled defensive barrier adjacent to them was detonated. It is small consolation that he suffered little; the explosion was absolutely massive, killing two Marines and severely wounding others.

Being killed by an IED does not make a warrior a hero, but Rowe was a hero because he had dedicated his life to serving his country, the Corps, and especially his Marines. He truly treated his Marines like his own children. Sometimes he showed them tough love, but he always showed them love. Six days after he was killed, I wrote a letter to his beautiful wife as I wept:

9 September 2004

Dear Dawn, I feel compelled to write and tell you how sorry I am to hear about your husband. He loved you and your children more than you will ever know. I could see it in his eyes whenever he spoke of you and your beautiful children. He also loved his Marines; they were his children also.

Alan had the same opinion as I when it came to training Marines. We agreed that we must train our Marines hard, so when a mother or wife asked us, did you do everything in your power to train my son to survive, we must be able to answer with a YES. Alan was one of the most professional Marines I have ever met. You and your children should be very proud of him. He absolutely loved being a Marine, as he loved his Marines and most importantly, you (his family).

Most people have critics; Not Alan. I never heard any man, enlisted or officer say anything other than praise for Alan. Alan was a professional, a warrior, and a loving father and husband and I will miss him very much! I am known as a hard Marine and some people think I do not care about anyone; they are wrong! Multiple times yesterday, I was unable to control my emotions and found tears in my eyes. My first thought when I heard the terrible news was, Oh my God, I feel so sorry for his family. You and your beautiful children flashed into my mind. I am so sorry for your loss.

Please know that Alan was an amazing Marine and one of the greatest warriors I have ever met. Alan died for his country; he was a true patriot. Please accept Nit's and my condolences.

Love, David K. Devaney, First Sergeant USMC

HM3 JUAN M. RUBIO

SMALL CRAFT COMPANY, 1ST BATTALION, 23RD MARINES,
31ST MARINE EXPEDITIONARY UNIT

FROM: SAN ANGELO, TEXAS

AWARDED THE SILVER STAR MEDAL FOR HEROIC ACTIONS ON
1 JANUARY 2005 DURING OPERATION IRAQI FREEDOM,
HADITHA, AL ANBAR PROVINCE, IRAQ

On the afternoon of 1 January 2005, HM3 Juan M. Rubio was working as the platoon corpsman for 2nd section, 4th platoon while conducting a riverine security patrol when he came under enemy fire from a concealed position on the riverbank. The boats immediately returned fire but could not dismount on the ground due to the lack of troops. The boats returned to base and picked up the remainder of the platoon and returned to the area to seek out, close with, and destroy the enemy. The patrol located the enemy ambush site and noticed marks where the enemy casualties had been dragged; at this point the enemy initiated an ambush by detonating an explosive device that seriously injured the radio operator and another Marine. The enemy then engaged the patrol with rocket-propelled grenades (RPGs), machine guns, and small arms, inflicting three more casualties. The patrol immediately began laying down suppressive fire on the enemy positions.

Rubio was called to assist the casualties. Unknown to anyone at this time, Rubio had himself sustained shrapnel wounds to the elbow and wrist. However, when called for, he immediately low-crawled over to the casualties under heavy and accurate enemy fire and began rendering field medical care. Rubio had several casualties to assist, and he made on-scene assessments of the casualties. While assisting one casualty, he was concurrently instructing the Marines who were assisting the other casualties. Undeterred by the intense enemy fire and bleeding from his own wounds, Rubio repeatedly exposed himself to enemy fire, took control of the situation for the duration of the firefight, and calmly continued to move from one casualty to another to provide medical care. Once all the casualties were stable enough to be transported, he assisted in moving the wounded Marines to the boat for medevac and continued to provide medical care until turned over to a higher echelon of medical care. Rubio ensured that all casualties were aboard the medevac helicopter and that he had done all he could before allowing medical personnel to treat his own injuries. Once all Marines were stabilized, he boarded the medical helicopter and was likewise transported to a higher echelon of medical care. Rubio demonstrated absolute resolve, dedication, and unselfish devotion to his Marines despite being injured and under accurate and heavy enemy fire.

According to GySgt Brian Vinciguerra, after LCpl Carl Fallen sustained a 7.62-mm gunshot wound to his shin, Rubio quickly assessed the wound, placing field dressings to protect it, and ensured the evacuation of this wounded Marine. Approximately forty-five minutes later, upon arrival of the ground quick-reaction force, the remaining Marines and boat crews moved to contact in the original area of engagement, putting ashore in the vicinity of the area where the first patrol broke contact. While investigating the area, they found several additional areas that looked to be weapons caches. At this time Vinciguerra heard a very loud concussion that seemed to be the impact of an RPG, followed by a long burst of automatic-weapons fire. Vinciguerra evacuated his position and moved forward with LCpl John Powell to provide covering fire. The platoon commander, 1stLt A. P. Thomas, returned to Vinciguerra's position and stated that there were an undetermined number of casualties on the other side of the pump house in the open.

The support elements of the platoon were assembled in a defilade position and were receiving heavy volumes of automatic-weapons fire and RPGs and could not move into the open to extract the casualties. It was at this time that Rubio, taking great personal risk, moved from his covered position and, under heavy fire, crawled to LCpl Timothy Parrello's position and dragged him back to the defilade position. He also assisted Capt. Jonathan F. Kuniholm, who had received a blast trauma to his right hand, in moving back to a covered position.

Once the casualties were in covered locations, Rubio, while under heavy small-arms and rocket fire, assessed the wounds and began immediate triage of the wounded. It was at this time that Vinciguerra was hit by RPG shrapnel in the right forearm and had to fall back to the casualty collection point. With three wounded Marines to attend to, Rubio delegated specific tasks to the platoon combat lifesavers, lance corporals Nicholas Shaffer and John Powell, who conducted initial treatment of Captain Kuniholm's right arm and Vinciguerra's wounds. During this period Rubio assessed the wounds of Lance Corporal Parrello, who had sustained the majority of the blast and concussion. It was initially thought that he had been lightly wounded, but as time progressed his condition deteriorated. Once Captain Kuniholm and Vinciguerra were stabilized, Rubio checked their vital signs and administered intravenous fluids to Kuniholm, who had lost a substantial amount of blood. When the small-unit riverine craft arrived on station, and while still under heavy fire, Rubio prepared the stretchers and the medevac boat to receive casualties. Once the casualties were loaded onto the boats and under way, Rubio commenced advanced life support on Lance Corporal Parrello. He continued to provide this support until they reached the battalion aid station on the top of the dam and it was determined that Rubio had also been wounded.

According to Thomas, during the entire firefight Rubio tried to stabilize the casualties, and it was determined that they had two urgent surgical casualties and one priority casualty. The boats pulled up to the bank to load the casualties, and Rubio continued to provide medical care—while still under heavy enemy fire—to the injured Marines. Lance Corporal Parello's lung had collapsed, and Rubio tried to keep him breathing. At this point he had already made his way to all three casualties and had ensured that they could be transported. Once they arrived at the FOB (forward operating base), all casualties were loaded in HMMWVs and transported to the battalion aid station (BAS) to await the medevac helicopters. When the helos landed and all casualties were loaded, Rubio had himself checked out by medical staff, and it was determined that he had shrapnel wounds in his elbow and leg. He was put on a helicopter and medevaced to Alpha Surgical. Rubio did not let his own injuries get in the way of performing his duties. He had to deal with multiple casualties but remained calm and, despite being injured, performed his duties in a superb manner. Although Lance Corporal Parrello died at Alpha Surgical, it was later determined that his death was due *not* to lack of medical attention, which was excellent, but to the nature of his wounds, which were too severe to be treated on site. The other two casualties were treated at Alpha Surgical and then transported to Germany. Rubio was returned to his platoon three days later.

Silver Star Medal Citation

The President of the United States of America takes pleasure in presenting the Silver Star to Hospital Corpsman Third Class Juan M. Rubio, United States Navy, for conspicuous gallantry and intrepidity in action against the enemy while serving as a Platoon Corpsman attached to the 4th Platoon, Small Craft Company, First Marine Division, I Marine Expeditionary Force, U.S. Marine Forces Central Command, in support of Operation Iraqi Freedom on 1 January 2005. During a dismounted patrol along the Euphrates River, 4th Platoon was ambushed in a complex attack by a well-emplaced and determined enemy. As Petty Officer Rubio and an assault element swept through the ambush site, insurgents detonated an improvised explosive device. Rocket-propelled grenades, machine gun, and small arms fire followed immediately after the explosion wounding three Marines. Realizing the severity of the Marines' wounds, and although bleeding profusely from wounds to his wrist and elbow, Petty Officer Rubio low-crawled across open terrain, exposing himself to enemy fire to provide triage. Working simultaneously on three urgent surgical casualties, Petty Officer Rubio coached his fellow Marines who were assisting other casualties as the volume of incoming fire intensified. Upon stabilizing the wounded for casualty evacuation, he directed the platoon to provide covering fire as he and several Marines began moving the casualties back towards the watercraft. Without regard for his own life, he once again exposed himself to the heavy and accurate enemy fire moving the Marines from the ambush site to the shoreline. By his bold leadership, wise judgment, and complete dedication to duty, Petty Officer Rubio reflected great credit upon himself and upheld the highest traditions of the United States Naval Service.

Information for this account is drawn from the U.S. Marine Corps "Award Summary of Action" (2005) and the Silver Star Medal Citation for Juan M. Rubio (2005), and witness statements of A. P. Thomas (2005) and Brian Vinciguerra (2005).

SSGT SIMON LOUIS SANDOVAL

COMPANY A, 1ST BATTALION, 4TH MARINES,
11TH MARINE EXPEDITIONARY UNIT (SPECIAL OPERATIONS CAPABLE)

HOME OF RECORD: COCHISE COUNTY, ARIZONA

AWARDED THE BRONZE STAR MEDAL WITH
COMBAT DISTINGUISHING DEVICE "V" FOR HEROISM FROM
4 THROUGH 27 AUGUST 2004 IN NAJAF, IRAQ

Najaf is widely considered the third holiest city in all of Shia Islam and is the center of Shia political power in Iraq. The Shia leader Muqtada al-Sadr had his head-quarters in the city, and he despised the Americans and coalitions, whom he considered occupiers.

During the 2004 Battle of Najaf SSgt Simon Louis Sandoval's fearlessness in combat and dedication to his Marines inspired his platoon to fight with tenacity and aggressiveness through one of the most intense battles in the Iraq War to that point.

On 5 August 2004 1/4 was ordered to attack and clear the Najaf cemetery, which is a two-kilometer by five-kilometer maze of buildings and crypts that limits visibility in many places to less than ten meters and offers the enemy numerous well-protected fighting positions from which to defend. Immediately after entering the Najaf cemetery, Sandoval's platoon was engaged by a heavy volume of small-arms fire from positions less than fifty meters away, by sniper fire from surrounding buildings, by 60-mm and 82-mm mortars, and by rocket-propelled grenades (RPGs) fired from less than one hundred meters. The mortar fire was so intense that the Q-36, counterbattery radar, registered more than one hundred mortar rounds fired at friendly troops during a twelve-hour period. While moving on the far left flank, Sandoval had a mortar land within fifteen feet of his position, and he laughed at the enemy's lack of accuracy and marksmanship. His courage in the face of danger and his warrior attitude proved instrumental in keeping Marines focused and aggressively pushing forward toward enemy positions while under heavy fire. Later he again displayed his calm, business-like demeanor under fire when a Marine in his unit broke his ankle. Sandoval quickly left his covered position and coordinated the evacuation team to move the Marine to the rear. Again Sandoval displayed great courage and aggressiveness when he ran up to a minaret twenty meters in front of friendly lines with his 9-mm handgun and a hand grenade and threw the grenade into the minaret so a squad could enter and clear the building. Sandoval then led a squad in clearing four other minarets from which his company had taken fire. The intensity of the Marine assault and quick action caused the militia occupying these positions to retreat. After leading the squad to clear these buildings, he returned to friendly lines and continued to lead his Marines fearlessly while under heavy enemy fire.

On 21 August 2004, immediately upon dismounting from their amphibious assault vehicles (AAVs) to move to the blocking positions, Sandoval's platoon came under heavy enemy fire. While en route to the blocking positions, the platoon took sniper fire from a variety of positions and had two RPG rounds impact in the center of the platoon. After the platoon had established its blocking positions, a Marine was shot in the foot. With no regard for his own safety and with heavy enemy and friendly fire being exchanged in all directions, Sandoval ran fifty meters to the casualty and led an evacuation team with the injured Marine back to the AAVs. Sandoval risked his life and safety to ensure that the wounded Marine was taken back to safety immediately.

On 25 August 2004 Sandoval gallantly led his Marines while fighting enemy forces in the Old City of Najaf during a company attack against a known militia stronghold. While moving with the platoon to attack and clear a four-story hotel, the platoon became heavily engaged in room-to-room and building-to-building fighting; the unit was taking small-arms, machine-gun, mortar, and RPG fire from three different directions. Additionally, the enemy dropped hand grenades from upper floor windows on Marines moving in the streets and threw grenades from window to window across the streets.

While the platoon was held up attempting to breach and make entry into its objective, an RPG impacted five feet in front of Sandoval's position; shrapnel injured him in the arm and shoulder. While the platoon was pinned down, enemy hand grenades took four other casualties, one of which was urgent and had to be taken back to the command element one hundred meters away for evacuation. Without any thought for himself or his own injuries, Sandoval got back on his feet and moved directly toward the casualty to organize a litter team. While Sandoval was doing this, his position took continuous enemy machine-gun fire from the alley in front of the casualty. After loading the casualty in the litter, Sandoval evacuated him to the casualty collection point under enemy fire and then returned to continue fighting with the platoon.

On August 26, after successfully clearing the objective building and establishing a defense, the platoon identified a number of enemy positions within one hundred meters of the platoon's defense. After seeing frequent enemy movement to the south of the hotel, Sandoval, along with another Marine, went down to the bottom of the building in an alley to ambush enemy fighters. Later that day, after clearing several buildings, Sandoval's patrol came under accurate and heavy machine-gun fire from the second story of a building seventy-five meters to the direct south. The patrol was forced to take cover in doorways and porches to avoid the heavy fire. Unable to advance any farther, the patrol stayed in its position, attempting to take out the enemy machine gun during the gun's pauses and reloads. After being pinned down for ten minutes and having no success killing the machine gunner, the patrol was ordered to break contact. Allowing the squad to move back to safe positions, Sandoval fearlessly suppressed the enemy position while standing in the middle of the alley. Only after all of his Marines had safely broken contact did he move back to a safe position. Sandoval bravely risked his own life while ensuring he was the last one out of the alley and all of his Marines had made it to safety.

Sandoval was one my sergeants in Company A, 1st Battalion, 7th Marines (1/7) during the invasion of Iraq and while we controlled Najaf in 2003. I do not think Sandoval liked me very much back then. I was constantly badgering him and the other patrol leaders about precombat inspections before each patrol. Well, I guess he really did listen to me because soon after the 2004 battle of Najaf, he contacted me via e-mail. Excerpts from the e-mail are below:

1st Sgt Devaney,

     I hope that all is going well for you where you are at now. I am doing well and have been in good health. If you don't already know, I am back here in Dewaneyah with ALPHA Company BLT 1/4. My Bn [Battalion] was the Bn fighting in Najaf from 4 Aug to 27 Aug. I am sorry to say I lost two good young Marines from my platoon in the battle for the Imam Ali Mosque in the Old City of An Najaf. Both their names were LCpl Alex Arrendado and PFC Nicholas Skinner. We had a memorial for them yesterday and it was a good one. Almost the whole camp, both Soldiers and Marines showed up to pay their respects and honor them both.

     I was injured by an RPG shot while I was fighting with my Marines in an alleyway. It was around 0200 on the 25 of Aug. I had some glass and shrapnel hit my left shoulder and 4 of the Marines that were with me were seriously injured. One of the Marines from Weapons Platoon had his jaw hanging off of his face 1st Sgt. After I was able to get myself together from the blast, I carried him all the way back to the Evacuation Position. It kind of hit me hard because this young Marine just kept on telling me to kill him by just using his tongue to speak. We took a lot of WIA's [wounded in action] in the Bn. and every Company took KIA's. God bless those Marines and our fallen brothers.

     My Marines fought with courage and valor. They killed a lot of Mother @#$%%'s in that 4 day battle. 1st Sgt, those 4 days made "Black Hawk Down" look like nothing. It's much different and I now know what it really feels like to listen to a round wiz next to your head. I had one of my Marines hit in the chest and his sappy plate saved his life and another Marine had his goggles knocked right off of his helmet. I tell you, there were a lot of close calls. Most of the time we were really lucky.

I have another SSgt that is with me here that knows you very well. His name is SSgt Brian Sommers (3rd Plt Sgt) and he was one of your students in a school you instructed. He says that you used to call him Sgt Major. I don't know if that rings a bell but we enjoy talking about you a lot. It makes us laugh our asses off when we are at chow talking shit about you and the times we spent under your leadership. You really have had a lot of impact on a lot of Marines 1st Sgt. So much impact that I am being put in for the Bronze Star with Combat V and I have also been put in for the Purple Heart. I would like to say that you had a lot to do with that 1st Sgt. Thanks for being the way you were with me when you had to be. Sometimes I needed that good kick to the balls. Take care and GOD bless 1st Sgt. I have never forgotten you.

R/S
SSgt Simon Louis Sandoval.

There are no words to adequately describe how proud I am of Sandoval.

Bronze Star Medal with Combat Distinguishing Device "V" Citation

For heroic achievement in connection with combat operations against the enemy as Platoon Sergeant, 1st Platoon, Company A, 1st Battalion, 4th Marine Regiment, 11th Marine Expeditionary Unit (Special Operations Capable), I Marine Expeditionary Force, from 4 to 27 August 2004, in support of Operation Iraqi Freedom II. While fighting Mahdi militia in the An Najaf cemetery, Staff Sergeant Sandoval displayed the highest levels of courage and leadership under continuous enemy fire. During this time, 1st Platoon had become pinned down by sniper fire from a group of five buildings. Leading a squad of Marines, Staff Sergeant Sandoval moved 50 meters forward of friendly lines to the buildings filled with insurgents with a grenade in one hand and his pistol in the other. After throwing the grenade into the first building, he fearlessly led Marines and cleared all the buildings. The attack of the Marines forced the enemy to retreat without a fight. Furthermore, he displayed an exceptional level of heroism in intense fighting during the battalion's main assault on the old town of Najaf. After a rocket-propelled grenade impacted in front of his position, injuring him with shrapnel, Staff Sergeant Sandoval courageously moved to a wounded Marine's position and evacuated him to safety. By his zealous initiative, courageous actions, and exceptional dedication to duty, Staff Sergeant Sandoval reflected great credit upon himself and upheld the highest traditions of the Marine Corps and the United States Naval Service. The combat distinguishing device is authorized.

Information for this account is drawn from the U.S. Marine Corps "Award Summary of Action" (2004) and the Bronze Star Medal Citation for Simon Louis Sandoval (2005). I am grateful to Sandoval for granting me permission to include his e-mail here.

2ND LT BRIAN MICHAEL STANN

WEAPONS COMPANY, 3RD BATTALION, 2ND MARINES,
2ND MARINE DIVISION

BORN: SCRANTON, PENNSYLVANIA

AWARDED THE SILVER STAR MEDAL FOR HEROIC ACTIONS
FROM 8 THROUGH 14 MAY 2005, KARABILAH, IRAQ

Serving as the commander of the task force reserve for Operation Matador from 8 to 14 May 2005, 2nd Lt Brian Michael Stann was tasked with seizing, sustaining, and reinforcing the battle position on the southern bank of the Euphrates River at the Ramana Bridge. En route to the objective, Stann led his reinforced platoon through an enemy gauntlet on three separate occasions, conducting a movement to contact along four kilometers of defended urban terrain with mutually supporting positions along the single road leading to the bridgehead. Stann's Marines defended the battle position and performed offensive actions under sustained fire from the enemy for over ninety-six hours. Intelligence analysts verified that insurgents and foreign fighters had constructed a deliberate defense in this area of Karabilah to protect the Ramana Bridge that spanned the Euphrates River and the road that led to Ramana. The bridge was key terrain for the enemy forces; as they controlled it for a year, the insurgents sympathetic to the foreign fighter influence had unimpeded cross-river movement. This limited multinational forces' access to the north banks of Ramana and created a foreign fighter safe haven. Thus the approach to the Ramana Bridge was mined, organized with deliberate enemy fighting positions in depth, littered with improvised explosive devices (IEDs), and patrolled by suicide-vehicle-borne IEDs (SVBIEDs). The last combat patrol in the area suffered a Marine killed in action in March 2005. The route to the bridgehead had not been successfully traversed in over a year and consequently was considered too dangerous to travel except under the most dire and extreme circumstances of absolute tactical necessity.

On 8 May 2005 at about 0430, Stann received his first movement order. 1st Mobile Assault Platoon (MAP), originally tasked with establishing the battle position, was delayed traveling a circuitous route from the west along the river. The action of establishing the battle position was synchronized as a key event with the effects of special operations units. When 1st MAP failed to meet the timeline and continued to report poor conditions and multiple vehicles stuck on their route, the task force commander ordered Stann and his Marines to rapidly seize the battle position from the south. In less than thirty minutes Stann prepared his platoon and departed Camp Al Qa'im en route to his objective.

Stann's platoon began receiving small-arms, rocket-propelled grenade (RPG), and machine-gun fire four kilometers from the objective. While maintaining the units' forward momentum, Stann skillfully directed the fire of his platoon, destroying each insurgent fighting position encountered. Fighting its way to the objective with heavy machine-gun and tank main-gun fire, Stann's platoon seized the bridgehead and established individual vehicle positions and their respective sectors of fire. It blocked possible enemy movement south from Ramana across the bridge, fought counterattacks from the southern avenue it had just traveled, and coordinated and awaited the link-up with Stann's adjacent MAP located three kilometers to the west and still hours away from the bridge.

Twenty minutes after occupation of the battle position, Stann's platoon received accurate and sustained indirect fire. Without a forward air controller on site, Stann rolled one radio to the tactical air direction net and coordinated with the rotary wing close-air support (RW/CAS) section overhead to talk the AH-1W Cobra gunship pilots onto observable enemy mortar firing positions south of his position. At approximately 1000 1st MAP arrived and assumed 2nd MAP's positions south of the bridge. The task was to conduct a relief in place so the task force could reconstitute its reserve element.

The increased friendly movement intensified the enemy fire, and as Stann's Marines pulled out of position, one of their attached tanks struck a large platform pressure-plate IED. The blast lifted the tank, permanently damaged the hull, creating a mobility kill, and severely injured its entire crew. Without hesitation and under intense enemy fire, Stann moved to the destroyed vehicle on foot, disregarding his personal safety. As enemy rounds snapped overhead, he initiated medevac procedures and personally extracted the most critically injured tank crew member from the vehicle. He designated a hasty casualty collection point (CCP) and terminally guided a UH-1N helicopter into the helicopter landing zone for the medevac. Once the medevac was complete and 1st MAP securely in position, Stann ordered his platoon to attack back along southern routes. He boldly planned to reduce the enemy's effective strength in an area he suspected he might fight in again. Running south through the gauntlet, Stann again controlled the disciplined fires of his platoon, engaging multiple enemy firing positions, negotiating roadblocks, and destroying an SVBIED that attempted to strike his trail vehicle on the outskirts of the built-up area. His audacity to draw the enemy out worked to his advantage. He and his MAP confirmed seven killed insurgents, some of whom were Arab foreign fighters. Stann was an eyewitness to the identification of foreign fighters with hoods, advanced body armor, and RPG-7 flechette-dart rounds—the darts that hit the reinforced windshields in twelve-inch patterns were pulled out for analysis after the movement.

On 9 May, after several convoy escort missions, Stann's platoon was ordered back to the bridgehead to supply the 1st MAP with ammunition and fuel; the option to deliver the supplies by helicopter was too great of a risk. The threat conditions permitted helicopters to land for urgent medevac requirements only. Traveling with two 7-ton medium truck vehicle replacements loaded with water, fuel, ammunition, and batteries, 2nd MAP arrived at the battle position without incident, but on the return trip they were ambushed with small arms and RPGs. Despite successfully killing all identified insurgents in the ambush site, Stann made the prudent judgment to egress south directly off their route into the desert to avoid decisive contact in the city along the route, thereby protecting his logistics vehicles.

On 10 May Stann was ordered to relieve the 1st MAP with his platoon on the Ramana Bridge battle position. With a mine-clearing detachment, an explosive ordnance disposal (EOD) detachment, an M1A1 tank section, and an M88 tank recovery vehicle attached, 2nd MAP again attacked into Karabilah. Making their final turn north to the battle position and bridge, the enemy ambushed the platoon with heavy RPG and machine-gun fire. Stann led with his tanks and directed their fire against the enemy's prepared positions. As the engagement intensified, the street filled with dust and smoke, and one of Stann's vehicle drivers became disoriented and turned down an alley off the route. Stann instructed the lost driver to turn around and retrace the vehicle's movement to rejoin the unit at the tail of the formation. His vehicle commander executed as instructed, and as the vehicle turned back onto the main road it was struck by a massive SVBIED speeding toward the end of the convoy. The blast destroyed the up-armored HMMWV and severely injured all of its crew. Moving to the blast, Stann calmly directed his platoon sergeant to request an aerial medevac, established a cordon around the destroyed HMMWV, and began medevac procedures. Knowing that he could not risk landing a helicopter in the heart of the enemy-controlled Karabilah, Stann established a mobile CCP inside the M88 tank recovery vehicle to protect and stabilize the casualties during the ground medevac to the designated helicopter landing zone at the bridge site. During the evacuation, two additional SVBIEDs swarm attacked the static formation and were destroyed by precise heavy machine-gun and M-1 (tank) main-gun fire. Once he had accountability of all casualties loaded aboard the M88 recovery vehicle, Stann personally led the movement to the medevac site. Hundreds of meters from the battle position at the bridge, the M88 struck a pressure-plate IED as well. This destroyed the M88, creating another tank recovery requirement. At the battle position, Stann supervised the final medevac of his Marines and the recovery of the destroyed tanks, and, with a forward air controller attached, he directed RW/CAS rockets and hellfire missiles onto enemy positions still firing at his platoon from the south—Stann remained at the battle position with one section of his platoon and the 1st MAP. He sent two M1A1 tanks towing the destroyed M1A1 and M88 back to Al Qa'im with the fire support of an AC-130 gunship overhead.

From 11 through 14 May Stann continuously displayed zealous initiative and endurance as the fighter-leader of the Marines at the Ramana Bridge in the continuous 360-degree contact with the enemy. Determined to force his platoon off the bridge, insurgent fighters engaged him from south and east of his position and north of the river. Day and night, Stann controlled the effects of his organic fires and coordinated the RW/CAS and eight precision-guided munitions from fixed-wing attack aircraft to destroy enemy strongpoints in the urban sprawl surrounding his position. For their protection, he required his Marines to remain inside their armored vehicles while he continuously ran to their positions, inspecting their sectors of fire and maintaining their fighting spirit. And he supervised the EOD team in its placement of cratering charges to temporarily deny the enemy a viable avenue of approach for the SVBIED threat.

On 14 May Stann received the order to withdraw his platoon from the blocking position. Exhausted after four days of nearly continuous fighting and no sleep, Stann patiently navigated his unit, bypassing the still dangerous built-up area to safely return his Marines and equipment to Camp Al Qa'im. Stann succeeded in accomplishing the task force deception plan through his aggressive actions south of the Euphrates River. He drew the enemy's focus in the vicinity of Karabilah and limited the enemy's initiative and ability to act elsewhere. This provided freedom of action to Task Force North during its exploitation and withdrawal phases.

SILVER STAR MEDAL CITATION

The President of the United States of America takes pleasure in presenting the Silver Star to SECOND LIEUTENANT BRIAN MICHAEL STANN, United States Marine Corps, for conspicuous gallantry and intrepidity in action against the enemy as 2d Mobile Assault Platoon Leader, Weapons Company, 3d Battalion, 2d Marines, Regimental Combat Team 2, 2d Marine Division, II Marine Expeditionary Force Forward in support of Operation Iraqi Freedom 04–06 from 8 May to 14 May 2005. During Operation Matador, Second Lieutenant Stann led his reinforced platoon on an assault through a foreign fighter and mujahedeen insurgent defense-in-depth to seize the Ramana Bridge north of Karabilah, Iraq. On three separate occasions, he traversed four kilometers of enemy occupied urban terrain in order to maintain his battle position. With each deliberate attack he controlled close air support and the direct fire systems of tanks and heavy machineguns destroying enemy positions along the route. At one point, the enemy massed on his platoon and fired over 30 rocket propelled grenades, machineguns, detonated two improvised explosive devices and attacked the unit with three suicide vehicle borne improvised explosive devices. Second Lieutenant Stann personally directed two casualty evacuations, three vehicle recovery operations and multiple close air support missions under enemy small arms, machinegun and mortar fire in his 360-degree fight. Inspired by his leadership and endurance, Second Lieutenant Stann's platoon held the battle position on the Euphrates River for six days protecting the task force flank and isolating foreign fighters and insurgents north of the river. Second Lieutenant Stann's zealous initiative, courageous actions, and exceptional presence of mind reflected great credit upon himself and upheld the highest traditions of the Marine Corps and the United States Naval Service.

Information for this account is drawn from the U.S. Marine Corps "Award Summary of Action" (2005) and the Silver Star Medal Citation for Brian Michael Stann (2006).

CPL JONATHAN T. YALE

Weapons Company, 2nd Battalion, 8th Marines,
I Marine Expeditionary Force

home of record: Burkeville, Virginia

Awarded the Navy Cross, posthumously, for heroic actions
on 22 April 2008, Ramadi, Iraq

LCPL JORDAN C. HAERTER

Weapons Company, 1st Battalion, 9th Marines,
I Marine Expeditionary Force

home of record: Southampton, New York

Awarded the Navy Cross, posthumously, for heroic actions
on 22 April 2008, Ramadi, Iraq

Cpl Jonathan T. Yale and LCpl Jordan C. Haerter were standing post together when they were killed while saving the lives of their brothers. On 22 April 2008, Yale and Haerter showed extraordinary heroism while standing post in the guard tower of the entry control point (ECP) into Joint Security Station (JSS) Nasser of east Ramadi. The Marines posted at this ECP are responsible for controlling access into the coalition forces and Iraqi police (IP) compound, which consists of a vehicle and equipment storage lot and multiple buildings used for IP operations and administration as well as the garrison for the partnering Marines.

At approximately 0745 a suicide-truck-borne improvised explosive device (STBIED) entered the vehicle entry control lane and drove through the barrier plan toward the gate. Realizing the vehicle had no intention of stopping, Yale engaged the vehicle with his M249 squad automatic weapon while Haerter engaged the vehicle with his M4 carbine. As a result of their steady and precise fires, the truck rolled to a stop ten meters from the entry gate and detonated more than two thousand pounds of explosives, as determined by Weapons Intelligence Team 5 (Camp Ramadi). The blast completely destroyed the ECP and guard tower and mortally wounded both Yale and Haerter. The explosion also caused extensive damage to the JSS's command operations center and the exterior of several buildings in the immediate vicinity.

The heroic actions of Yale and Haerter prevented the STBIED from breaching the front gate of JSS Nasser and protected the lives of the fifty Marines and IP present at the station that day. Recognizing the danger to their fellow Marines and partnered IP, Yale and Haerter fearlessly gave their lives in defense of others.

The brave actions of these two Marines were later referenced in a speech given by Lt Gen John Kelly, USMC, to the Semper Fi Society of St. Louis, Missouri, on 13 November 2010. This was four days after his son, 1st Lt Robert Kelly, USMC, was killed by an improvised explosive device while on his third combat tour.* During his speech General Kelly spoke about the dedication and valor of the young men and women who step forward each and every day to protect us. During the speech, he never mentioned the loss of his own son. He closed the speech with the moving account of the last six seconds in the lives of two young Marines who died with rifles blazing to protect their brother Marines:

> I will leave you with a story about the kind of people they are . . . about the quality of the steel in their backs . . . about the kind of dedication they bring to our country while they serve in uniform and forever after as veterans. Two years ago when I was the Commander of all U.S. and Iraqi forces, in fact, the 22nd of April 2008, two Marine infantry battalions, 1/9 "The Walking Dead," and 2/8 were switching out in Ramadi; one battalion in the closing days of their deployment going home very soon, the other just starting its seven-month combat tour.

---

* 1st Lt Robert M. Kelly of the 3rd Battalion, 5th Marines, 1st Marine Division was awarded the Purple Heart for wounds received on 9 November 2010, Helmand Province, Afghanistan.

Two Marines, Corporal Jonathan Yale and Lance Corporal Jordan Haerter, 22 and 20 years old, respectively, one from each battalion, were assuming the watch together at the entrance gate of an outpost that contained a makeshift barracks housing 50 Marines. The same broken down ramshackle building was also home to 100 Iraqi police, also my men and our allies in the fight against the terrorists in Ramadi, a city until recently the most dangerous city on earth and owned by Al Qaeda.

Yale was a dirt-poor mixed-race kid from Virginia with a wife and daughter, and a mother and sister who lived with him and he supported as well. He did this on a yearly salary of less than $23,000.

Haerter, on the other hand, was a middle-class white kid from Long Island. They were from two completely different worlds. Had they not joined the Marines, they would never have met each other or understood that multiple Americas exist simultaneously depending on one's race, education level, economic status, and where you might have been born. But they were Marines, combat Marines, forged in the same crucible of Marine training, and because of this bond they were brothers as close, or closer, than if they were born of the same woman.

The mission orders they received from the sergeant squad leader I am sure went something like, "Okay, you two clowns, stand this post and let no unauthorized personnel or vehicles pass. You clear?" I am also sure Yale and Haerter then rolled their eyes and said in unison something like, "Yes, Sergeant," with just enough attitude that made the point without saying the words, "No kidding, sweetheart. We know what we're doing."

They then relieved two other Marines on watch and took up their post at the entry control point of Joint Security Station Nasser, in the Sophia section of Ramadi, Al Anbar, Iraq.

A few minutes later a large blue truck turned down the alley way—perhaps 60–70 yards in length—and sped its way through the serpentine of concrete jersey walls. The truck stopped just short of where the two were posted and detonated, killing them both catastrophically. Twenty-four brick masonry houses were damaged or destroyed. A mosque 100 yards away collapsed. The truck's engine came to rest two hundred yards away knocking most of a house down before it stopped. Our explosive experts reckoned the blast was made of 2,000 pounds of explosives.

Two died, and because these two young infantrymen didn't have it in their DNA to run from danger, they saved 150 of their Iraqi and American brothers-in-arms.

When I read the situation report about the incident a few hours after it happened, I called the regimental commander for details as something about this struck me as different. Marines dying or being seriously wounded is commonplace in combat. We expect Marines regardless of rank or MOS [military occupational specialty] to stand their ground and do their duty, and even die in the process, if that is what the mission takes. But this just seemed different. The regimental commander had just returned from the site and he agreed, but reported that there were no American witnesses to the event—just Iraqi police. I figured if there was any chance of finding out what actually happened and then to decorate the two Marines to acknowledge their bravery, I'd have to do it as a combat award that requires two eye witnesses, and we figured the bureaucrats back in Washington would never buy Iraqi statements. If it had any chance at all, it had to come under the signature of a general officer.

I traveled to Ramadi the next day and spoke individually to a half-dozen Iraqi police, all of whom told the same story. The blue truck turned down into the alley and immediately sped up as it made its way through the serpentine. They all said, "We knew immediately what was going on as soon as the two Marines began firing." The Iraqi police then related that some of them also fired, and then to a man, ran for safety just prior to the explosion.

All survived. Many were injured . . . some seriously. One of the Iraqis elaborated and with tears welling up said, "They'd run like any normal man would to save his life." What he didn't know until then, he said, and what he learned that very instant, was that Marines are not normal. Choking past the emotion he said, "Sir, in the name of God no sane man would have stood there and done what they did. No sane man. They saved us all."

What we didn't know at the time, and only learned a couple of days later after I wrote a summary and submitted both Yale and Haerter for posthumous Navy Crosses, was that one of our security cameras, damaged initially in the blast, recorded some of the suicide attack. It happened exactly as the Iraqis had described it. It took exactly six seconds from when the truck entered the alley until it detonated.

You can watch the last six seconds of their young lives. Putting myself in their heads, I supposed it took about a second for the two Marines to separately come to the same conclusion about what was going on once the truck came into their view at the far end of the alley. Exactly no time to talk it over, or call the sergeant to ask what they should do. Only enough time to take half an instant and think about what the sergeant told them to do only a few minutes before: " . . . let no unauthorized personnel or vehicles pass." The two Marines had about five seconds left to live.

It took maybe another two seconds for them to present their weapons, take aim, and open up. By this time the truck was half-way through the barriers and gaining speed the whole time. Here, the recording shows a number of Iraqi police, some of whom had fired their AKs, now scattering like the normal and rational men they were—some running right past the Marines. They had three seconds left to live.

For about two seconds more, the recording shows the Marines' weapons firing nonstop . . . the truck's windshield exploding into shards of glass as their rounds take it apart and tore into the body of the son-of-a-bitch who is trying to get past them to kill their brothers—American and Iraqi—bedded down in the barracks totally unaware of the fact that their lives at that moment depended entirely on two Marines standing their ground. If they had been aware, they would have known they were safe . . . because two Marines stood between them and a crazed suicide bomber. The recording shows the truck careening to a stop immediately in front of the two Marines. In all of the instantaneous violence, Yale and Haerter never hesitated. By all reports and by the recording, they never stepped back. They never even started to step aside. They never even shifted their weight. With their feet spread shoulder width apart, they leaned into the danger, firing as fast as they could work their weapons. They had only one second left to live. The truck explodes. The camera goes blank. Two young men go to their God. Six seconds. Not enough time to think about their families, their country, their flag, or about their lives or their deaths, but more than enough time for two very brave young men to do their duty . . . into eternity. Those are the kind of people who are on watch all over the world tonight—for you.

We Marines believe that God gave America the greatest gift he could bestow to man while he lived on this earth—freedom. We also believe he gave us another gift nearly as precious—our soldiers, sailors, airmen, Coast Guardsmen, and Marines—to safeguard that gift and guarantee no force on this earth can ever steal it away. It has been my distinct honor to have been with you here today. Rest assured our America, this experiment in democracy started over two centuries ago will forever remain the "land of the free and home of the brave" so long as we never run out of tough young Americans who are willing to look beyond their own self-interest and comfortable lives, and go into the darkest and most dangerous places on earth to hunt down, and kill, those who would do us harm.

God Bless America, and . . . SEMPER FIDELIS!

NAVY CROSS CITATION FOR CORPORAL YALE

The President of the United States of America takes pride in presenting the Navy Cross (posthumously) to CORPORAL JONATHAN T. YALE, United States Marine Corps, for extraordinary heroism while serving as an Anti-Tank Missileman, Mobile Assault Platoon 4, Weapons Company, Second Battalion, Eighth Marines, Regimental Combat Team 1, I Marine Expeditionary Force (Forward) in support of Operation Iraqi Freedom on 22 April 2008. While Corporal Yale and a fellow Marine manned a sentry post at the entry control point (ECP) for Joint Security Station Nasser in Ramadi, Iraq, a tank truck suddenly began to rapidly negotiate the serpentine concrete obstacles leading to the ECP. Corporal Yale and his fellow Marine quickly recognized the threat of a suicide bomber driving a truck capable of carrying a large quantity of explosives and posing a major threat to the more than 50 Marines and Iraqi policemen in the Joint Security Station. Corporal Yale immediately engaged the truck with precise fire from his M249 squad automatic weapon, while his fellow Marine opened fire with his M4 rifle. Ignoring the grave personal risk, Corporal Yale and his fellow Marine continued their accurate fires, stopping the truck a few feet from their positions. At that instant the suicide bomber detonated approximately 2,000 pounds of explosives contained in the truck, leveling the ECP and mortally wounding Corporal Yale. The courageous actions of Corporal Yale in resolutely defending his post against an imminent threat undoubtedly helped save the lives of more than 50 Marines and Iraqi policemen at Joint Security Station Nasser that day. By his outstanding display of decisive leadership, courageous actions and total devotion to duty, Corporal Yale reflected great credit upon himself and upheld the highest traditions of the Marine Corps and the United States Naval Service.

NAVY CROSS CITATION FOR LANCE CORPORAL HAERTER

The President of the United States of America takes pride in presenting the Navy Cross (posthumously) to LANCE CORPORAL JORDAN C. HAERTER, United States Marine Corps, for extraordinary heroism while serving as a Rifleman, 3d Platoon, Weapons Company, First Battalion, Ninth Marines, Regimental Combat Team 1, I Marine Expeditionary Force (Forward) in support of Operation Iraqi Freedom on 22 April 2008. While Lance Corporal Haerter and a fellow Marine manned a sentry post at the Entry Control Point (ECP) for Joint Security Station Nasser in Ramadi, Iraq, a tank truck suddenly began to rapidly negotiate the serpentine concrete obstacles leading to the ECP. Lance Corporal Haerter and his fellow Marine quickly recognized the threat of a suicide bomber driving a truck capable of carrying a large quantity of explosives and posing a major threat to the more than 50 Marines and Iraqi policemen in the Joint Security Station. Lance Corporal Haerter immediately engaged the truck with precise fire from his M4 rifle, while his fellow Marine opened fire with his M249 squad automatic weapon. Ignoring the grave personal risk, Lance Corporal Haerter and his fellow Marine continued their accurate fires, stopping the truck a few feet from their positions. At that instant the suicide bomber detonated approximately 2,000 pounds of explosives contained in the truck, leveling the ECP and mortally wounding Lance Corporal Haerter. The courageous actions of Lance Corporal Haerter in resolutely defending his post against an imminent threat undoubtedly helped save the lives of more than 50 Marines and Iraqi policemen at Joint Security Station Nasser that day. By his outstanding display of decisive leadership, courageous actions and total devotion to duty, Lance Corporal Haerter reflected great credit upon himself and upheld the highest traditions of the Marine Corps and the United States Naval Service.

Information for this account (excluding Lt Gen John Kelly's speech) is drawn from the U.S. Marine Corps "Award Summary of Action" (2008) and the Navy Cross Medal Citation for Jordan C. Haerter (2010), and from the U.S. Marine Corps "Award Summary of Action" (2008) and the Navy Cross Medal Citation for Jonathan T. Yale (2010).

I am grateful to LtGen John Kelly for granting permission to include the text of his 13 November 2010 speech here.

CASUALTY ASSISTANCE CALLS OFFICERS

CPL JOHN R. STALVEY

Scout Sniper Platoon, 3rd Battalion, 6th Marines

home of record: Brunswick, Georgia

Awarded the Purple Heart Medal
after being killed in action
3 October 2005, Karabilah, Iraq

I have made multiple combat tours and I have been shot at, bombed, Rpged, and so on, but none of the sensations I have felt in combat compare to the fear I felt when traveling on a CACO call. The CACO is the casualty assistance calls officer assigned by Headquarters Marine Corps for active-duty deaths of Marines. Although I was brought up Catholic and attended a Catholic school, I have never been as religious as I was on my way to inform Cpl John Stalvey's family of his death in combat. I prayed almost constantly during the almost ninety-minute ride to Brunswick, Georgia, from Savannah.

At about 0900 on 3 October 2005 my most terrifying combat mission began. I received a call from Headquarters Marine Corps casualty branch. They informed me that I would be the CACO for the family of Cpl John R. Stalvey from the 3rd Battalion, 6th Marines' Scout Sniper Platoon. At 1000 our CACO team departed Savannah for Brunswick, Georgia. While en route to the Stalvey residence, we called the Glynn County police for assistance. We linked up with the patrol vehicle at 1145 and briefed the officer on our requirements. At 1205 we arrived at Crystal Merillat's (John's mother) house. When we were approaching the front door, her daughter Cristen pulled up in her car. As she passed us, I confirmed the name of the resident. We stepped into the living room and Cristen called to her mother. When Crystal saw us standing in her house, she knew her son was dead. I was unable to give my canned speech as taught. After a few minutes of Crystal and Cristen hugging and crying, I asked them to sit down so I could explain the circumstances behind Stalvey's death.

I told them that he had been killed at about 0540 local time by an improvised explosive device (IED). Stalvey was the driver of a highly mobile multiwheeled vehicle. The other three Marines in the vehicle were all injured, but I had no specific details on their injuries.

At 1315 we called Stalvey's father's workplace and coordinated with his supervisor to make notification. The local police escorted the CACO team to the Gulf Stream Aerospace Corporation in order to notify Stalvey's father, William "Billy" Stalvey. At 1325 I made notification. Peter, Billy's supervisor, informed us that we could leave and he would take care of Billy. We then returned to Savannah.

On 4 October from 0700 until 0940, I coordinated with multiple agencies. At 1100 our administrations chief and I arrived at Crystal's house to meet with the family and fill out administrative paperwork. Crystal asked about Stalvey's "hog's tooth." A hog's tooth is actually a bullet given to scout sniper students right before they graduate; they wear them around their necks on a cord. I explained that she may never see it again, and then I gave her my hog's tooth from around my neck. At 1730 we departed the house and continued coordination until 2100.

On 5 October the CACO team conducted coordination duties from 0530 to 1100. At 1230 I arrived in Brunswick to complete paperwork and visit with the family. The family treated me as if they had known me forever and requested that I give a speech at the funeral; I was honored. At 2130 I received a call from the mortuary affairs representative at Dover Air Base with information that Stalvey's remains had arrived. I immediately called the family with news of the arrival.

The next day began much like the previous: CACO coordination from 0530 to 1100. At 1230 I presented Stalvey's Purple Heart to John's mother and visited with the family. Again the family treated the CACO team like part of the family. They even apologized for the CACO team having to go through the ordeal with them.

But there was bad news. At 1730 I received a call from Dover telling me that Stalvey's remains were not complete; the explosion had separated some parts from his body, and without a signature on the disposition document, the remains would not be released. At 1830 I explained to the family that some remains were not recovered. The mother and father agreed to receive the body with missing body parts. The Dover rep informed me that remains could be in by early afternoon the next day. I arrived in Savannah and made phone calls to inspector/instructor (I&I) staff to be on standby for pick-up of remains.

On 7 October I conducted coordination until 1100, when I headed back to Brunswick. At 1630 the family and I&I staff left Stalvey's house for the funeral home. At 1930 the Georgia state patrol provided an escort from the funeral home to the Florida border. At 2030 the Florida troopers continued the escort to Jacksonville Airport. At 2100 we arrived at the airport. The plane was delayed multiple times. I apologized to the Florida state trooper for all of the delays, and he replied, "I retired from the Army with twenty-six years of service. I will not leave my brother behind." This statement floored me. Later I found out the trooper stayed on duty for hours after his shift to honor Stalvey. What a great patriot.

At 2400 our convoy moved to the cargo security area for vehicle searches. On 8 October at 0040, the plane pulled into the skyway. At 0100 Stalvey's remains were unloaded by ceremonial detail while the family watched from the tarmac. At 0130 the Florida trooper escorted us to the Georgia border. At 0200 the Georgia state police picked up the escort all the way to the funeral home. Once in Glynn County three county police cars joined the escort and we arrived at the funeral home at 0310. The ceremonial detail moved Stalvey's remains into the funeral home. At 0400 the I&I staff and I headed back to Savannah.

On 9 October coordination continued until 1430, when I arrived at John's house to visit with the family. At 1600 we coordinated with the funeral director for viewing procedures, and Sgt Michael Kudro, who escorted Stalvey from Dover to Jacksonville, had Crystal sign for the only item to return with Stalvey's remains, his hog's tooth. At 1630 the I&I Marines began honor guard duty at the front doors of the funeral home, at the memorial guest book, and at the casket, keeping fifteen-minute rotations. One guard was dressed in a Ghillie suit (sniper uniform) to honor Stalvey's sniper military occupational specialty. At 2100 the viewing ended and the team headed back to Savannah.

On 10 October at 0700 the funeral details for Savannah and Beaufort Marine Corps Air Station moved to Brunswick. At 0910 we conducted final rehearsals and coordination at Faith Baptist Church. At 1000 the funeral began.

I have given speeches around the world and to very large and diverse crowds. I do not get nervous when giving speeches, but this day was different. This was not a speech; I was eulogizing a fallen warrior. When I stepped up to the podium I just stood there, unable to speak—for how long I do not know. I remember yelling at myself in my mind to speak, just speak. Below are excerpts from my speech at the funeral.

CACO SPEECH

It is truly my honor to be chosen as a speaker at this funeral for Cpl John R. Stalvey. On day one they hated me and I wanted to just disappear. On day two they disliked me very much. On day three they treated me like I was a long-time friend of the family.

This is a great American family: Crystal, thank you for the stories about John, your faith in me, and your understanding. Billy, thank you for your strength and understanding. Matthew, thank you for all of the stories about John. Cristen, thank you for the stories and of course the cookies and milk. Lauren, thank you for all of the stories in the airport and for making me understand the many similarities between John and me (eye of the tiger). AP, you have been my sounding board and guiding light; thank you, sir.

We are not only here to mourn John's death; we are here to honor his memory and celebrate his life. John died knowing love: the love of his family and friends. John was also honored by the police officers that escorted us on Friday night, and by the airport personnel that saluted him or had their hands over their hearts when John came off of the plane.

I do not apologize for any tears because warriors weep at funerals; John has earned our tears. Corporal John R. Stalvey has been called names in the last week: Marine, Corporal, Warrior, Hero, Scout Sniper, but I think the most fitting is Guardian Angel! John became a scout sniper because while he was conducting combat operations in Afghanistan he saw that the scout snipers were always there to protect the infantry and he wanted to be a guardian angel for the war-fighters. There are three kinds of people in the world: Sheep, most of society; Wolves, who prey on the Sheep; and Sheepdogs, the protectors of the Sheep. John was certainly a Sheepdog. He cared more about others than he cared about himself.

John died a warrior's death. People die every day due to DUI, car accidents, disease, etc. John will from this day on be known as our Guardian Angel. When someone gives his life for your life, you must not waste it. Let me say that again: If someone buys your life at the price of his life, *you do not dare waste it*. Your moral, sacred responsibility is to lead the fullest, richest, best life you can. Although I never met John, I feel as if I knew him. He was not only my fellow warrior and Marine; he was a Marine Scout Sniper and my brother in arms.

Irony:

— I, the CACO, I am also a Marine Scout Sniper.
— The vault John will be buried in was donated by a former Marine.
— Georgia State Police officer was a corporal.
— The Florida state trooper had spent twenty-six years in the army, but always loved Marines (he stayed with us for over five hours on his own time).
— The weather was terrible almost right up until John's plane landed.
— We were led over the tarmac by a former Marine corporal.
— As we were cruising along at 85 mph to the funeral home I noticed we were on the Purple Heart Highway.

— One of the police officers escorting us into the
funeral home was John's cousin.

This is just to name a few!

John 15:13: "Greater love has no man than this: that he
give his life for his friends."

Lord, please bless John and all of us on this memorable
day.

Semper Fidelis, John; you are still our Guardian Angel.

At 1130 the service was complete, and Stalvey's casket was
removed from the church and placed in a limousine by the
Beaufort funeral detail. At 1220 the family arrived at the cemetery with a police escort. Marines lined the road with an honor
detail on the street entering the cemetery. Another honor detail
was at the gravesite.

At 1230 the graveside ceremony began. The preacher gave
a short speech and then turned the service over to the Marines:
21-gun salute (3 volleys of seven rifles); "Taps" (played by the
Marine wearing the Ghillie suit); single shot fired by scout
sniper as flags were being handed to presenters; simultaneous
American flag presentations to Stalvey's mother and father. The
I&I staff decided to give a third flag to John's girlfriend. All the
Marines attended the reception.

On 6 May 2006 we held a gravesite memorial service, this
time to help the 3/6 Scout Sniper Platoon with closure. Even
in 2011, almost six years after John's death, I still heard from
family members by e-mail. Following are some significant
letters:

Mr and Mrs Stalvey,
My name is Sgt Hunter Sorrells. John was a dear friend
and one of the finest Marines that I have ever met. John was
one of the first people I met after boot camp in School of
Infantry. I can remember praying that I would meet some
good solid Christian men in the Corps and was worried
that that would not happen when your son came up and

introduced himself to me. John's friendship was something that is very dear to me, and myself and Sgt Jeremy Riddle thought that John would make a great addition to our Sniper Plt. He was an immediate success with the senior Marines and juniors in our ranks. It is a great loss not only to yourselves, the Marine Corps, and our platoon but to the Sniper community as a whole. John's memory will burn forever in all of our memories.

John was an usher and part of the sword detail in my wedding back in April. My wife and I will remember him standing so proudly among the other NCOs for the arch swords. John was a devout follower of Christ and an amazing young man and there is no doubt that he is sitting at the right hand of our lord at this moment praying for a sense of peace to fall over us all. You should be proud of your son. He made a huge impact on everyone's life that he was able to touch and for this I am eternally grateful . . .

Yours truly
Sgt Hunter Sorrells

Dear First Sergeant Devaney,

Crystal told me that you had another CACO assignment. We were all crushed, thinking of what you will have to go through again. Steffani just let me know that it is a wife, 7 months pregnant with a little boy. My heart has broken all over again.

I just wanted to remind you that "pain shared is pain divided." Remember when you are making the lonely drives to and from this precious wife's home, we are with you in spirit. Please tell her that another Marine family grieves deeply with her. It's funny, since John has died, every Marine I see, I feel we are somehow connected. I've had to restrain myself from walking up and hugging these complete strangers.

I also wanted to share this with you: In one of your letters to Crystal and her kids, you mentioned that you wondered if we thought you were unprofessional because you couldn't contain your emotions. Well, to be perfectly honest with you, it was your compassion and concern that won us over. Somehow, knowing that you and Officer Dempsey shared in our pain, made it easier. Words are cheap but your "emotions" were true and genuine. Please know that your presence as a Marine was not compromised in any way. You are the Marine that John would have become most like.

I know you're swamped with work. I apologize for the long email. I wanted to just let you know that we are praying for you. I'm glad to hear Nit is better. We would love to meet her one-day. You should have received your copy of the letter I wrote to President Bush. I meant every word. Thank you again for taking such great care of my sister and Matt and Cristen. Remember that you and Officer Dempsey are part of our family now. Please let us know how we can help.

Sincerely,
Melinda Merillat [Stalvey's aunt]

Dear GySgt Reidsma,

My name is Crystal Merillat and I am the very proud Mom of Cpl John Stalvey. I am writing because 1st Sgt David Devaney forwarded me the e-mail from you about your recommendation to dedicate the main schoolhouse building for the scout snipers to John. I know that it is uncertain as to if [it] will happen but I just wanted to say "THANK YOU" for what you have done. Wow, this is such an honor! When I read the E-mail, I was stunned for a moment to think that someone would want to do this and at the same time I was so proud of John.

During the time John was in Afghanistan, it became his dream to be a Scout Sniper and "Guardian Angel" to his fellow marines. When he told us of the news that he had been accepted into Sniper School, he was so excited and everyday was to prepare until time to go. My son, daughter and myself visited with him one weekend when he was back at Camp LeJeune. The whole weekend we heard stories of Sniper training. According to him it was the greatest thing in the world and I had no doubt that he would make it. He spoke very highly of you and his other instructors. After graduation, he came home for a visit and he was telling me about the meaning of the hogs tooth that he so proudly wore around his neck. It was funny because I just wasn't getting it at first and we laughed about my interpretation of it. Now he couldn't wait to go to Iraq as a Sniper. He had lived his dream and for that I am thankful.

We were sitting at the table a couple of days after John's death with 1st Sgt Devaney finalizing all the paperwork and I told him that if there were anything that I would hope would come back from Iraq, it would be his hogs tooth. He of course didn't know and he took the one he was wearing from his neck and gave it to me. I then placed it in my son's hand. Later when John's body arrived with his escort, Sgt Eric Kudro, 1st Sgt Devaney told me that one thing had come back with his body and that was his HOGSTOOTH. I will always cherish it.

I just want to say Thank You for what you are doing to train our future snipers and for your service to our country. I know that John was very proud to serve with you and all his Marine Corps brothers.

Sincerely,
Crystal Merillat

Hello 1st Sgt (David)!

Just wanted to drop you a line, got off the phone with the folks in Georgia just now, and they told me how much they appreciate you keeping up with them, your messages, thoughts and concerns, etc.

I am saddened to hear of your new CACO assignment. Melinda told me that a young wife and mother of two have been left to grieve. Please convey to that family my sincere and deepest sympathy and condolences. Most people can't say, "I know how you feel" and mean it. Our family can, although our relationship to John was different than husband and wife, of course. But I lost a young man as close to me as my own son—I drove him to the recruiter's office, a move that ended up in his death, so I have a special connection to the loss. But, I promise you, I will pray for that young widow and her family. There is much for her to face, as you know, and we all are aware of the fact that you have a tremendous responsibility on your shoulders to try and comfort and support that family of a fallen patriot. God bless you and give you strength and wisdom in this new assignment.

Thank you, 1st Sgt, for what you've done in my own life by your example and fortitude. Thank you for your kindness, thank you for your compassion, thank you for your sincerity, thank you for giving of yourself to strangers, thank you for being used by Almighty God to help people who hurt. I will never forget you, sir. I treasure the book you gave me, as well as the "hog's tooth"—I wear it every day, and will do so until God calls me home. I've had the opportunity to write several editorial-type pieces as a result of our tragedy, and I hope that hearts have been touched and people lifted up and encouraged by them. God bless the USMC. Semper Fi, my friend.

A. P. Merillat

24 October 2005

Dear Crystal,

I have been writing this letter for a couple of weeks now. I just can't put into words how I feel about you and your family. I hoped I would never be called upon to be a CACO, but on the 3rd of October that is exactly how my Monday started. When I received the call, my heart started racing; how could I look a mother in the eyes and tell her that her son was killed? It was a lonely ride for me, even though I was with three other Marines in the van. I was praying that the good Lord would allow me to be compassionate and professional.

When I saw your face and you saw mine, we were both crushed with pain and sorrow. I felt your pain more than you could ever know. This has been the most emotional event of my life. I would rather be back in combat than have to ever be a CACO again. I have never shed so many tears before; I even found tears in my eyes as I took that lonely ride to Brunswick each day.

You made my job easier, yet harder. You made my job easier because I enjoyed being around all of you and I loved helping in every way I could. Every day my mind raced, trying to think of what I could do to ease your pain and honor John. Honoring John was easy. He was a Marine, a scout sniper and my brother warrior. My job was harder because I became emotionally attached to you and your entire family. I am stronger because of you; thank you. I can't help thinking that I made things harder on you because I was so emotional. I tried so hard to read John's Purple Heart Citation like a professional warrior, but I had much trouble getting the words out of my mouth. I have been accused of not having any feelings for any other human being; it is my environment.

I will never forget you and I thank you for treating me like I was a part of your family. I will never forget how you held my arm so tightly when John's casket came off of the plane, or when we stood outside the church; it made me proud. I felt as if I were your Guardian Angel, at least for those moments in time. I was on an emotional roller coaster and could feel all of your pain. "Pain shared is pain divided."

You amazed me with your strength. When I saw you move to Matthew, when he was in so much pain, I was moved. His pain was more important than your own. Each time a family member needed help, you thought of them before yourself. You even apologized to me, because you felt bad for me, having to be the CACO. You again amazed all of my Marines and me when after the viewing, you presented each of us with the two poems; mine are proudly displayed in my office right now. I am still touched and honored that you allowed me to speak at John's funeral. I give public speeches all the time, but this was different. I was unable to speak at first. I said many prayers, asking God to help me give a good speech in honor of your son and my brother, John. I hope I did well! (John 15:13: "Greater love has no man than this: that he give his life for his friends." "John is still our Guardian Angel.")

Crystal, please know that John was an outstanding Marine and a great warrior. John died for his country; he was a true patriot and our guardian angel. Please accept my condolences.

Love, David K. Devaney
First Sergeant USMC

This account is drawn from my CACO event chronology. I am grateful to A. P. Merillat, Crystal Merillat, Melinda Merillat, and Hunter Sorrells for granting me permission to include their e-mails here.

SSGT JOEL P. DAMERON

Explosive Ordnance Detachment, 8th Engineer Support
Battalion, 2nd Force Service Support Group,
II Marine Expeditionary Force

home of record: Ellabell, Georgia

Awarded the Bronze Star Medal with Combat
Distinguishing Device "V," posthumously, for heroism on
30 October 2005, Amiriyah, Iraq

Just days after completing the main portion of my casualty assistance calls officer (CACO) work with the services for Cpl John R. Stalvey, I received my second Operation Iraqi Freedom CACO call. I had just returned home from a run, and my wife told me that Headquarters Marine Corps (HQMC) had called with a CACO call, this time for Joel Dameron, who had been killed by an improvised explosive device. I remember pacing in circles and telling my wife, "I cannot do this anymore." She stopped me right there and said, "You have to, Baby, no one else can do it better than you."

On 30 October 2005 at 1700, the HQMC casualty branch called my government phone with a CACO call. I was to be the CACO for the parents, but I was relieved that I was not the CACO for the wife; she lived at Camp Lejeune, North Carolina. My CACO team departed for his parents' house at 1800. When I stepped out of the vehicle, Dameron's father asked, "Which one is it?" I was baffled. He informed me that Joel's brother was with the 26th Marine Expeditionary Unit, and he was also in Iraq. He then informed us that he was separated from Joel's mother and gave us directions to her house. Escorted by a Georgia state trooper, we arrived at her house at 2040. During the notification, Joel's mother showed me a photo of a lovely young lady, Dameron's wife. I selfishly thought, *Thank God I do not have to make notification to her*. We returned to the reserve center in Savannah at 2330. At 2400 personnel at HQMC were informed that Dameron's wife, Logyn, was at her father's house in Pembroke, Georgia. While I was at home taking a shower, HQMC called again to order me to make notification to Logyn, who was seven months pregnant.

At 0045 on 31 October, I recalled the CACO team, this time including our Navy hospital corpsman due to Dameron's wife's pregnancy. I made notification to Logyn in the early hours of the morning, while her young son held onto her and said, "What is wrong, Mommy?" I felt as low as low could go!

Over the next several days I coordinated events and visited with the family. On 4 November I learned that Dameron's body was not complete; therefore, I had to get consent from Logyn to receive Dameron's remains incomplete. Just after the Marine Corps Birthday Ball that night, I received a call from HQMC informing me that Dameron's remains would arrive in Jacksonville, Florida, the next day.

On 5 November the CACO team met at the funeral home in advance of the Purple Heart presentation. A Bryan County sheriff's deputy and a Georgia state trooper escorted us to the Florida state border for our drive to Jacksonville to escort Dameron's remains to the funeral home. We had a planeside ceremony as Dameron was taken off the plane, and then we departed for Georgia. As we crossed the state line, the Florida trooper passed us at a high rate of speed. Ahead on I-95, I saw the Florida trooper standing on the side of the road saluting, and a Georgia Bureau of Investigation bomb squad truck joined our convoy.

On 6 and 7 November we conducted rehearsals for the funeral, and the visitation was held that evening. During the entire visitation, we kept honor guards at the front doors and at the registration book, and another guard at the casket.

The funeral was held on 8 November at 1500. The church was completely filled with friends, family members, and many Marines and other service members. After the funeral the Marines left for the cemetery and lined themselves up every few meters; they saluted the flag-draped casket as it went by, and then they formed into a platoon and marched to the gravesite. The graveside ceremony began at 1615: prayers, 21-gun salute, "Taps" with live bugler, and a dual flag presentation—one to Logyn and one to Dameron's mother.

On 6 January 2006 the rest of Dameron's remains arrived at the Savannah airport. As I walked through the airport with the urn, I was amazed by all the people who stopped to put their hands over their hearts in respect for Dameron. As we departed the airport, I noticed a young soldier from the 3d Infantry Division saluting while tears rolled down his face; that is respect. We held a very small graveside ceremony on 10 January to bury the cremated remains at the base of Dameron's casket.

Below is a summary of Dameron's actions for which he was awarded the Bronze Star Medal with Combat Distinguishing Device "V."

While assigned as part of an explosive ordnance disposal (EOD) detachment in support of Regimental Combat Team (RCT) 7, stationed in Al Asad, Iraq, from 1 September to 28 October 2004, SSgt Joel P. Dameron demonstrated exceptional performance in neutralizing explosive hazards to the friendly forces in the area. Supporting and responding to various emergency response calls including unexploded ordnance (UXO), improvised explosive devices (IEDs), and operations that played a key role in reducing the threat of hostile enemy insurgents within the area, Dameron responded to 15 emergency response calls resulting in the destruction of 13 IEDs and more than 523 UXO items.

On 15 October 2004, for operations against terrorist insurgents in Hit, Dameron assisted in locating and rendering safe eight IEDs consisting of thirty high-explosive artillery projectiles hidden along alternate supply route Golden. While responding to a forward element of 1/8 that had found an IED, EOD technicians identified another IED located at a chokepoint for vehicle and foot traffic. Dameron stopped the EOD vehicle in front of the IED and directed the security vehicles back from the intended trap. Dameron then assisted in manually disarming the IED, tracing out the command wires and disconnecting them from the cordless phone base station used as the firing device. After ensuring the device was rendered safe, Dameron started a sweep for secondary devices. During this sweep, he located yet another device hidden in a trash pile. The second device was apparently set up to target EOD technicians working on the first IED and was pointing in their direction. Without the use of remote devices, and at great personal risk, Dameron quickly located the arming wires and rendered the device safe before any harm could befall his fellow Marines.

On the same day, while waiting in a supposed safe area for an IED to be destroyed, Dameron discovered a set of wires running out of the road ten feet behind the EOD team. Without regard for his personal safety and just seconds before a controlled detonation, Dameron ran to the IED and manually disconnected the device before diving back to the safety behind his own vehicle just as the controlled detonation sent fragments of metal flying past him. Dameron put his personal safety at risk several times by quickly responding to disarm IEDs located within an established safe area. Because of the urgent need to disarm these devices and protect Marines in the immediate vicinity, Dameron had to operate without the aid of any remote means several times. The fact that no Marines were harmed by IEDs during this operation reflects directly on Dameron's heroic actions and keen devotion to duty.

While in support of RCT-1 Operation Al Fajr (the siege of Fallujah, from 8 through 30 November 2004, Dameron assisted the EOD effort in destroying or rendering safe 518 IEDs, discovering and clearing 3 IED manufacturing houses, and destroying 60 caches consisting of 25,024 pieces of ordnance. Dameron also played a vital role in clearing 2 bridges that proved to be key terrain for RCT-1. These actions were all accomplished under hostile fire and compressed timelines. The fact that it was done without injury to any Marines from RCT-1 stands as testimony to his superior skill, training, professionalism, and valor. His selfless actions decisively impacted the safety and mobility of RCT-1 and directly contributed to the overall accomplishment of the mission.

Returning to Iraq to serve his second tour in support of Operation Iraqi Freedom, Dameron served as an EOD technician in direct support of RCT-8 in Camp Fallujah. Dameron was instrumental in preparing all Fallujah EOD teams for the mission at hand. With his wealth of knowledge and experience, he was continuously assigned new and inexperienced team members, both junior and senior to him, to train and develop while operating in this high operational tempo environment. He maintained a flawless record of mission accomplishment with no injuries to any of his team members. While supporting RCT-8, Dameron rendered safe forty-four IEDs, and eight vehicle-borne IEDs, prosecuted and destroyed twenty-one enemy weapons caches, and conducted six postblast investigations. All of these accomplishments were achieved when he was a sergeant; he was posthumously promoted to staff sergeant.

Bronze Star Medal with Combat Distinguishing Device "V" Citation

For heroic achievement in connection with combat operations against the enemy while serving as Technician, Explosive Ordnance Disposal Platoon, Combat Service Support Battalion-1, 1st Force Service Support Group (Forward), I Marine Expeditionary Force (Forward) from September 2004 to February 2005, and as Technician, Explosive Ordnance Disposal Company, 8th Engineer Support Battalion, 2d Force Service Support Group (Forward), II Marine Expeditionary Force (Forward) from September 2005 to October 2005 in support of Operation Iraqi Freedom 04–06. Throughout this period, STAFF SERGEANT DAMERON's superior technical skill, determination, and thorough understanding of enemy tactics, techniques, and procedures proved critical as he successfully accomplished hundreds of explosive ordnance disposal missions involving the recovery and disposal of numerous improvised explosive devices. On numerous occasions, during more routine explosive ordnance disposal operations as well as during the high intensity Operation Al Fajr, he selflessly and knowingly exposed himself to great personal risk by conducting very dangerous manual disruptions of improvised explosive devices in order to protect those around him and provide for their mobility in offensive operations. Staff Sergeant Dameron's selfless, heroic actions ensured the safety of his fellow Marines during intense combat operations against insurgent forces. His valorous actions continued throughout until 30 October 2005 when, while on patrol, he made the ultimate sacrifice and gallantly gave his life for his country. Staff Sergeant Dameron's total effectiveness, forceful leadership, and loyal devotion to duty reflected great credit upon him and upheld the highest traditions of the Marine Corps and the United States Naval Service.

Information for this account is drawn from the U.S. Marine Corps "Award Summary of Action" (2005) and the Bronze Star Medal Citation for Joel P. Dameron (2005), and from my own CACO event chronology log (2005).

AFGHANISTAN

GYSGT BRIAN M. BLONDER

Force Reconnaissance Platoon attached to 2nd Battalion, 7th Marines, 1st Marine Division

home of record: Deer Beach, Florida

Awarded the Navy Cross for heroic actions on 8 August 2008, Shewan City, Bala Baluk District, Afghanistan

In the late 1990s I was the chief instructor of the III Marine Expeditionary Force Special Operations Training Group's reconnaissance and surveillance course. I had the pleasure of meeting and training a very quiet but proficient young Marine named Brian Blonder. Just days after receiving the Navy Cross, he came to Weapons Training Battalion to shoot some rounds from our weapons. After shooting he went to the Scout Sniper Instructor School to give a speech. It was one of the best speeches I have ever heard at the school. It is always good when we can get a combat veteran scout sniper to speak to our students. Not only is Gunnery Sergeant Blonder a war hero, but he is also an amazing leader. His words to the scout sniper students were very powerful. Although almost every student we have at our scout sniper school is a combat veteran, Blonder was able to get through to these warriors. He is a soft-spoken man, but he speaks with incredible power. During his speech he spoke of the importance of understanding that scout snipers are a combat support unit, and of the importance of not forgetting that we support the infantryman, not the other way around. Scout snipers have long had an elitist reputation that rubs some people the wrong way. He reminded the students that they are not special, but that their mission is. Most important, he reminded the students that being "too cool for school" is a good way to upset their leadership, which causes many problems. "Do your job and be proud, but do not flaunt it."

On 8 August 2008 Blonder successfully reduced a major Taliban stronghold during an eight-hour battle against a numerically superior force, thus opening a major supply route to coalition forces that had previously been under complete control of the Taliban. The city of Shewan has historically been a Taliban safe haven used to plan and stage attacks on coalition forces in the Bala Baluk district. Shewan was home to several of the major insurgent leaders in the battalion area of operations and housed approximately 250 full-time fighters serving under the leadership of at least 8 mid-level Taliban commanders. Several forces had attempted to enter the village in order to open up Route 517 to coalition convoys, but many of these attempts were repelled and resulted in numerous friendly deaths and casualties. Enemy control over Route 517 isolated coalition and Afghan national forces in the city of Farah from the rest of the district, dramatically restricting coalition and Afghan forces' ability to accomplish their mission. The provincial governor of Farah deemed the security of Route 517 his highest priority. It has been opened to coalition convoys since the battle for Shewan due to Blonder's decisive leadership and his keen tactical direction of his platoon in closing with and destroying Taliban forces.

Blonder's unit was conducting a deliberate clearing operation of the city of Shewan when a 4-man enemy rocket-propelled grenade (RPG) team ambushed the platoon. The RPG traveled between 2 highly mobile multiwheeled vehicles (HMMWV) about 50 meters away. Blonder scanned for the rocket's point of origin and was able to identify 3 enemy fighters attempting to ambush the vehicle element of the platoon with RPG and PK (Russian-made medium machine gun) fire. He directed the platoon's machine gunners to fix the enemy with their fire while he maneuvered with a team to destroy them. As he bounded toward the enemy, he was able to observe one of the RPG gunners aiming his weapon at an HMMWV approximately 150 meters away. Blonder fired 2 rounds from his M4 from the standing, killing the RPG gunner with a single round to the head before the enemy combatant could fire. Surprised and confused at the platoon's coordinated attack, the remainder of the RPG team broke from its position and stopped fighting. Blonder continued to bound with a team toward the enemy, driving the remainder of the RPG team to the west toward another team that was waiting for them. The 2 teams were able to kill an additional 2 fighters. Blonder's superior marksmanship, quick thinking, and decisive action stopped the enemy's attempt to ambush the platoon and thus kill or wound any Marines.

At this point in the battle sounds of machine-gun fire and explosions indicated that Company G's 2nd Platoon (Golf 2) was in contact. The platoon quickly moved to link up with Golf 2 when Blonder observed an RPG gunner engage the platoon from two hundred meters to the north of his HMMWV. He dismounted from his vehicle and chased the enemy fighter sixty meters to the north until he came under accurate and controlled alternating fire from at least two medium machine guns. He dropped to a knee but was forced into a prone position because of the heavy volume of fire. Enemy fire continued to impact within a foot of his position as he crawled behind a foot-high piece of microterrain. While still receiving extremely accurate small-arms and continuous medium machine-gun fire, Blonder moved forward in alternating bounds with his battle buddy into a shallow irrigation ditch. He attempted to move east through the trench in order to conduct a flanking attack on the enemy, but the trench petered out into an open, flat cemetery, and he was forced to withdraw back into the trench. Mounted and dismounted elements of the platoon attempted to flank the enemy to relieve pressure on Blonder and the rest of the dismounts, but these attempts were repelled, and an HMMWV was destroyed in the process as more and more enemy fighters and machine-gun positions revealed themselves. The crew of the downed vehicle immediately dismounted and began taking heavy grazing fire from the tree line.

They were in an extremely vulnerable and exposed position, trapped behind microterrain next to a burning vehicle in an open field two hundred meters away from a prepared enemy defense and were unable to escape. The enemy had drawn the platoon into the two-hundred-foot-wide frontage of a well-prepared enemy defense with numerous fighting positions built into a series of irrigation trenches that ran through a tree line. These positions were mutually supporting and had interlocking fields of fire. Blonder continued to suppress the enemy positions to his north until the Marines in the kill zone had been recovered and the platoon used close-air support to suppress the enemy positions and withdraw from the trenches. Blonder attempted to raise the platoon commander on the radio, but one of the handsets in the burning vehicle was keyed and was effectively jamming all communications. He was unable to see anything from his position in the irrigation ditch, so he stood up, disregarding the enemy fire that was impacting around him. Blonder exposed himself to heavy enemy machine-gun and RPG fire at great risk to his own personal safety in order to coordinate individual Marines' suppression of the enemy trench system that was pinning down the Marines in the kill zone. Blonder's quick thinking and decisive action enabled the platoon to effectively focus its fire and suppress the enemy fighting positions engaging the Marines in the kill zone.

After Blonder unsuccessfully attempted to raise the vehicles outside of the kill zone, he ran more than fifty meters under fire to the closest vehicle and directed the movement of the platoon's seven-ton truck to act as an armored screen to facilitate the withdrawal of the Marines still pinned down in the irrigation ditch. He did so under sustained enemy machine-gun and RPG fire with total disregard for his own safety. His actions at this critical point in the battle directly contributed to safely retrieving the Marines from the kill zone and saving their lives. Once the Marines were recovered, the platoon withdrew outside of small-arms range and Blonder prepared the platoon to conduct a counterattack on the trenches. He collected the ammunition, casualty, and equipment report from the assistant team leaders and redistributed ammunition and personnel as required. He met with the platoon commander and team leaders, and together they came up with a course of action for a counterattack.

The mounted portion of the platoon conducted a feint attack on the western portion of the trench in order to draw the enemy's focus while Blonder led the dismounted element of the platoon on a flanking attack on the eastern trench. Due in large part to the platoon feint, close-air support, and heavy mortar fire, Blonder was able to quickly close with and establish a foothold in the eastern trench, but he met with significant enemy resistance as his team assaulted west through the trench in order to clear the ambush site. Blonder took countless volleys of machine-gun and RPG fire from a well-entrenched and prepared machine-gun position to the north as his element attacked the enemy's left flank in order to clear the ambush site. The devastating effect of his vicious assault caused the collapse of the enemy's left flank. Blonder rallied his Marines and maintained pressure on the enemy forces as he led them further into the enemy trench system. He was able to fight his way to a position 150 meters away from the compound but was repelled by another fortified machine-gun position that was surrounded by an open field. The grazing fire from this weapon system made it impossible to approach the compound without first destroying the machine gun. Blonder relayed a fire mission from one of his team leaders to the forward air controller and requested that numerous air strikes be conducted "danger close" (so close that the impacts could endanger him and his men) to his position.

Blonder's aggressive, selfless actions and initiative were instrumental in the success of the mission at great personal risk. He was personally responsible for killing 3 enemy fighters while he led the dismounted element of the platoon on numerous attacks on enemy fortified positions as they fought to clear a numerically superior Taliban force from a complex trench system and numerous hardened battle positions in the 8-hour battle for Shewan. While the long duration and dispersed nature of the battle made it nearly impossible to accurately estimate the overall number of enemy combatants, multiple-source intelligence reporting indicates that there were more than 100 enemy fighters and fewer than 500. Some reports have indicated that there were approximately 250 Taliban fighters involved in the battle. In addition, the enemy force fired more than 100 RPGs, 3 107-mm rockets, 5 82-mm mortar rounds, and countless medium machine-gun rounds at the platoon. Despite these overwhelming odds, Blonder's recon platoon and 2 infantry squads were able to kill more than 50 Taliban and wound numerous others before crushing the Taliban resolve and driving them from the battlefield. Blonder's tactical ability, superior marksmanship, and aggressive fighting spirit inspired the platoon to continually advance on the enemy despite being vastly outnumbered. Blonder was a driving force during the 8-hour battle, and his bold, decisive leadership allowed the platoon to gain and maintain the momentum against the enemy fighters until they were destroyed. Blonder's valorous actions helped reduce a major enemy stronghold, destroying several Taliban cells in the process, and opened Route 517 up to coalition and Afghan National Security Force convoys.

Navy Cross Citation

The President of the United States of America takes pleasure in presenting the Navy Cross to Gunnery Sergeant Brian M. Blonder, United States Marine Corps, for extraordinary heroism in action against the enemy while serving as Platoon Sergeant, Force Reconnaissance Platoon, Second Battalion, Seventh Marine Regiment, Marine Corps Forces Central Command (Forward) on 8 August 2008 in support of Operation Enduring Freedom. Gunnery Sergeant Blonder was leading a dismounted patrol through the city of Shewan when his platoon came under intense rocket propelled grenade, mortar and machinegun fire that destroyed a vehicle and trapped several Marines in the kill zone 150 meters away from the enemy. Gunnery Sergeant Blonder exposed himself time and again to heavy fire as he coordinated the suppression of the enemy so that the Marines could be recovered. Later in the battle, Gunnery Sergeant Blonder personally led a flanking attack on the enemy trench system through countless volleys of machinegun and rocket propelled grenade fire. He continued to press the attack as the platoon penetrated further into the trenches in order to defeat the enemy. Gunnery Sergeant Blonder's tactical ability, superior marksmanship and aggressive fighting spirit inspired the platoon to continually advance on the enemy despite being highly outnumbered. He was a driving force during the eight-hour battle and pushed the platoon to gain and maintain the momentum against the enemy until they were destroyed. Gunnery Sergeant Blonder's valorous actions helped reduce a major enemy stronghold as his platoon killed over fifty enemy fighters, destroying several Taliban cells and opening the highway in Shewan to Coalition convoys. By his bold leadership, wise judgment, and complete dedication to duty, Gunnery Sergeant Blonder reflected great credit upon himself and upheld the highest traditions of the Marine Corps and the United States Naval Service

Information for this account is drawn from the U.S. Marine Corps "Award Summary of Action" (2008) and the Navy Cross Medal Citation for Brian M. Blonder (2008), and from multiple personal interviews with Blonder at Quantico, VA, 2011.

SGT LUCAS J. CHAFFINS

1st Force Reconnaissance Company,
1st Reconnaissance Battalion, I Marine Expeditionary Force

born: Coventry, Rhode Island

Awarded the Bronze Star Medal with Combat
Distinguishing Device "V" for heroic actions from
16 June through 10 October 2010, Afghanistan

Sgt Lucas Chaffins served with the 3rd Platoon, Force Reconnaissance Company, 1st Reconnaissance Battalion operated in support of Operations New Dawn and Tor Shezada, both suboperations of Marjah-focused Operation Moshtarak. The operations focused around Marjah, particularly the Trek Nawa area.

From 16 June to 18 July 2010 Chaffins' platoon operated for thirty-two straight days behind the forward line of enemy troops (FLET) in the previously uncontested Taliban stronghold of central Trek Nawa, Helmand Province. Chaffins conducted thirteen patrols, including zone and area reconnaissance as well as ambushes and disruption operations through this treacherous terrain, in order to map the human and physical terrain of this area, about which little to nothing was known, as well as to disrupt enemy operations in support of hold/build operations in Marjah. Chaffins displayed effectiveness and proficiency under stress on close to twenty occasions of fighting with enemy forces by providing effective suppressive and destructive fire with his M240B.

On 16 June 2010 at 0250, Chaffins inserted with his platoon via a CH-53 into an area that was well regarded as an enemy stronghold. The platoon was to be inserted several kilometers behind the FLET. At 0715 an enemy force totaling approximately 40 individuals attacked the platoon with heavy, accurate, and coordinated small-arms fire (SAF), including machine-gun fire. At 0719, with accurate SAF impacting near the platoon from multiple directions, the on-scene commander declared troops in contact (TIC). Chaffins positioned himself and his M240B medium machine gun at a north/south-running, 3-foot-high wall, which spanned approximately 30 meters. Realizing the importance of his weapon as 1 of the only 2 machine guns in the platoon, Chaffins worked with the Marines to his left and right to identify enemy firing positions at approximately 300 meters to his east and provided effective suppression. He coordinated his fires with his adjacent Marines and devised a system that used automatic fire from his weapon timed with SAF from his adjacent Marines to effectively gain fire superiority over the enemy. When the enemy's fire ceased from one position and started from another, he relocated himself to ensure he could bring his machine-gun fire to bear. Chaffins braved incoming direct fire to haul the cumbersome weapon into optimal position to return fire. Between 0715 and 0900, Chaffins twice exposed himself by dashing in a low crouch approximately 25 feet between 2 positions in order to position himself next to his fellow Marines, who had better situational awareness on the current enemy position. After coordinating with the Marines there, Chaffins employed his automatic weapon, suppressing enemy fighting positions. Once the enemy at that position was suppressed, Chaffins moved again approximately 25 feet back to his original position to resynchronize his fire. It was during this time that Chaffins' weapon malfunctioned, firing only in single-shot mode. He quickly conducted immediate and remedial action while remaining exposed to enemy fire in a valiant and successful effort to maintain positive identification of the enemy fighters and their locations, but his machine gun would not return to burst-fire mode. While engaging enemy fighters at distances of 300 to 600 meters to his east in this unconventional yet adaptive manner, Chaffins killed one enemy fighter at a range of approximately 350 meters and suppressed other enemy positions. When fighting subsided around 0930, Chaffins conducted elaborate remedial action to his weapon and rectified the problem; therefore, he was once again ready to engage with automatic fire.

At approximately 1000 the volume of enemy fire increased to the point that the on-scene commander reopened TIC.

Chaffins' accurate fire allowed the other Marines to orient on his tracer rounds and mass fire. During this second TIC period Chaffins moved himself and his weapon once again, dashing as bullets zipped by approximately twenty feet along the same wall in order to synchronize fire and suppress enemy forces. Once again his accurate fire helped to suppress the enemy threat, and TIC was closed at approximately 1230.

At 1800 enemy forces attacked the platoon with massed fire from three directions, subsequently triggering the third TIC declaration of the day. The primary enemy threat was assessed to be coming from the southeast. Chaffins dashed approximately seventy-five feet while rounds snapped past him to position himself where he could best suppress the threat. Once again deterring the enemy from orienting on his position, he quickly aligned himself with a spotter and synchronized his fire for mass effect. After suppressing the enemy to the southeast and the threat from that area subsided, Chaffins moved again, this time approximately sixty feet to the north.

By 1905 the platoon had neutralized the enemy threat and the on-scene commander closed the TIC. Throughout the eleven-and-a-half-hour engagement, regardless of the amount of incoming fire, Chaffins showed great courage and personal initiative by positioning himself and his M240B where they, in harmony with the platoon's other weapon systems, could best destroy or suppress enemy personnel. Along with enabling him to provide effective fire, his courageous movements also motivated his fellow Marines and prevented the enemy from targeting him and his machine gun.

On 27 June 2010, while conducting zone reconnaissance from a temporary patrol base (PB) in Trek Nawa, Marines observed what appeared to be enemy personnel emplacing improvised explosive devices (IED) on the side of a major road. The observers estimated the distance from observation point to target at well more than one thousand meters. Chaffins quickly climbed to the rooftop position to provide critical sniper fire onto the IED emplacers. Using the scope of the .50 caliber special-application scoped rifle (SASR), he oriented himself onto the suspected enemy forces. The nature of insurgent tactics meant that they usually attempted to make hostile actions appear as innocent ones. From thorough studies of and previous firsthand experience with the enemy's tactics, techniques, and procedures, Chaffins knew that one of their techniques was to feint farming to emplace IEDs in order to attempt to confuse observing friendly forces, who are known to operate under strict rules of engagement (ROE). Chaffins, due to superior attention to detail and expert skill with his optics, discerned that he was observing hostile acts, not innocent ones. However, Chaffins also noticed what appeared to be women and children approximately two hundred meters from the enemy fighters. He conveyed his observations and confirmed them with his two spotters. Chaffins was careful not to fire prematurely and risk inflicting civilian casualties. He confirmed the presence of three enemy fighters and, with his spotter, established engagement criteria and target precedence. While communicating his observations and intentions, Chaffins simultaneously received targeting data such as range, wind calls, and elevation holds, and he adjusted his rifle, optic, and point of aim accordingly. On order, Chaffins pressed the trigger, sending the .50 caliber round to its target, striking one of the enemy fighters. The other fighter next to him frantically looked around, seemingly in shock or disbelief and unaware where the shot had come from. Chaffins had raced into position and in doing so had not taken the time to secure hearing protection. As a result, he tore his eardrum while taking this shot. Unfazed by the violence and trauma to his ear, by the dust that choked his every breath, and by a now frantically moving target, Chaffins displayed unparalleled focus and effectiveness under stress by quickly reacquiring sight picture and target and squeezing the trigger, taking a second shot. This shot violently struck the second enemy fighter, who instantly dropped out of sight. Chaffins reacquired sight picture and searched for a third target. Working with his spotters, he identified the third enemy fighter poking his head over a terrain feature, attempting to observe Chaffins' position while maintaining personal cover and concealment. Chaffins, understanding that the third fighter would inevitably flee out of the field of view, quickly sighted in on target and squeezed the trigger. Due to the limited exposure of his third target, Chaffins grazed the enemy fighter, causing injury. The man eventually crawled out of sight. Chaffins fired these precision shots from a range of approximately 1,200 meters. His ability to employ the weapon system at such a range while simultaneously communicating with his spotters demonstrated his unparalleled tactical proficiency as well as superior effectiveness under stress. Future engagements with Afghan nationals revealed that the enemy fighters were frustrated with the distance from which they could be engaged as well as their inaccurate perceptions of American forces' ROE. In other words, the enemy thought that friendly forces were helpless to defend and deter against such IED emplacement. Chaffins' actions killed two enemy fighters and wounded one. In addition, he prevented them from emplacing IEDs on the main thoroughfare of the area and deterred other enemy fighters from attempting to do the same thing. This had a profound impact on the enemy, significantly disrupted enemy operations in the area, and helped to maintain the security of the road for usage by Afghan nationals.

From 16 June to 18 July 2010 Chaffins helped 3rd Platoon to cover and collect on approximately twenty-eight square kilometers in addition to engaging with approximately fifty local nationals and searching and reporting on seventy-two compounds. Chaffins' actions directly contributed to the complete disruption and confusion of the Taliban command-and-control network in Trek Nawa. The Taliban were forced to find alternate routes in and out of Marjah.

From 27 July to 27 August 2010 3rd Platoon operated in support of Operations Tor Shezada and New Dawn, both sub-operations of Operation Moshtarak. Operating alone and once again in Taliban territory previously uncontested by coalition forces, the platoon performed a total of sixteen patrols in which it generally executed multiple tasks/missions, including four mounted displacements, eight dismounted displacements, eleven reconnaissance missions (either zone or area), and two interdiction operations. Since every mission contributed to doing so, disruption of enemy forces was a duration mission that concurred with every operation the platoon undertook. The nearest friendly forces were generally two to four kilometers away. 3rd Platoon was responsible for inflicting an estimated twenty enemies killed in action (EKIA) and three enemies wounded in action (EWIA), covering and collecting on twenty square kilometers, engaging with twenty-three Afghan nationals, employing indirect fire and/or close-air support (CAS) on six occasions, and searching and reporting on thirty-four compounds.

On the evening of 3 August 2010 3rd Platoon displaced from PB Christopher and patrolled three kilometers through chest-deep canals and knee-deep mudded farm fields into Trek Nawa to conduct zone reconnaissance in order to map the human and physical terrain as well as to disrupt the enemy's flow into Marjah. On the morning of 4 August 2010 3rd Platoon task-organized into two independent elements (Alpha and Bravo), occupied two temporary PBs, and established force protection measures. At 0800 the Battalion Jump informed 3rd Platoon that, through unmanned aerial system (UAS) assets overhead, Battalion Jump Marines were observing a flurry of suspicious activity in the form of approximately thirty people scurrying and gathering items, possibly weapons and contraband. The UAS observed this activity approximately 150 meters southwest of 3rd Platoon. The platoon's Alpha element quickly assembled a ten-man patrol whose task would be to confirm the suspicious activity by unknown personnel as either hostile or nonhostile.

Chaffins was part of the three-man element tasked with security of the temporary PB while the ten-man foot patrol maneuvered out to investigate the suspicious activity. Chaffins manned a loophole in the wall of the compound, which provided maximum force protection but limited field of view and elevation. Quickly realizing that his ability to provide overwatch and security to support his fellow Marines was limited at the loophole he manned, he and a buddy climbed atop a twelve-foot roof, hoisting three cumbersome weapons with them: the SASR, the designated marksman rifle, and the M240B medium machine gun. Chaffins and his buddy forfeited cover and concealment in order to ensure they could provide maximum overwatch for their fellow Marines. Shortly after the maneuver element arrived at its objective, enemy forces conducted an RPG-initiated attack against the maneuvering patrol as well as the compound that Chaffins was occupying. Heavy and accurate SAF impacted at both friendly positions. The mission to confirm what type of activity was being observed had been accomplished. The patrol engaged with precision fire. The on-scene commander declared TIC, and CAS checked in on station. However, due to the presence of women and children, whom the enemy was employing as human shields, 3rd Platoon was unable to provide air-delivered ordnance. The enemy attacked both the maneuver patrol and the temporary PB where Chaffins was located. After returning fire and confirming enemy locations, the maneuver patrol proceeded to retrograde back to the temporary PB and consolidate. Chaffins persistently engaged enemy forces at ranges from four hundred to eight hundred meters, combining with his partner to kill an estimated ten enemy fighters. In addition to neutralizing and suppressing enemy threats in support of the maneuvering patrol, Chaffins and his fellow scout sniper on overwatch further enhanced the situational awareness of the maneuvering patrol by relaying the direction, distance, and activities of the enemy forces and atmospherics. The maneuvering patrol, realizing that to further close with the enemy would mean overextending and thereby losing mutual support, decided to reconsolidate at Chaffins' position. Despite the fact that he remained in an open position and under constant accurate SAF and machine-gun fire, Chaffins held his position and continued to engage, suppress, and destroy enemy forces, thereby helping to facilitate the foot patrol's safe movement back to the rally point. While the patrol moved to consolidate, Chaffins' overwatch partner sustained a gunshot wound to the right shoulder. Chaffins and his partner yelled down to the third Marine that one of them was hit and was coming down. Chaffins helped lower the wounded Marine off the roof and then, under the weight of full personal protective equipment, risked injury by jumping down from the twelve-foot rooftop to assist in medically treating the wounded Marine.

Once on the deck, Chaffins worked diligently to stop the bleeding from the gunshot wound. Working with the third Marine present, he helped to remove the wounded Marine's personal protective equipment and blouse, stuffed pressure dressing into the wound and applied pressure to control the bleeding, conducted a sweep of the body for additional wounds, and ensured that the Marine was breathing and maintained a good airway. During the stressful situation Chaffins helped to keep matters calm by talking and joking with the wounded Marine and the other first responder. His actions as a first responder undoubtedly helped to save the life of his fellow scout sniper. When the maneuver patrol consolidated back at the compound, Chaffins helped conduct patient turnover with the platoon corpsman. Chaffins' bold and decisive actions were critical in ensuring the security of the maneuvering patrol as well as the destruction and neutralization of enemy forces. His proactive nature, courage, and selfless concern for his fellow Marine, as well as his calm, collected manner under fire were instrumental in building the overall situational awareness for the maneuvering patrol. His courageous and timely actions resulted in approximately ten EKIA and multiple EWIA between Chaffins and his overwatch partner.

On 21 August 3rd Platoon established a temporary PB/ blocking position on a key enemy line of communication. The platoon employed itself in a low-profile manner to avoid detection by the enemy. This position enabled the platoon to interdict Afghan nationals and enemy forces by surprise as they attempted normal travel along this key route. While vigilantly standing his post, Chaffins skillfully employed his basic knowledge of the Pashto language to stop and then search twelve people that day. His proficiency with basic Pashto enabled the platoon to successfully halt and control traffic and search 100 percent of personnel and vehicles that passed by. Ultimately, due to Chaffins' and other Marines' adept use of vigilance and their cultural and language knowledge, along with excellent situational awareness of their surroundings, 3rd Platoon was able to detain three individuals suspected of shooting at adjacent friendly forces approximately thirty minutes prior.

On 23 August 2010 3rd Platoon's Alpha element (3A) conducted an area reconnaissance in the Dinai Shatsu Shash area of Marjah in order to confirm the presence of enemy fighters at a mosque and madrassa, as well as to observe and report on patterns of life in the area. Chaffins, once again remaining alert in the performance of his duties, watched over his sector, employing Pashto verbal commands when required and obtaining high-quality photographs of persons of interest and atmospherics as they moved in and out of his sector. His efforts helped to identify the civilian key leadership of the area and possible Taliban hiding among them and to identify atmospherics and pattern of life in the area.

Intelligence reporting from higher and adjacent units reported that the Taliban leaders of the area had ordered their fighters to stop using the side of Marjah in which 3rd Platoon operated and instead to take the long route to infiltrate into Marjah and avoid the risk of running into the platoon. The enemy was significantly disrupted, and Chaffins' bold and decisive actions against the enemy and his consistently positive attitude throughout all operations, were contagious throughout the platoon and significantly impacted mission accomplishment. His detailed and astute reporting helped to build the platoon's situational awareness, thereby directly enabling the platoon to take rapid, decisive action against the enemy. His courage under fire and effectiveness under stress set an example for all Marines of the platoon to emulate.

BRONZE STAR MEDAL WITH COMBAT DISTINGUISHING
DEVICE "V" CITATION

For heroic service in connection with combat operations against the enemy while serving as Machine Gunner, 3d Platoon, Force Reconnaissance Company, 1st Reconnaissance Battalion, 1st Marine Division (Forward), I Marine Expeditionary Force (Forward) Afghanistan, from 16 June 2010 to 10 October 2010 in support of Operation Enduring Freedom. On 16 June 2010, SERGEANT CHAFFINS and his platoon were attacked from multiple directions upon helicopter insertion to the Trek Nawa sector of the Marjah District. He exposed himself to enemy fire on five occasions in order to reposition his weapon and provide suppressive fires and protect the platoon's vulnerable defensive position during an ensuing fire fight lasting more than 11 hours. The endurance and fortitude he displayed in action throughout this sustained period of engagement is a testament to his courage and selflessness. On 4 August 2010, as a patrol from his platoon maneuvered toward suspected enemy forces, he forfeited cover and concealment to climb on a rooftop and provide overwatch. When the enemy attacked and the patrol became pinned down, he provided a base of devastating fire, killing ten enemy and enabling his fellow Marines to safely retrograde. As the patrol returned toward the platoon's base of operations, his overwatch partner was struck in the back by enemy small arms fire. Lowering the wounded Marine from the roof, he then dropped to the ground in order to provide cover and conduct first responder medical treatment, ultimately saving the Marine's life. By his extraordinary guidance, zealous initiative, and total dedication to duty, Sergeant Chaffins reflected great credit upon himself and upheld the highest traditions of the Marine Corps and the United States Naval Service.

Information for this account is drawn from the U.S. Marine Corps "Award Summary of Action" (2010) and the Bronze Star Medal Citation for Lucas J. Chaffins (2010).

SFC NATHAN CHAPMAN

1ST SPECIAL FORCES GROUP

BORN: ANDREWS AIR FORCE BASE

AWARDED THE BRONZE STAR MEDAL WITH
COMBAT DISTINGUISHING DEVICE "V" FOR HEROIC ACTIONS
AND THE PURPLE HEART MEDAL AFTER BEING KILLED IN ACTION
4 JANUARY 2002, GARDEZ AREA WEST OF KHOST, AFGHANISTAN

SFC Nathan Chapman was born on 23 April 1970 on Andrews Air Force Base and was killed in action on 4 January 2002 in the Gardez area west of Khost. Chapman was a great American and a personal friend. He was a member of 1st Special Forces Group and was the first American soldier to be killed in combat during the war in Afghanistan. Although Chapman served most of his twelve-and-a-half-year career with the 1st Special Forces Group at Fort Lewis, Washington, since the war on terrorism he had been assigned to the 5th Special Forces Group at Fort Campbell, Kentucky. He was directing troop movements from the back of a flatbed when he was shot; a CIA paramilitary operations officer from the special activities division was also wounded. Chapman was posthumously awarded the Purple Heart Medal and the Bronze Star Medal. Forward Operating Base Chapman was named after Sergeant First Class Chapman.

Although Chapman was an extremely professional and dedicated soldier, he was a wise guy. He had a way of lightening things up no matter how tense a situation was. I met him when he was assigned to Operational Detachment Alpha 135/6. The teams were combined to work as a sniper group. Although Chapman was an 18E (communications specialist), I knew him because he was a superior sniper. On occasion he assisted the urban sniper course and reconnaissance and surveillance (R&S) course at the Special Operations Training Group of the III Marine Expeditionary Force. He and I also deployed together during Operation Vector Balance Mint to Malaysia.

According to Chapman's close friends, Mark Carey and Jason Koehler, Chapman and the CIA officer were ambushed as they left a meeting with tribal leaders in Afghanistan's Paktia Province, near where U.S. warplanes had struck several al-Qaida and Taliban targets recently. The firefight took place about 1600 Friday, north of where U.S. warplanes struck an al-Qaida compound Thursday and again Friday. Chapman and the CIA officer were working with Afghan leaders near the town of Khost, not far from the Pakistan border, to gain information on the whereabouts of al-Qaida members. Shortly after leaving a meeting with the Afghans, the Americans were ambushed by small-arms fire, including light-machine-gun and rifle fire. The CIA officer suffered a serious chest wound in the fighting, though his injuries were not considered life threatening; both were removed from the area by U.S. forces.

Chapman was a highly decorated combat veteran whose awards and decorations include the Bronze Star Medal with Combat Distinguishing Device "V" for heroic actions and the Purple Heart Medal for combat wounds, the Meritorious Service Medal, the Army Commendation Medal with oak leaf cluster, the Army Achievement Medal with three oak leaf clusters, the Humanitarian Service Medal, the United Nations Medal, the Kuwait Liberation Medal, the Southwest Asia Service Medal with bronze service star, the Armed Forces Expeditionary Medal with arrowhead, the Army Good Conduct Medal (3rd Award), the Armed Forces Service Medal, the Joint Meritorious Service Unit Award, the Army Superior Unit Award, the Combat Infantryman Badge second award, the Master Parachutist Badge, the Parachutist Combat Badge with bronze service star, the Special Forces Combat Divers Badge, the Special Forces Tab, the Ranger Tab, and the Royal Thai Army Parachutist Badge.

Chapman's award citation is not included here because all Special Forces award summaries of action are classified to ensure that no classified information is accidentally disseminated. All information for this account was obtained through e-mail interviews with Mark Carey and Jason Koehler in 2003.

MSGT TANOS CHAVEZ

Explosive Ordnance Detachment, 2nd Battalion,
7th Marines, 1st Marine Division

HOME OF RECORD: INTENTIONALLY WITHHELD

Awarded the Bronze Star Medal with Combat
Distinguishing Device "V" for heroic actions from
April through November 2008,
Sangin District of Helmand Province, Afghanistan

During combat operations Master Sergeant Chavez led his explosive ordnance disposal (EOD) team during more than 105 responses to the location of improvised explosive devices (IED) in support of Company E 2/7, the Afghan National Army (ANA), and companies from 2nd Battalion, the Parachute Regiment, British Army. Chavez responded to multiple IED finds, IED strikes, and unexploded ordnance finds, and he participated in numerous company-level offensive operations, including movements to contact, cordon and searches, and raids. The impact of his work altered the IED and counter-IED landscape for all of northern Helmand Province. Through Chavez's efforts, countless coalition and Afghan National Security Forces soldiers' lives were saved and new enemy IED tactics were discovered and defeated.

During Company E 2/7's two-day tactical ground movement to occupy the Sangin District center, conducted 10–11 June 2008, Chavez safely executed two postblast analyses, after vehicles in the movement were attacked by pressure-plate IEDs (PPIED) occurring within fifty meters of each other. Showing complete mastery of his occupational specialty, Chavez was able to quickly determine the IED emplacers' TTPs (tactics, techniques, and procedures), leading him to discover a third PPIED emplaced in the immediate area, which was subsequently reduced. During the remainder of the movement, Chavez identified and reduced three more IEDs using manual approaches due to terrain limitations on his robot. The PPIEDs were clearly targeted toward Company E's ground movement elements and scheduled route of travel. Chavez ensured that the British battle group controlling the battle space became educated to the adapting IED threat, and at his recommendation, British forces altered their logistical movements and routes to become less susceptible to the threat.

On 19 June the Company E commander's personal security detachment (PSD) and EOD received information from a reliable intelligence source that enemy forces had emplaced an IED along a canal path south of the district center. Chavez coordinated with the PSD platoon commander to ensure security was in place and then moved up to identify the device. Due to terrain limitations, Chavez had to approach the IED on foot. While sweeping for the device, enemy forces initiated a command-wire-initiated IED (CWIED) while he was positioned within five meters of the device. Despite sustaining a Grade I concussion, Chavez swept the surrounding area and then exploited the site to glean information regarding the enemy's TTPs for IED employment. Chavez's exploitation revealed enough nuances in the enemy's IED TTPs to allow coalition forces and Afghan National Security Forces to successfully target the IED emplacers and triggerman in that area while avoiding threat areas.

On 5 August, when a British forces patrol reported finding an IED south of the Sangin District center near the Helmand River, Chavez's EOD team and PSD responded to the discovery. Chavez exploited the device manually and discovered it to be a victim-operated IED (VOIED) consisting of twenty-five pounds of homemade military explosive outfitted with an antipersonnel mine tilt fuse that was encased in thin plastic. Chavez's find, a tilt-switch-initiated IED, was the first of its kind reported in Regional Command South, Afghanistan. Seven hours later, Chavez and his EOD team, along with PSD, responded to an IED find by a patrol in a neighborhood. Once again, terrain limited his ability to conduct a manual approach on the IED; however, his exploitation revealed a second tilt-switch-initiated VOIED. These findings and the subsequent communication of his exploitation reports to higher and adjacent units prevented other units in northern Helmand Province from initiating similar enemy devices.

On 15 August Chavez led his EOD team in their response, along with PSD, to a reported IED find by a British forces patrol south of the Sangin District center in an area known as the Green Zone. While en route to the IED site, enemy forces initiated a CWIED attack on the PSD patrol, resulting in one priority U.S. Marine Corps casualty. Within seconds of the attack, Chavez moved rearward to the blast site, sweeping the area for secondary devices. After completing the sweep, he conducted a quick postblast analysis, revealing a daisy-chained CWIED consisting of five separate shot holes with eleven total pieces of military ordnance. Upon conclusion of the postblast analysis, EOD and PSD continued their maneuver toward the British IED find. Due to terrain limitations and the requirement to respond on foot, Chavez exploited the device manually and determined it to be a VOIED specifically targeting EOD personnel. The device consisted of a collapsing circuit with three separate main charges placed in locations where EOD and close security personnel would likely take cover during an explosive reduction of the IED. Chavez's technical proficiency allowed him to recover the device in its complete form. FBI officials reported that this was the first recovery of a collapsing circuit IED since 1975.

While reducing the device, EOD and PSD were attacked by enemy forces with accurate small-arms fire and rocket-propelled grenades (RPGs). Upon being engaged, Chavez stopped his exploitation, cleared the area of friendly forces, and returned fire onto the enemy's position, knowingly exposing himself to the danger of incoming rounds in order to effectively suppress their position. Chavez's accurate fire enabled PSD to maneuver against the enemy positions and break the enemy attack.

An hour after completing the exploitation of the collapsing circuit VOIED, an adjacent patrol in Haji Nizamuddin village was attacked by an IED, causing two priority casualties. Chavez's EOD team and PSD immediately pushed out on foot to exploit the IED site. Once again Chavez conducted his exploitation manually and determined the IED to have been a daisy-chained CWIED with four shot holes and five pieces of military ordnance. Later that night, when 3rd Platoon patrol discovered an IED, Chavez responded with EOD and PSD for the third time that day. Due to terrain, Chavez again completed a manual approach to the IED and exploited it, revealing a radio-controlled initiated IED. Chavez's exploitations, reporting, and recommendations were instrumental in instigating an increase in man-portable electronic countermeasures within northern Helmand Province.

On 10 September Chavez and his EOD team were part of a Company E combined movement to contact with the ANA soldiers and their British Army mentors in the villages of Barakzai and Khanan. A planned canal crossing failed when the bridge chosen for the crossing was deemed insufficient to support coalition forces. The fallback plan called for crossing the canal at a known IED site. A platoon of ANA soldiers pushed across the bridge to post far-side security, and Chavez led his EOD team up to the exposed bridge to quickly sweep it for IEDs. Chavez identified an IED on the bridge and prepared to reduce it. At this time, enemy forces attacked the ANA platoon on the far side of a canal with a heavy volume of small-arms and RPG fire. Enemy fire also targeted the bridge itself. Under heavy and accurate fire, Chavez unhesitatingly moved up to the IED location and placed a drop charge on the IED. Still under heavy fire, Chavez made his way to cover, initiated the drop charge, and then exposed himself again to heavy enemy fire to ensure that the IED had been removed.

Once the bridge site had been cleared of IEDs, Chavez led his EOD team to a position on the bank of the canal where they put effective suppression on the enemy positions despite accurate return fire. Company E PSD then joined the EOD team, and together they achieved enough effective suppression to allow the company commander for Company E to send elements of 2nd Platoon across the canal bridge. While elements of 2nd Platoon cleared the enemy firing positions to the south, enemy forces from the north once again took the bridge site under heavy fire. Chavez repositioned his EOD team and put accurate fire from his M4 rifle and M203 grenade launcher onto the enemy positions. Exposing himself to enemy fire, Chavez identified targets for the PSD machine-gun team to engage and coordinated with a nearby ANA unit to move into position to suppress the enemy. After enemy forces from the north had withdrawn, Chavez's EOD team supported Company E elements as they cleared south of the crossing site. Once friendly forces had cleared the villages of Barakzai and Khanan, another crossing site had to be cleared before friendly forces could cross back to the eastern side of the canal. Chavez personally led his EOD team from the front in identifying and reducing a remote-controlled IED while under confirmed enemy observation. Chavez's fearless work enabled friendly forces to continue the attack and then safely retrograde upon conclusion of the movement to contact.

On 30 September a squad from 3rd Platoon, Company E located a possible IED in the neighborhood of Wishtan. Chavez and his EOD team responded to the scene with the Company E PSD. As Chavez closed on the possible IED, enemy forces initiated the CWIED when Chavez was approximately 1 to 3 meters from the device. Despite sustaining a Grade III concussion, Chavez immediately cleared the area of friendly forces, swept the area for follow-on devices, and conducted a thorough post-blast analysis. In doing so, Chavez was able to identify the enemy firing point, which was more than 150 meters from the blast site. Once his exploitation was complete, Chavez led his EOD team back to the district center before allowing medical personnel to check him over. The extent of his injuries required that he remain on light duty for more than two weeks.

BRONZE STAR MEDAL WITH COMBAT DISTINGUISHING DEVICE "V" CITATION

For heroic achievement in connection with combat operations against the enemy while serving as Staff Non-Commissioned Officer in Charge, Explosive Ordnance Disposal Detachment attached to 2d Battalion, 7th Marines, Marine Corps Forces, Central Command (Forward) from 8 April 2008 to 5 November 2008, in support of Operation Enduring Freedom. MASTER SERGEANT CHAVEZ responded to over 100 improvised explosive device related contingencies throughout the deployment, distinguishing himself through his tactical acumen and unyielding commitment to defeating the enemy forces in the northern Helmand Province of Afghanistan. In particular, he recovered a collapsing circuit device as well as a complex victim operated improvised explosive device; both types of devices had never been recovered in Afghanistan. His recommendations were instrumental, enabling friendly forces to avoid and subsequently reduce attacks from similar apparatus. On 10 September 2008, during a combined movement to contact, Master Sergeant Chavez unit was forced through an area containing a known improvised explosive device. Despite facing imminent contact, he led his team to the crossing site to confirm emplacement of the enemy threat. While preparing to reduce the device his position was attacked by a heavy volume of enemy small arms fire and rocket propelled grenades. With complete disregard for his welfare, he remained in a vulnerable position, reducing the improvised explosive device. Knowingly exposing himself to enemy fire, he returned to the blast site a second time to confirm its reduction. Master Sergeant Chavez's dynamic direction, keen judgment, and inspiring devotion to duty reflected great credit upon him and were in keeping with the highest traditions of the Marine Corps and the United States Naval Services.

Information for this account is drawn from the U.S. Marine Corps "Award Summary of Action" (2008) and the Bronze Star Medal Citation for Tanos Chavez (2008), and from multiple personal interviews with J. D. Thompson, one of Chavez's old teammates, at Quantico, VA, 2011.

HM3 PETER A. GOULD

Weapons Company, 3rd Battalion, 1st Marines,
1st Marine Division

born: Syracuse, Kansas

Awarded the Silver Star Medal
for heroic actions on 1 July 2010, Garmsir District,
Helmand Province, Afghanistan

On 1 July 2010 HM3 Peter Gould was serving as the 2nd Section corpsman, 81-mm Mortar Platoon; they were conducting a security patrol. At 0650 the patrol received four individually fired shots from the tree line 350 meters to its direct west. The patrol consolidated and maneuvered its first fire team to the north, close to a berm, to use as a position of overwatch and cover, while the second fire team moved south in an attempt to flank the enemy. Once each element had moved approximately 100 meters, the enemy opened fire with rifles and machine guns from a tree line to the west, 300 meters away, as well as from an east-to-west running tree line to the southwest 400 meters away. The fire was accurate and impacted within 5 meters of the patrol in all positions. Gould, while under a heavy volume of enemy fire, was serving as part of the security element and, at the direction of his squad leader, was actively engaging the enemy to the west with his M4 carbine. As the engagement continued, the enemy force grew to an estimated 35 to 40 Taliban fighters who actively engaged the 13-man patrol with an extremely high level of accurate small-arms, medium machine-gun, and RPG fire from the west, southwest, and south. Greatly outnumbered and taking fire from 3 directions, Gould continued to return fire with the rest of his patrol, maneuvering back to consolidate in a covered and concealed position to the east, which provided a better position of advantage with good fields of fire and the ability to better assess the developing situation. As the patrol maneuvered to the east, it received increasingly accurate small-arms

fire from the tree line 250 meters to the south of their position. During the movement, Gould continued to actively employ his M4 against enemy forces to the southwest.

As the patrol approached a covered position, a Marine was shot in the left leg at the back of the thigh. Upon hearing the call of "Corpsman!" Gould selflessly and unhesitatingly, with complete disregard for his own personal safety, exposed himself to heavy and accurate enemy small-arms and medium machine-gun fire, running across an open area to assess the casualty. With rounds snapping around him, he conducted the initial assessment and helped carry the casualty back into a covered and concealed position where he could begin medical care. Gould then quickly applied the appropriate intervention and, never losing sight of the tactical environment, continuously advised the squad leader and section leader of the status of the casualty and treatment rendered. Simultaneously, he calmly reassured the wounded Marine despite being under an increasing amount of enemy fire directed at their position.

When it was determined that the volume of fire was too great at that position and that the casualty had to be moved to a safer location for evacuation, Gould assisted in carrying the patient through a field to the east in an attempt to get the casualty out of the line of fire. Moving through a vineyard under heavy and effective enemy small-arms and medium machine-gun fire, Gould showed a complete disregard for his personal safety and continuously reassured the casualty. As the patrol bounded east, the aid and litter team stepped on a victim-operated improvised explosive device, wounding three more men and causing additional injuries to the first casualty. Gould was one of those seriously injured in the blast; he received fragmentation to his neck and face and was severely bleeding. Gould quickly assessed his own wounds, instructed a Marine to place his finger into the large wound on his neck to slow the bleeding, and began simultaneously assessing the other wounded.

Once done with his initial assessment of the casualties and while still under heavy and effective enemy fire, Gould calmly directed the other Marines in the squad to render the appropriate continuous aid to the casualties. Despite his own severe injuries, Gould continued to provide guidance and instruction to the Marines who were applying tourniquets to the other wounded Marines, one of whom was missing both legs. Additionally, he continued to advise another Marine on applying pressure dressings to another wounded Marine. He also continued to direct the treatment of his own injuries. Amidst the chaos and carnage of the most recent event, the increasing volume of small-arms and machine-gun fire snapping all around them, and his own critical condition, Gould's heroic attention to duty and presence of mind was a calming force to all those involved as he issued clear instructions to the caregivers, reassured the wounded, and continually updated his squad and section leader on the status of their Marines. He continued to provide aid, advice, and comfort throughout the next hour until completion of the medevac. Reluctantly, Gould was among the last to be evacuated.

Throughout the deployment, Gould displayed a tremendous level of courage and attention to duty under fire, and his actions on 1 July 2010 undoubtedly saved numerous Marines' lives. His steadfast dedication to the care of his men, presence of mind in extreme adversity, and complete disregard for his own personal safety gave convincing testament to his character and ability as a true hero and brother to whom nothing was more important than his comrades in arms. A warrior whose true measure was in his dedication to saving lives and who would fight to protect them even at the expense of his own, Gould is a hero. His actions have continually exemplified the ideals and standards above and beyond expectations, showcasing the ideals of the U.S. Navy corpsman. The sense of pride that the Marines have when talking about Gould speaks volumes of his natural abilities as a leader and his devotion to providing the best medical care humanly possible. His humility, courage, loyalty, and proficiency serve as an example for others to emulate.

Silver Star Medal Citation

The President of the United States of America takes pleasure in presenting the Silver Star to Petty Officer Third Class Peter A. Gould, United States Navy, for conspicuous gallantry and intrepidity in action against the enemy while serving as Corpsman, Weapons Company, Third Battalion, First Marines, Regimental Combat Team 7, First Marine Division (Forward), I Marine Expeditionary Force (Forward) Afghanistan, on 1 July 2010 in support of Operation Enduring Freedom. During a security patrol, Hospital Corpsman Third Class Gould's squad was engaged from three different directions by an enemy force estimated at between 35 to 40 Taliban fighters. When one of the Marines from the patrol was shot in the leg and with complete disregard for his own safety, Hospital Corpsman Third Class Gould exposed himself to accurate, medium machine gun and small arms fire to retrieve the wounded Marine and apply medical aid. With the order to move to another location to evacuate the casualty, he again exposed himself to enemy fire that was increasing in volume and accuracy to assist in the movement. While transporting the casualty, the unit struck an improvised explosive device, critically wounding three Marines and causing Hospital Corpsman Third Class Gould to sustain severe fragmentation injuries to his neck and face. Quickly instructing a Marine to stop the bleeding coming from his neck with direct pressure and while still under effective fire, he turned his attention to his wounded comrades, directing appropriate steps in assessing injuries and rendering life saving aid, to include the application of tourniquets and cardio pulmonary resuscitation. His inspirational actions and mental toughness under intense enemy fire led directly to saving at least one Marine's life that day. By his bold leadership, wise judgment, and complete dedication to duty, Hospital Corpsman Third Class Gould reflected great credit upon him and upheld the highest traditions of the United States Naval Service.

Information for this account is drawn from the U.S. Marine Corps "Award Summary of Action" (2010) and the Silver Star Medal Citation for Peter A. Gould (2010).

CPL MARTIN GRAHAM

Company B, 1st Battalion, 6th Marines, 24th Marine
Expeditionary Unit, International Security Assistance Force

born: Winchester, Virginia

Awarded the Navy and Marine Corps Achievement Medal
with Combat Distinguishing Device "V" for heroic actions
on 10 May 2008, Garmsir District, Helmand Province,
Afghanistan, in support of Operation Azada Wosa.

During April 2008 1st Battalion, 6th Marines was tasked to attack and destroy insurgent forces in the Garmsir District of Helmand Province, Afghanistan, in order to clear a route through the area for the 24th Marine Expeditionary Unit forces to occupy Forward Operating Base Rhino and reestablish Government of Islamic Republic of Afghanistan control. The Garmsir battle space had been under the occupation and control of Taliban forces for two years. The area was a series of strongholds anchored in and around a canal system where the enemy had repelled two separate coalition battalion-size attacks to regain the area. The insurgents numbered at various times from two hundred to six hundred fighters. These fighters included Afghan Taliban and foreign Pakistan, Baluch, and Waziristan tribal fighters supported by financiers and facilitators, using weapons that crossed the border from Pakistan and Iran.

Company B's task was to conduct a heliborne insertion and seizure of key passage points through the Garmsir area of operations. On 10 May 2008 the 1st and 2nd Squads were tasked with investigating a possible weapons cache. While moving through an open poppy field, the squads received a barrage of enemy automatic fire. Corporal Graham instinctively returned fire while maneuvering his team to a covered position in a nearby compound. While at the hasty defensive position, Graham guided his automatic rifleman, armed with an M249 squad automatic weapon (SAW), onto the enemy's position, allowing

2nd Squad to exit a kill zone. In the process of defending the compound, Graham quickly handled two persons of interest who were nearby when the situation unfolded and ensured their safety while the fighting ensued.

On 20 May 2008 Graham's squad was tasked with conducting a night-clearing mission of a key piece of enemy terrain. The village was a known Taliban position and point of origin for machine-gun, small-arms, and rocket fire. As his squad was moving across a compartmentalized danger area, enemy automatic fire opened up from two positions approximately one hundred meters away. Graham was with the first team that entered the compound from which the Marines were taking fire. Leading his team, he cleared the left half of the compound by employing a hand grenade. Once the northern half of the compound was clear, Graham moved his team to the southwestern corner, closing the distance to the enemy to less then fifty meters. Here he was positioned with his automatic rifleman (SAW) and effectively designated sectors of fire, and he gave on-the-spot corrections while identifying targets. In between bursts from his SAW gunner, Graham frequently moved to a firing position, on top of a wall, to suppress the enemy bunkers with 40-mm grenades. Despite impacts in his vicinity, his concentration allowed for multiple direct hits. Upon secondary searches conducted the following morning, two RPG launchers, five warheads, and hundreds of small-arms rounds were discovered; a blood trail leading out of the compound was also present. Graham's tenacity and aggressive actions allowed his squad to successfully fight through an enemy ambush. Graham's initiative and fighting spirit under fire were essential to his squad's success. His dedication and leadership to his squad members and peers is above reproach.

According to a witness statement by LCpl Ryan Murray:

> On 20 June 2008, first squad moved through many compounds clearing every room as they went. Moving North along a poppy field our squad took contact from the West. Instantly firing back, we maneuvered to a compound and Cpl Graham cleared the first room with a fragmentation grenade. The rest of the squad moved

past us and started taking more fire. Without any hesitation Cpl Graham shot two well-placed M-203 rounds (40mm Grenades) over the wall exactly where I saw the muzzle flashes coming from. Cpl Graham clearly put his life before the teams' by exposing himself first into the compound. Cpl Graham showed no hesitation from the moment we took contact, thus giving us fire superiority right away.

LCpl Dylan Mills stated the following about the events of 20 June 2008:

After the squad was tasked to clear out the compound we quickly entered from the East clearing the first few buildings. Shortly after that we were engaged from a building a 100 meters away. Without hesitation Cpl Graham pushed up clearing a compound with a grenade. Then from 50 meters, at another position the squad was engaged again. While engaging the enemy Cpl Graham placed well aimed M-203 shots into the enemy's position in between SAW bursts to overwhelm the enemy's assault; during the engagement enemy rounds impacted all around us. Due to Cpl Graham's actions, the enemy had no chance to move on the squad and we were able to quickly gain fire superiority and close in on them.

Navy and Marine Corps Achievement Medal with Combat Distinguishing Device "V" Citation

Heroic achievement while serving as team leader, 1st Squad, 1st Platoon, Company B, Battalion Landing Team 1st Battalion, 6th Marines, 24th Marine Expeditionary Unit, II Marine Expeditionary Force, International Security Assistance Force, Garmsir District, Helmand Province, Afghanistan, from 28 April 2008 to 15 August 2008 in support of Operation Azada Wosa. In the early morning of 20 May 2008, 1st Platoon conducted a clearance operation of a company objective. While moving through the village, fire erupted from Corporal Graham's flank. He immediately led two teams into a nearby compound and established a base of fire allowing the third Team to exit the kill zone. As fire shifted onto his position, Corporal Graham led an assault into the enemy's compound personally employing his rifle and throwing hand grenades. After consolidation, enemy fire again erupted from another compound. Corporal Graham engaged the enemy with multiple rounds from his grenade launcher that impacted on the enemy's position. Corporal Graham's daring and courage under fire reflected great credit upon himself and were in keeping with the highest traditions of the Marine Corps and the United States Naval Service.

Information for this account is drawn from the U.S. Marine Corps "Award Summary of Action" (2009) and the Navy and Marine Corps Achievement Medal Citation for Martin Graham (2009), from eyewitness statements of Dylan Mills (2008) and Ryan Murray (2008), and from multiple personal interviews with Graham at Quantico, VA, 2010.

LCPL BRADY A. GUSTAFSON

Company G, 2nd Battalion, 7th Marines, 1st Marine Division

home of record: Eagan, Minnesota

Awarded the Purple Heart Medal for his wounds and
Navy Cross for Heroic actions on
21 July 2008, Shewan Village, Afghanistan

On 21 July 2008 Lcpl Brady A. Gustafson served as a turret (machine) gunner in the lead vehicle, a mine-resistant ambush-protected vehicle (MRAP), of a four-vehicle mounted patrol in Farah Province, Afghanistan. As the patrol moved through the village of Shewan, multiple enemy rocket-propelled grenades (Rpgs) and medium machine-gun positions fired upon it, some as close as twenty meters. The ambush was initiated by an armor-piercing RPG round that penetrated the right side of Gustafson's MRAP, striking him in the right leg, resulting in traumatic injury and partial loss of his leg below the knee. The impact of the RPG knocked the driver unconscious, rendering the vehicle temporarily immobile and in the kill zone.

Without hesitation, and with complete disregard for his severe injuries, Gustafson remained in the turret; he immediately established positive identification of several enemy machine-gun positions and returned fire with his M240B machine gun while a Marine applied a tourniquet to his injured leg. Simultaneously, Gustafson reported to the vehicle commander that the patrol's second vehicle, behind his, had sustained two direct RPG impacts, rendering it immobile. As Gustafson continued to engage the enemy, the driver of the MRAP regained consciousness and put the MRAP in reverse, using the vehicle as a means to push the disabled vehicle out of the enemy's kill zone. While the driver moved both vehicles, Gustafson braved the effects of shock and remained in the turret, suppressing enemy positions with accurate machine-gun fire. By the time they reached the end of the kill zone, the rear vehicle had become engulfed in flames. Gustafson's fire allowed the Marines in that vehicle to dismount and escape while under intense enemy fire.

Continuing to ignore his wounds and while still receiving intense enemy fire, Gustafson reloaded his machine gun. Only after his fellow Marines had evacuated the burning vehicle did he allow himself to be removed from the turret to receive medical treatment.

NAVY CROSS CITATION

The President of the United States of America takes pleasure in presenting the Navy Cross to LANCE CORPORAL BRADY A. GUSTAFSON, United States Marine Corps, for extraordinary heroism while serving as Turret Gunner, Lead Vehicle, 3d Squad, 2d Platoon, Company G, Second Battalion, Seventh Marines, Marine Corps Forces, Central Command (Forward), in support of Operation Enduring Freedom on 21 July 2008. In the village of Shewan, Afghanistan, Lance Corporal Gustafson's squad was ambushed from multiple positions by enemy insurgents with rocket-propelled grenades and medium machine gun fire. The attack was initiated by a rocket-propelled grenade that pierced the hull of his mine resistant ambush protected vehicle and struck him, resulting in severe traumatic injury to his right leg. Despite bleeding profusely, Lance Corporal Gustafson quickly identified enemy positions and engaged them with accurate fire from his M-240b machine gun while a tourniquet was applied to his leg. When the vehicle to their rear was disabled by further rocket-propelled grenade fire, he directed his driver to push the vehicle out of the enemy's kill zone, and shortly thereafter the vehicle was engulfed in flames. Although medium machine gun fire continued to impact around him, Lance Corporal Gustafson remained steadfast, returning concentrated fire on the enemy. His effective suppression allowed the Marines behind him to safely dismount and exit their burning vehicle. Lance Corporal Gustafson braved the effects of shock and reloaded his weapon twice, firing more than 400 rounds, before he allowed himself to be pulled from the turret and receive medical treatment. By his bold actions, daring initiative, and total devotion to duty, Lance Corporal Gustafson reflected great credit upon himself and upheld the highest traditions of the Marine Corps and the United States Naval Service.

Information for this account is drawn from the U.S. Marine Corps "Award Summary of Action" (2008) and the Navy Cross Medal Citation for Brady A. Gustafson (2008).

CPL LARRY D. HARRIS JR.

Weapons Company, 3rd Battalion, 1st Marines,
1st Marine Division

home of record: Thornton, Colorado

Awarded the Silver Star Medal, posthumously, for heroic
actions on 1 July 2010, Garmsir District, Afghanistan

On 1 July 2010 81-mm Mortar Platoon, 3rd Battalion, 1st Marines was conducting a security patrol in the Laki area of Garmsir District. Laki was, at the time, the southernmost location of any coalition forces in the Garmsir District, which had once been under complete control of the Taliban. Laki had been the scene of the toughest and most consistent heavy fighting of 3/1's deployment. Every patrol that ventured into the area was at high risk and certain to make contact.

At 0650 Cpl Larry D. Harris' patrol received four individual shots from a tree line 350 meters to its direct west. Knowing the enemy in this area often attempted to bait units into an ambush, Harris immediately and aggressively maneuvered his team across an open field in an attempt to outflank the suspected enemy position from the north and not be drawn into an anticipated kill zone. As his team closed by bounding toward the enemy position, the enemy opened fire from the tree line to the west 300 meters away and from an east-to-west running tree line to the southwest 400 meters away. The enemy small-arms and medium machine-gun fire was heavy and accurate and increasing in volume. Rounds impacted within 1 to 2 meters of Harris' team; snapping tree branches could be heard overhead.

During this time Harris established positive identification of the hostile targets, directed the fire of his team along with that of the M240 gunner attached to his team, and boldly stood in a fully exposed position to engage the enemy with his M203 40-mm grenade launcher. Once he determined that the volume of enemy fire was too great for his small team to handle in the open field, he led his team east to a covered and concealed position, where he would be able to link up with his squad leader and determine the best course of action, all the while continuing to direct the fire of his team against the enemy. An estimated thirty-five to forty Taliban fighters had been actively engaging the thirteen-man patrol throughout this time with an extremely high volume of accurate small-arms, medium machine-gun, and RPG fire, which was now coming from the west, southwest, and south.

While leading his team to the east, Harris exposed himself numerous times in the open field so that he could better engage the enemy with his M203 to facilitate the movement of his team out of the kill zone. As the team bounded back, the M240 machine gunner was shot in the leg. At this point, to assess the casualty and to minimize his exposure to further injury, Harris and the squad corpsman immediately sprinted back into the open field with complete disregard for their own safety in order to retrieve the injured Marine. Harris, while under fire and still exposed, courageously hoisted the Marine on his back and carried him to a defilade position in the squad's position, where the corpsman could provide appropriate medical aid. While this was taking place, the accuracy and volume of enemy fire continued to increase, with rounds impacting in and around the compound the squad was currently holding. The enemy also maneuvered toward the compound in an attempt to surround and isolate them from the company's fixed positions. The squad leader then made a decision to continue to move east to a more secure location from which the wounded Marine could be evacuated. At that point Harris picked up the casualty and transported him with the aid of the litter team to a safer location near a patrol base. With complete disregard for his own safety, and again exposing himself to the high volume of small-arms and medium machine-gun fire, Harris broke the cover of the compound and moved quickly through a vineyard to the next compound to the east with the casualty on his back. As he moved through the vineyard, he struck a victim-operated improvised explosive device. Harris absorbed the majority of the blast and suffered critical wounds to his lower extremities. By absorbing the blast, he undoubtedly saved the life of his casualty for the second time that day. The injuries sustained in this attack would ultimately prove fatal; Harris succumbed to his wounds on the scene.

Through his actions, Harris displayed his steadfast devotion to duty and heroic dedication to the care of his fellow Marines. With complete disregard for his personal safety, on several occasions he exposed himself to heavy enemy fire in order to engage the enemy in support of the movement of other Marines or to personally evacuate a wounded Marine to safety. Without his bold and selfless actions, there is no doubt that the squad would have incurred more casualties as a result of the large number (forty) of enemy forces and automatic weapons fire coming from multiple directions. His loyalty and allegiance to his Marines should serve as an example for others to emulate. Harris clearly understood the consequences of and risks associated with his decisions, selflessly devoting his life to the defense of his country and his brothers. Harris' selfless service to his country, the Marine Corps, and, most important, his fellow Marines exemplifies the attributes that make him a hero, warrior, and patriot in every sense. His unwavering and persistent dedication to the accomplishment of the assigned mission and the safety of his fellow Marines cannot be questioned. He gallantly gave his life for his country.

SILVER STAR MEDAL CITATION

The President of the United States of America takes pride in presenting the Silver Star (posthumously) to CORPORAL LARRY D. HARRIS, JR., United States Marine Corps, for conspicuous gallantry and intrepidity in action against the enemy while serving as Fire Team Leader, 3d Squad, 81 Millimeter Mortar Platoon, Weapons Company, Third Battalion, First Marines, Regimental Combat Team 7, First Marine Division (Forward), I MEF (Forward) Afghanistan, on 1 July 2010 in support of Operation Enduring Freedom. During a patrol in Garmsir District, Helmand Province, Corporal Harris' Squad was engaged by sporadic enemy fire from the west. As he boldly maneuvered his men to outflank and close with the enemy, about 40 enemy fighters engaged Corporal Harris' squad with heavy and accurate small arms and medium machine gun fire. Consistently exposing himself to the effective fire, Corporal Harris expertly controlled his team and personally suppressed the enemy with rifle and 40-millimeter grenade fire to facilitate the movement of his team to a covered position. When the squad's machine gunner was shot in the leg, Corporal Harris immediately moved from his covered position while still under heavy fire, with complete disregard for his own safety, to reach the casualty and carry him to a defilade position. When the decision was made to move the casualty for evacuation, Corporal Harris unhesitatingly picked up the wounded Marine and carried him to the medical evacuation site, once again exposing himself to effective enemy fire from multiple directions. As he moved through a vineyard while carrying the wounded Marine, Corporal Harris struck an improvised explosive device, absorbing the majority of the explosion with his body. Although his injuries would prove fatal, Corporal Harris ultimately saved the life of the wounded Marine. By his bold leadership, wise judgment, and complete dedication to duty, Corporal Harris reflected great credit upon himself and upheld the highest traditions of the Marine Corps and the United States Naval Service.

Information for this account is drawn from the U.S. Marine Corps "Award Summary of Action" (2010) and the Silver Star Medal Citation for Larry D. Harris Jr. (2010).

CPL WILLIAM D. HIETT

Embedded Training Team, 2nd Battalion (Kandak),
3rd Brigade, 201st Corps, Afghan National Army

born: San Antonio, Texas

Awarded the Navy and Marine Corps Commendation Medal
with Combat Distinguishing Device "V," 8 August 2009,
Surobi District, Uzbin Valley, Eastern Afghanistan

During August of 2009, with the approach of only the second Afghan national elections and a heavy murder and intimidation campaign by enemy fighters to dissuade citizens from voting in his area of operations, Cpl William D. Hiett's embedded training team (ETT) endured three significant engagements with enemy elements. Throughout this period Hiett remained steadfast, showing courage and bravery in instances of enemy attacks and presence that ultimately allowed the Afghan citizens in his area of operations to vote safely.

At 0040 on the morning of 8 August 2009, Hiett reported "incoming" as an SPG-9 rocket propelled its way inside of Combat Outpost (COP) 42, nearly destroying the Afghan National Army (ANA) ammunition depot. After alerting the other three ETT members at this position and the ANA contingent, Hiett made his way to the northern wall inside the COP and took up a defensive position with his personal weapon and both thermal and night-vision optics. Hiett searched and assessed for a point of origin for the SPG-9 launch for five minutes, after which the enemy launched a coordinated and accurate rocket-propelled grenade (RPG) and rocket attack on this ANA and ETT-only COP from multiple positions. With multiple RPGs sailing past his position, Hiett immediately returned fire and marked the enemy point of origin with his M249 squad automatic weapon. This oriented several ANA Kalashnikov 7.62 × 54R–mm (PKM) medium machine-gun positions to suppress the enemy positions as well, while the other ANA soldiers prepared the main guns of the BMPs (tracked/armored fighting vehicle) for further counterattack on the enemy positions. Within minutes the enemy fired two additional timed RPGs, which exploded directly over the COP, spraying the whole area with shrapnel. Immediately following this barrage, the enemy increased the volume of fire on the northern and northwestern observation posts (OPs) with PKM and RPG fire in an attempt to overrun these positions.

Upon seeing what the enemy's intent was, Hiett immediately ran to the ETT ammo supply point while the enemy was still firing RPGs overhead and extracted an MK-19 (40-mm automatic machine gun) from a fighting position to set up a supplementary position to aid in the defense of the two OPs under attack. Hiett would ensure that the enemy could not advance any farther to the OPs. Carrying the heavy machine gun up a hill in the dark to a position that could effectively range the enemy attackers, and with minimal assistance moving ammo, Hiett had the weapon system assembled and ready to engage enemy elements moving on the OP in minutes. Due to the previous suppression and communication given by Hiett, his ANA soldiers were conducting an aggressive defense of their OPs and pushing the enemy out. With the enemy attack on the OPs halted, Hiett fired many well-placed bursts from the MK-19 along a hilltop that the enemy was using to egress from the location.

Hiett's aggressive efforts spearheaded the successful counterattack of twenty to thirty enemy fighters attempting to overrun two OPs at the ANA and ETT-only COP 42. With his immediate suppressive fire delivered by his squad automatic weapon and later by moving an MK-19 to a supplementary fighting position, all while under a barrage of enemy rockets and RPGs, Hiett was able to bring ETT fire support to bear while his ANA soldiers took heavy and effective fire, and he was able to break the enemy's attack on the position.

Enemy fighters intent on disrupting the elections and discrediting the fledgling Afghan government conducted a heavy murder and intimidation effort to dissuade the citizens in southern Kapisa Province from casting their votes. Enemy fighters distributed letters at night, posted threatening propaganda at polling locations, and increased their attacks ahead of these most important elections. Along with his partnered ANA company, Hiett devised a comprehensive election security plan and conducted a wide range of inner and outer cordons, presence patrols, and operations to provide security for the vulnerable polling sites. After the planning and preparation for this election security mission was complete, Hiett again answered the call and performed valorously on 20 August 2008 while performing the election security mission.

On election day, at approximately 1130, the first rocket in a volley of five landed 150 meters from the polling site for which Hiett was providing dismounted security. As the additional rockets came in, Hiett immediately remounted his vehicle, obtained the enemy point of origin, and planned a counterattack on the numerous enemy positions to suppress their fire and keep the Afghan citizens safe at the polling site. The decision by the ANA and ETT ground force commanders was made to maneuver toward the enemy position to engage them. As the ANA and ETT element moved north on main supply route Vermont toward the enemy positions, Hiett and his ANA element branched off the main supply route and moved toward the tree line to further close with the enemy. As Hiett's element maneuvered through the tree line, it took RPG and small-arms fire from a garden approximately 200 meters away. Hiett once again manned an MK-19 and was in a position where he had positive identification on 3 personnel firing on the ANA soldiers. Hiett effectively engaged these fighters with multiple bursts of the MK-19, effectively suppressing and eliminating the enemy fighters. Upon eliminating that particular threat, an ANA element 400 meters to the north of his position began to take heavy small-arms and RPG fire as well as frequent mortar rounds. Hiett, along with the ANA company commander, made his way northeast to assist the forward element with additional fire support.

While maneuvering through the fields and gardens heading northeast to the forward element that was taking heavy fire, the ANA soldiers informed Hiett that they had taken a casualty in the tree line near that engagement. Hiett went forward into the tree line with another ETT and a small ANA element to find the casualty and evacuate him. While en route to retrieve this casualty, Hiett and his ANA comrades ran into a wall of small-arms fire coming seventy-five meters from the northwest. The ANA soldiers engaged; once Hiett maneuvered into position to assist with the MK-19, he delivered effective fire on this enemy location as well. As the enemy location was engaged and fire from that position ceased, Hiett and his ANA comrades continued in their quest to link up with the wounded ANA soldier. After finding him and upon seeing that both an ETT corpsman and an ANA medic were rendering aid to the urgent surgical ANA casualty, Hiett, with the ANA company commander, continued toward the forward ANA location that was under heavy fire.

After finally reaching the forward element, the ANA platoon commander at that position identified a point-of-origin site where they had been receiving RPG, small-arms, and mortar fire. Within minutes of reinforcing this forward position, the enemy attacked from these positions once again, and Hiett immediately engaged the first compound from which RPGs came, while the ANA element was able to suppress two other positions simultaneously. After the dust and smoke had settled, there were no further movements or fire from the compound. Minutes later, Hiett and his ANA element obtained positive identification on an enemy mortar team approximately 1,500 meters to the north as they began to send mortar rounds in the vicinity of their position. Once again Hiett, in tandem with ANA machine gunners, effectively suppressed and eliminated the enemy threat.

After the destruction of the enemy mortar position, there was no more fire from enemy elements. After these engagements, Hiett and other ETTs present continued communicating with close-air support assets (U.S. Army OH-58 Kiowa Warriors) that had since checked on station to assess the area and attempt to locate any other enemy elements. Through the duration of these engagements on election day, there was only one ANA casualty. Due to the courage and aggressiveness of Hiett and his team of fellow ANA and ETT, the urgent surgical casualty remained safe from further injury and was promptly treated by ANA and U.S. personnel, which ultimately saved his life.

Hiett demonstrated aggressiveness, courage, bravery, and technical and tactical proficiency by leading his ANA men forward in the face of enemy fire and by bringing his MK-19 to bear on numerous enemy positions. Due to these valorous efforts, the enemy assaults were repelled on every occasion, and there were no injuries to noncombatants or innocent villagers. Despite the increased enemy threats and even enemy attacks on the polling site, Afghan villagers were so encouraged by the security conditions that Hiett and his ANA men had set that they continued to vote in the hopes of a better Afghanistan.

While under heavy enemy threat and a spike in enemy attacks during the period of 8 August 2009 through the national elections on 20 August 2009, Hiett remained steadfast and courageous throughout many enemy engagements. Showing tactical acumen under fire and effectively maneuvering himself and his ANA comrades into advantageous positions from which to engage the enemy with his MK-19 and ANA crew–served weapons, he suppressed and eliminated multiple enemy positions during engagements.

I am glad that Hiett (now a sergeant) has been recognized for his heroic actions, but I do wish that he had received a higher award, such as a Bronze Star with "V" device. Sergeant Hiett is a member of the Marine Corps combat shooting team and works as foreign weapons instructor when not competing or training. Hiett has never complained about his award; on the contrary, he is very proud of it, as he should be. I just wish there was a way to ensure that warriors receive the appropriate awards for their actions.

NAVY AND MARINE CORPS COMMENDATION MEDAL WITH COMBAT DISTINGUISHING DEVICE "V" CITATION

For heroic achievement in the superior performance of his duties while serving as the 2d Company Advisor, 2d Battalion (Kandak), 3d Brigade, 201st Corps, Afghan National Army, Surobi District, Uzbin Valley, Eastern Afghanistan, on 8 August 2009, in support of Operation Enduring Freedom. During this period, CORPORAL HIETT courageously repelled over 20 determined enemy fighters trying to over-run Combat Outpost 42 and multiple observation posts in the area. Under intense, concentrated rocket and small arms fire, Corporal Hiett immediately coordinated fires within the Afghan National Army and continuously resupplied fighting positions with ammunition. Corporal Hiett risked his life by charging towards the observation post while under heavy enemy fire with a MK-19. Corporal Hiett suppressed the enemy and manned an outpost that was being overwhelmed by anti-Coalition militia fire and was in danger of being over-run. Corporal Hiett's actions reflected great credit upon himself and were in keeping with the highest traditions of the Marine Corps and the United States Naval Service.

Information for this account is drawn from the U.S. Marine Corps "Award Summary of Action" (2009) and the Navy and Marine Corps Achievement Medal Citation for William D. Hiett (2010), and from multiple personal interviews with Hiett at Quantico, VA, 2011.

1ST SGT ERNEST K. HOOPII

COMPANY C, 1ST BATTALION, 6TH MARINES (BATTALION LANDING
TEAM 1/6) 22ND MARINE EXPEDITIONARY UNIT
(SPECIAL OPERATIONS CAPABLE)

BORN: MAUI, HAWAII

HEROIC ACTIONS ON 3 JUNE 2004

I met Ernest Hoopii—or, as his friends call him, "Hoop"—during the first sergeant's course held at Quantico, Virginia, in the summer of 2003. Hoop is a difficult person to figure out—on the one hand, he is a gentle man who genuinely loves his Marines; on the other hand, he is a fierce warrior one would not wish ever to upset.

During August 2004 he was deployed to Afghanistan when LCpl James Gould was shot in the leg by a 7.62 × 54–mm round. Advancing along a steep, rocky hillside in pursuit of anticoalition militia fighters during an offensive against enemy fighters in south central Afghanistan, Gould had been shot by an enemy sniper hidden in a cave on the hillside opposite a small valley. Meanwhile, other Marines from Company C poured rifle fire at the anticoalition milita sniper's cave until the matter was finally settled with a hand grenade. With the enemy suppressed, the full focus of the platoon turned to its wounded Marines. The evacuation of the wounded, especially Gould, became perhaps the most difficult part of the day. Gould was unable to bear weight on his severely wounded leg, and the area was inaccessible to helicopters; the use of a litter down the steep, rocky slopes was out of the question. Realizing the desperate situation Gould was in, without hesitation Hoopii dropped his body armor, handed off his rifle, and picked up the wounded Marine. Hoop carried Gould down the mountain on his back for almost two hours, stopping only a couple of times for brief breaks. When I asked Hoop about "the hump," he stated, "That was the hardest hump of my life, [but] hey, you do what you got to do to take care your boys." In the end, Gould was evacuated to Kandahar Airfield, where he made a full recovery.

Information for this account is drawn from multiple personal interviews with Ernest K. Hoopii at Al Asad Air Base, Al Asad, Iraq, 2008.

SGT BRANDAN JANSEN

Weapons Company, 3rd Battalion, 4th Marines,
1st Marine Division

born: Colorado Springs, Colorado

Awarded the Navy and Marine Corps Commendation Medal
with Combat Distinguishing Device "V" for heroic actions,
October–December 2009, Now Zad, Afghanistan

Sgt Brandan Jansen demonstrated extraordinary leadership, courage, and proficiency on three separate occasions while operating as a combined anti-armor team (CAAT) section leader in Now Zad, Afghanistan.

On 23 October 2009, while conducting quick-reaction force operations, Jansen maneuvered on an enemy force in an area commonly referred to as "Pakistani Alley." While maneuvering, the second vehicle in the section detonated an improvised explosive device (IED), immobilizing the vehicle and yielding one priority casualty. Jansen identified the enemy position and suppressed enemy forces with heavy machine guns, simultaneously coordinating the evacuation of the priority casualty and collection of serialized equipment from the immobilized vehicle. Jansen evacuated the casualty back to the forward operating base, Caffereta, then returned to the immobilized vehicle to maintain security. He maintained positive control of his section and engaged enemy forces for approximately eight hours while waiting for the evacuation of the immobilized vehicle. His tactical proficiency and maturity as a leader freed his platoon commander to coordinate close-air support and indirect fire assets.

On 28 October 2009 Jansen's capabilities as a leader were on display once again when his CAAT section reacted to evacuate five scout snipers who had been critically wounded after an IED detonation. In the absence of his platoon commander, Jansen received a briefing on the situation and tasking, and he quickly departed to lead his section and the shock trauma platoon vehicles to the location of the casualties. While moving to the friendly casualties, his section hit an IED that immobilized one of his vehicles. Jansen immediately executed a bump plan (moving personnel around to different vehicles) and continued to pursue mission accomplishment. He dismounted his vehicle and led his Marines to evacuate the five urgent casualties from a compound while taking accurate direct and indirect fire from enemy forces. He was able to stay focused on the mission despite losing one of his own Marines to an IED while attempting to evacuate the wounded snipers. After ensuring that the wounded snipers were evacuated to the next echelon of medical care, he maintained security at the blast site and facilitated a postblast analysis with Marines of the explosive ordnance detachment. During the initial actions at the scene of the casualties, Jansen was the senior tactical commander on the scene, outranked only by medical personnel and the Lima Company first sergeant with the shock trauma platoon. Jansen took command of the situation and remained involved in all elements of the casualty evacuation. The actions of Jansen and his Marines saved the lives of four urgent casualties.

On 4 December 2009 Jansen's section participated in Operation Cobra's Anger. Jansen's section was tasked with establishing a support-by-fire position in order to neutralize enemy forces in the vicinity of Pakistani Alley. The support-by-fire position was located approximately five hundred meters north of Lima Company, First Platoon. At approximately 1530 CAAT Black received medium machine-gun fire from a building located three hundred meters to its northeast. Jansen immediately initiated suppression on the building in order to prevent enemy forces from advancing south. The enemy resistance increased by engaging CAAT Black with indirect fire and an RPG, which came within meters of destroying Jansen's vehicle. Jansen quickly provided his platoon commander with vital information about the enemy force, allowing him to call for indirect fire on the enemy. Simultaneously, Jansen conducted coordination with a Danish Leopard II main battle tank. While facing increasing resistance from enemy forces, Jansen marked their location with an MK-19 heavy machine gun. This allowed the main battle tank to locate the enemy force and destroy the threat with a 120-mm high-explosive antitank round. Jansen's bias for action and elevated situational awareness destroyed enemy forces to the north, allowing the Cobra's Anger main effort platoon to accomplish its mission unimpeded by enemy forces.

The fearless leadership of Jansen played a significant role in determining the outcome of almost every major operation in Now Zad during this period. He demonstrated tactical proficiency and lethality in his actions while employing his section to destroy enemy forces. He also demonstrated unrivaled courage and selfless devotion to his fellow Marines. The scout snipers who survived the described events on 28 October 2009 are a direct reflection of the courageous actions performed by Jansen and his Marines.

In a personal interview, I asked Jansen about the mission to rescue the wounded scout snipers. He told me:

> When I saw the path to the sniper team was too narrow for my vehicles, I left a couple team members with the vehicles, for security, and I took nine of my Marines and went down the road. The Marines got in stacks and we made our way to the downed sniper team. En route to [the] snipers' location, LCpl Cody Stanley, just in front of me, stepped on a pressure plate that threw him against the wall and left him mortally wounded. We tried to get him back to vehicles, but he succumbed to his injuries on the way.

Jansen and his Marines pushed on with the mission and found the sniper team while receiving accurate and intense fire. The corpsman on site did what he could at the scene, but these snipers needed a much higher level of care. Having only one stretcher, Jansen and his Marines had to make the dangerous trip four times from the incident site to the evacuation vehicles; all of the snipers were rescued.

Jansen is currently one of my Marines, working as a member of the Marine Corps combat shooting team and as a foreign weapons instructor when not competing or training. Jansen is one of the best combat shooting instructors I have ever observed in my thirty years of service.

NAVY AND MARINE CORPS COMMENDATION MEDAL WITH COMBAT DISTINGUISHING DEVICE "V" CITATION

For heroic service while serving as Section Leader, Combined Anti-Armor Team 2, Weapons Company, 3d Battalion, 4th Marines, Regimental Combat Team 7, Marine Expeditionary Brigade-Afghanistan, from October to December 2009 in support of Operation Enduring Freedom. SERGEANT JANSEN regularly demonstrated bravery and tactical acumen under fire during combat operations in Now Zad. On 28 October, he led his Marines down a narrow alley known to contain improvised explosive devices in order to save the lives of four seriously wounded Marines. Sergeant Jansen demonstrated superior situational awareness and tactical proficiency on 4 December, when he coordinated with a Danish Leopard II Main Battle Tank by marking target with fires so the tank could destroy the enemy. Sergeant Jansen's initiative, perseverance, and total dedication to duty reflected credit upon him and upheld the highest traditions of the Marine Corps and the United States Naval Service.

Information for this account is drawn from the U.S. Marine Corps "Award Summary of Action" (2009) and the Navy and Marine Corps Commendation Medal Citation for Brandan Jansen (2010), and from multiple personal interviews with Jansen at Quantico, VA, 2011.

CPL JASON D. JONES

Embedded Training Team 5-3, 3rd Kandak, 2nd Brigade,
201st Corps, Regional Corps Advisory Command

born: San Angelo, Texas

Awarded the Silver Star Medal for heroic actions on
13 July 2008, Patrol Base Wanat, Afghanistan

On 13 July 2008 Cpl Jason D. Jones risked his life and by doing so saved the lives of soldiers and Marines. His courage and leadership on the battlefield served as an example to his fellow Marines, Afghans, and soldiers during the battle. At 0400 the newly established Combat Outpost Kahler came under attack from approximately 115 to 130 anti-Afghan force (AAF) fighters. The AAF that attacked did so in a coordinated manner from multiple positions, including nearby buildings, homes, tree lines, and the village mosque. At times the AAF was within ten meters of the coalition forces' positions, firing accurate and heavy direct and indirect fire. The courage of this Marine undoubtedly allowed the coalition forces to maintain control of Combat Outpost Kahler and repel a well-synchronized and numerically superior force.

When the attack began, Jones was at the embedded training team (ETT) fighting position along with two other Marines. The three Marines immediately began to engage AAF fighters, and after some time being completely pinned down, Jones noticed a rocket-propelled grenade (RPG) round impact an up-armored highly mobile multiwheeled vehicle (HMMWV), which caused it to catch fire. Soon after the impact, the anti-tank missiles within the vehicle exploded from the heat of the fire. Jones then noticed that one Afghan National Army (ANA) soldier was wounded as a result of the destroyed vehicle. At this point Jones saw the soldier begin to crawl and could tell that he was badly injured. Of his own accord, without hesitation or regard for his life and under intense accurate AAF fire, Jones ran toward the wounded soldier's position. Another Marine, after observing Jones' initiative, immediately followed him to the wounded soldier's position. AAF fire was directly impacting along his route of travel and around both positions. They then dragged the soldier back through the AAF fire to the fighting position, where Jones assessed the soldier's medical needs. The ANA soldier had burns to more than 25 percent of his body, with major lacerations to the lower extremities and a gunshot wound just above his buttocks. Jones immediately took charge of the situation and treated the gunshot wound and burns using supplies from the ETT combat life-saving bag. He applied tourniquets to both of the soldier's legs to stop the extensive bleeding. He also packed gauze into the gunshot wound on the ANA soldier's buttocks, with the aid of the ETT interpreter. His calm and deliberate actions were a direct example to his fellow Marines, inspiring them into action. Without his initiative and calm demeanor, the soldier would not have been rescued. Jones' actions undeniably saved the life of this ANA soldier.

Shortly thereafter, the team received word from an observation post (OP) that they had a number of killed in action and wounded in action and needed immediate reinforcement. Upon hearing the situation of the soldiers at the OP, Jones told his fellow Marines that they had to go up there. He immediately picked up the M240B machine gun and ammunition to take to the OP. Seeing the amount he had to carry, another Marine, of his own accord, decided to accompany Jones to OP Topside. They traversed approximately 130 meters of rough uphill terrain while exposed to heavy AAF fires. The M240B that Jones brought to the OP, in concert with the additional troops, was instrumental in turning back the AAF assault on the OP. His main objective at the OP was to provide additional suppressive fire to help the troops that were still at the OP. He exposed himself countless times to AAF fire in order to retrieve weapons systems and ammunition from fallen comrades, and he again exposed himself to fire to treat wounded soldiers. His situational awareness while under fire remained completely intact, allowing him to calmly ensure weapons were functional, attend to wounded, and coordinate the placement of weapons systems. After treating multiple wounded soldiers, Jones found himself out of tourniquets. For one U.S. soldier that he came across Jones used the belt around his waist to stop the bleeding of a gunshot wound to the leg, and he aided in providing an IV in order to maintain the soldier's blood pressure.

According to the Army first sergeant from Chosen Company, 1SG Scott Beeson:

> Cpl Jones was all over the place at the OP, when any-one got hurt and had to pull off [the OP] he moved under heavy fire to ensure that we were not leaving any holes for the AAF to get in. He used any and all weap-ons systems around him in order to continue fighting. Cpl Jones in particular was a hero in my book and I am pretty sure he saved my life a couple of times. As the fighting died down, Cpl Jones' resolve did not fade and he continued to assist in the medical evacuation of sol-diers and Marines.

Jones distinguished himself throughout the course of this battle, and any one of these heroic acts deserves high recogni-tion. He was calm and scrupulous in his actions. He retrieved wounded soldiers while under intense accurate hostile fire and expeditiously attended to their medical needs. The OP was almost overwhelmed with multiple wounded soldiers and several already killed, but he did not hesitate to take the initia-tive and lead a fellow Marine to reinforce that OP before it was completely overrun. His example inspired those around him into action. He risked his life in the face of heavy and accurate AAF fire on more than one occasion during the engagement. However, it was his calm resolve, leadership, and action that set him clearly above his peers in courage and valor. The tre-mendous courage and selfless gallantry of Jones showcased his commitment and dedication to his fellow Marines and soldiers. Not only did his actions directly save lives and repel the AAF, but his leadership on the battlefield also inspired those around him of all ranks to continue to fight.

SILVER STAR MEDAL CITATION

The President of the United States of America takes pleasure in presenting the Silver Star to CORPORAL JASON D. JONES, United States Marine Corps, for conspicuous gallantry and intrepidity in action against anti-Afghan forces as a Mentor, Embedded Training Team 5-3, Regional Corps Advisory Command-Central, 201st Corps, Afghan National Army, in support of Operation Enduring Freedom, on 13 July 2008. Embedded with two other Marines in an Afghan National Army platoon manning vehicle patrol base Wanat alongside a reinforced U.S. Army platoon, Corporal Jones and the coalition forces came under an intense coordinated predawn attack from an estimated 200 anti-Afghan forces. He calmly returned suppressive fires while encouraging the Afghan National Army soldiers to deliver well-aimed defensive fires. Seeing a seriously wounded Afghan National Army soldier in the open, he and another Marine ran across 35 meters of open ground to drag him back to their position where Corporal Jones treated his life threatening wounds. When the U.S. Army squad manning an observation post was in danger of being overrun after suffering heavy casualties, he and a fellow Marine crossed 130 meters of fire swept ground with an M-240b machinegun and ammunition that proved vital to repelling the attack. Corporal Jones constantly exposed himself to grenades and fires from the attackers as he provided lifesaving first aid to several of the wounded U.S. soldiers. By his bold initiative, undaunted courage, and complete dedication to duty, Corporal Jones reflected great credit upon himself and upheld the highest traditions of the Marine Corps and the United States Naval Service.

Information for this account is drawn from the U.S. Marine Corps "Award Summary of Action" (2008) and the Silver Star Medal Citation for Jason D. Jones (2009), and from a witness statement from Scott Beeson (2008).

CPL MARC A. MADDING

EMBEDDED TRAINING TEAM 5-4, 201ST CORPS,
AFGHANISTAN NATIONAL ARMY,
COMBINED JOINT TASK FORCE PHOENIX, U.S. ARMY

BORN: POINT PLEASANT, NEW JERSEY

AWARDED THE BRONZE STAR MEDAL WITH COMBAT DISTINGUISHING
DEVICE "V" FOR HEROIC ACTIONS ON 23 DECEMBER 2008,
KORENGAL OUTPOST, KUNAR PROVINCE, AFGHANISTAN

Cpl Marc A. Madding was assigned to the Korengal Outpost serving in a staff sergeant's billet, mentoring and advising an Afghan National Army (ANA) company under some of the most severe enemy conditions in Afghanistan. On 23 December 2008 Madding and another embedded training team (ETT) were advising an ANA platoon conducting a joint operation in the village of Darbart in the Korengal Valley. The ANA platoon had established a security position in northern Darbart while elements of Bravo Company, 1/26 Infantry, U.S. Army, were conducting a key leader engagement in the southern part of Darbart. The Army had also set up a machine-gun and sniper position on a hill to the west of the village. At approximately 0825 the U.S. Army elements began their egress out of the village.

The main Army element moved north across a river into the village of Ali Bad. The ANA soldiers remained in their security position in northern Darbart for the overwatch position to break down and link up with them. As the overwatch element was contouring along the hill, the ANA/ETT and U.S. Army overwatch began receiving a heavy volume of accurate PKM (machine-gun) fire from Honcho Hill. Madding immediately ran from ANA position to ANA position to ensure that the ANA soldiers were directing their fire at the correct location and using proper fire discipline.

Moments after the engagement began, the team leader of the overwatch position broadcast over the radio that he had three wounded soldiers. A U.S. Army platoon commander called over the radio and asked the ETT element if it had a medic. Since it did not, Madding and the other ETT member volunteered to go to the Army position and provide medical attention. They took two ANA soldiers with them and moved under heavy enemy PKM fire from two positions, uphill five hundred meters to the Army casualty collection point (CCP). Upon entering the CCP, Madding and the other ETT first assessed the casualties and the security positions. They placed the soldiers in more secure positions and incorporated the two ANA soldiers into the security plan. The three wounded soldiers were all urgent surgical casualties. Two soldiers had gunshot wounds to the knees and one received a gunshot wound to the back, one inch from his spine. He was also suffering from internal bleeding. Madding identified the most critical patient and immediately began applying first aid. He quickly controlled the bleeding and directed another U.S. Army soldier to maintain pressure on the bandage that he had applied. Madding then moved to the next patient. While he was providing medical attention to the second patient, he called in a split indirect fire mission on two enemy PKM positions, suppressing the enemy. He then organized a litter team to transport the patients to the medevac helicopters and gave them instructions on transporting the patients.

Madding continued suppressing the enemy by directing 120-mm mortars until Apache aircraft arrived on station. When the medevac helicopters arrived, they lowered a flight medic into the CCP. Madding informed the flight medic of all the injuries and the patients' statuses. He then assisted in hoisting the casualties onto the helicopter, which hovered seventy-five feet above the ground. Once the medevac was complete, Madding led the remaining U.S. Army and ANA soldiers to the ANA security position and organized them all into three elements so they could cross the river and link up with the other U.S. Army elements. His exceptional planning and motivation and his unwavering professionalism, combined with his combat leadership and superior mentoring and advising skills, undoubtedly saved the lives of three U.S. Army soldiers and set a tremendous example for the ANA soldiers as well as his fellow ETT team members to emulate.

BRONZE STAR WITH COMBAT DISTINGUISHING DEVICE "V" CITATION

The President of the United States of America takes pleasure in presenting the Bronze Star Medal with Combat "V" to CORPORAL MARC A. MADDING, United States Marine Corps, for heroic achievement in connection with combat operations against the enemy as an Embedded Advisor, Embedded Training Team 5-4, 201st Corps, Afghanistan National Army, on 23 December 2008, in support of Operation Enduring Freedom. While on a combined patrol with the Afghanistan National Army, Embedded Training Team and elements of Viper Company, 1/26 U.S. Army, Corporal Madding selflessly exposed himself to intense enemy fire to assist a U.S. Army element that sustained three casualties. As the overwatch position came under fire, three U.S. Army soldiers received gunshot wounds. Corporal Madding and another Embedded Training Team member ran 500 meters uphill, across open terrain through heavy enemy fire and established security around the wounded soldiers. Corporal Madding then assessed the casualties and began to administer aid to the most serious casualty who received a gunshot wound to his back. After administering aid to the soldier, he then conducted a call for fire (split mission), which suppressed two enemy fighting positions. Then Corporal Madding requested an urgent medevac for the three "urgent surgical" casualties. With the help of another Embedded Training Team, Corporal Madding continued to hold security until the medevac helicopter arrived and hoisted all three soldiers to safety. Once the soldiers were evacuated, Corporal Madding and his fellow Embedded Training Team linked up with their patrol and continued with their mission. Corporal Madding's total effectiveness, forceful leadership, and loyal devotion to duty reflected great credit upon himself and were in keeping with the highest traditions of the Marine Corps and of the United States Naval Service. (Corporal Madding is authorized to wear the Combat "V".)

Information for this account is drawn from the U.S. Marine Corps "Award Summary of Action" (2008) and the Bronze Star Medal Citation for Marc A. Madding (2009).

CPL DAKOTA L. MEYER

Embedded Training Team 2-8, Regional Corps Advisory
Command 3-7, Combined Joint Task Force 82.

born: Columbia, Kentucky

Awarded the Medal of Honor for heroic actions on
8 September 2009, Ganjgal Village, Sarkoni District,
Kunar Province, Afghanistan,
along the Afghan–Pakistani border

I have read every Medal of Honor citation in Marine Corps
history, and the story of then-Cpl Dakota Meyer (later promoted to sergeant) is the greatest story of heroic actions
I have ever heard of. I know Dakota; he is a very nice young man
who claims he is not a hero. I disagree. It takes tremendous courage to run toward the sound of the gun one time; Dakota ran
toward the sound of the gun *five* times. When someone asked
Meyer if he thought he was going to die that day, he responded
with, "I did not think I was going to die, I knew I was going to
die." He told me that that is why he fought so ferociously that
day; he was going to kill as many enemy troops as he could, and
he was going to save as many friendly personnel as possible
before he died. His is an incredible story of immense courage.

The Ganjgal Valley is an area that is rugged, steep, compartmentalized, and dotted with small villages with terraced
agriculture fields. The enemy was about forty to sixty insurgents fighting from well-fortified positions within Ganjgal
Village and from the mountains above Ganjgal Valley along a
prepared ambush, with a one-kilometer kill zone. The weather
on 8 September 2008 was sunny, clear, and in the low 80s.

Embedded Training Team (ETT) 2-8, with elements of 1st
Kandak, 2nd Brigade, 201st Corps of the Afghan National Army
(ANA) and 2nd Kandak of the Afghan Border Police (ABP),
moved into the Ganjgal Valley, Kunar Province, Afghanistan, to
execute Operation Buri Booza II (Dancing Goat II). Their mission was to conduct a key leader engagement with the village

elders of Ganjgal Village and to photographically document any military-age males found in the village.

Although the patrol was entering Ganjgal Valley to discuss security and development plans with the elders, it had prepared to respond to enemy contact based on past operations in the area. According to the plan developed during the preceding days, the unit was organized into four elements: an observation post, a quick-reaction force (QRF), a dismounted patrol, and a security element that was located at the objective rally point (ORP). Task Force Chosin provided a squad of scouts that manned the observation post overlooking the village of Dam Darye and a platoon that was mounted in highly mobile multiwheeled vehicles (HMMWV), mine-resistant ambush-protected vehicles, and armored security vehicles at the mouth of Ganjgal Valley.

The combined ETT/ANA/ABP unit crossed the line of departure at 0300 and traveled in HMMWVs and unarmored pickup trucks from the main route, up an unimproved jeep trail to the east, toward Ganjgal Village. The ORP was established about an hour later and dismounted, leaving behind the vehicles with a security element of the ANA, SSgt Juan Rodriguez-Chavez, and Corporal Meyer. The remaining ANA and ABP units, together with their Marine and Army advisers, continued to the village on foot. Three Marines and one Navy corpsman were forward with the lead of the column, and three Marines and two soldiers were located in the middle of the column with the combined ANA/ABP command element. The ABP were to isolate Ganjgal to the east and south, allowing the ANA element to enter the village to conduct a key leader engagement and document any military-age males.

As the patrol climbed the valley floor toward Ganjgal, all of the lights of the village went out at about 0520. At about 0530 the lead element was caught in a deliberate, complex ambush near the village of Ganjgal. The ambush was initiated with a furious volley of rocket-propelled grenades (RPGs), mortars, and machine-gun fire from PKM, DSHKA (12.7-mm × 108 heavy machine gun), at least one recoilless rifle, and various small arms. Subsequent fire from both flanks joined this initial fire against the lead element of the patrol. At this point the enemy

positions formed a U-shaped kill zone measuring approximately one kilometer in length. As the enemy engaged the
patrol from three sides, other anti-Afghan forces continued to
move parallel to the patrol in an attempt to completely envelop
it. Under the assault of this murderous fire, the ANA soldiers and
ETT members took cover in the terraced landscape, returned
fire, and attempted to call for indirect fire and air support. For
reasons unknown at the time, air support was denied. With no
air support available, indirect fire was called on the hills surrounding the village. Initial suppression of enemy positions
was successful. However, the enemy continued to maneuver
against the patrol as well as fire from buildings within Ganjgal.
Subsequent fire missions were called to support against these
new positions but were questioned because of the proximity
to the village. The forward-most Marine advisers requested
smoke to screen the withdrawal of the lead elements. Finding
that smoke was unavailable, two on-call targets were fired with
one round each of white phosphorous before the supporting
mortars were ordered to cease fire. The white phosphorous
rounds were ineffective and did not provide sufficient smoke
to screen movement. While casualties mounted, the patrol
remained pinned down without support for two hours.

Frustrated by the desperate radio traffic and the lack of
supporting arms, and witnessing the enemy actions firsthand from their relatively safe location at the ORP, Meyer
and Rodriguez-Chavez repeatedly asked permission to enter
the kill zone but were denied due to the unstable situation.
The ETT advisers in the lead element of the patrol reported
that they were fighting from inside a house on the edge of
Ganjgal and were in danger of being cut off from the rest of
the unit. Requests for helicopter medevac were sent over the
radio. Seeing that the patrol's organic fires were ineffective to
cover a withdrawal, Meyer disregarded his own safety and initiated a plan to move into the kill zone in an attempt to link
up with the Marines who were in danger of being cut off, as
well as support the evacuation of mounting casualties. Meyer's
plan called for Rodriguez-Chavez to serve as driver of Meyer's
HMMWV. Meyer, despite being junior in rank, easily assumed
the role of vehicle commander in the vehicle's turret, from

which he directed Rodriguez-Chavez around obstacles and toward the patrol pinned down in the kill zone. Rodriguez-Chavez did not hesitate to help execute this extraordinary rescue mission, but it was Meyer's initiative that set the plan in motion.

Unable to convince the ANA soldiers in the ORP to go with them, Meyer manned the MK-19 machine gun and, with Rodriguez-Chavez driving, moved east into the valley. In the face of overwhelming RPG, mortar, and machine-gun fire, Meyer, with no supporting arms or additional troops, directed the vehicle deeper into the kill zone. Some of the impacting RPG and mortar rounds exploded within 5 meters of the lone HMMWV, bracketing it and impacting in the road in front of the vehicle. Undeterred, Meyer and Rodriguez-Chavez continued into the valley. En route to support the encircled advisers at the lead of the column, they found 5 wounded ANA soldiers along a trail and evacuated them back to a location about 150 meters to the west that provided them with better cover and concealment.

After dropping off this first group of wounded ANA soldiers, Meyer and Rodriguez-Chavez turned around and returned to the kill zone in an attempt to link up with the Marines in the lead element of the column. At this point they encountered elements of a QRF on the side of the road. Meyer dismounted to talk to the crew of a lone QRF HMMWV to convince them to come with him into the valley. The crew refused on the grounds that they did not have permission to go with them. Undaunted, Meyer remounted his HMMWV, informed Rodriguez-Chavez that they would still drive in alone, and resumed engaging the enemy with the MK-19 as they drove deeper into the valley. After firing multiple cans of ammunition, the MK-19 developed a stoppage that Meyer could not remedy, and he quickly switched to the adjacent mounted M240 machine gun to continue to suppress enemy firing at him.

Again they encountered four more wounded ANA soldiers, including a company first sergeant. They loaded the HMMWV with the casualties and returned to the same point where they dropped off the previous group of wounded ANA men. The ANA first sergeant frantically insisted that the situation was too dangerous in the valley and that they should not return. After dropping off the ANA first sergeant and other Afghan soldiers, Meyer and Rodriguez-Chavez decided to return to the ORP to switch out vehicles and attempt to get more firepower. At this point radio communication was lost with the Marine advisers at the head of the column.

At the ORP, Meyer jumped out of the HMMWV and remounted the nearest idle gun-truck with a .50-cal machine gun. Rodriguez-Chavez got in to drive the truck. As they drove into the kill zone again, the enemy machine-gun fire intensified. Personnel from the overwatch positions in the mountains on the north side of the valley reported via radio that the enemy was encircling the column and that Meyer and Rodriguez-Chavez were in danger of being surrounded. The overwatch positions began to fire at the enemy who were attempting to flank the lone HMMWV. The enemy closed with the HMMWV until they were below the angle of the machine-gun barrel.

Unable to depress the gun low enough, Meyer, demonstrating incredible presence of mind, switched to his M4 and continued engaging from the turret, killing at least one enemy with a head shot as Rodriguez-Chavez was evaluating the worsening terrain. Rodriguez-Chavez told Meyer that the HMMWV might get stuck in the rough terrain ahead. Meyer acknowledged this risk and indicated he understood that getting stuck would mean probable death. In spite of this, Meyer clearly stated his intention to press deeper into the kill zone by remarking, "I guess we'll die with them." Rodriguez-Chavez resumed forward movement and immediately took effective machine-gun fire from the south. Meyer switched back to the .50 cal and deftly suppressed the enemy position. Rodriguez-Chavez spotted a yellow smoke grenade and drove toward it in an effort to help find embattled Americans.

At this point members of the main element of the patrol came into view. They were all on foot, crossing open terrain and struggling to evacuate a wounded U.S. Army sergeant first class who had been wounded in the face and neck. Meyer provided suppressive fire as Rodriguez-Chavez drove cross-country and closed the distance. Rodriguez-Chavez maneuvered the HMMWV between the enemy and the group of friendly personnel in order to shield the personnel from the incoming direct fire. Throughout this maneuver, Meyer placed effective fire into the enemy positions with his .50 cal and, when that weapon eventually went down, his M240 machine gun. By this time Meyer had transitioned fluidly between four different weapon systems, including three varieties of crew-served weapons that he employed single-handedly, demonstrating an imperturbable combat mindset and an unusually high degree of tactical competence under great pressure. He would later employ a fifth weapon system: his M203 grenade launcher.

Once the ETT advisers reached a point of relative safety, Meyer and Rodriguez-Chavez drove their HMMWV deeper into the valley in search of the four U.S. advisers with whom they had lost radio contact. As they approached the village, Meyer notified Rodriguez-Chavez that the .50-caliber machine gun now had a malfunction that could not be fixed and that they should return to the ORP to switch to yet another HMMWV with a working heavy machine gun. As Rodriguez-Chavez began to turn the vehicle around, they took accurate RPG and mortar fire, and Meyer sustained a laceration to his arm. Meyer assured Rodriguez-Chavez that he was well enough to continue. Rodriguez-Chavez succeeded in turning the vehicle around amid the bursting rounds and drove toward the ORP.

When they encountered what appeared to be more wounded Afghan soldiers lying prone, Meyer dismounted the vehicle and went over to assess the ANA men up close; all the while, rounds impacted near his feet. After discovering that these Afghan soldiers were all dead, Meyer remounted the HMMWV and they headed back to the ORP.

Meyer and Rodriguez-Chavez returned to the position where they dropped off the wounded ANA soldiers, which had by now become the casualty collection point (CCP). The condition of the HMMWV turret, with its fresh pock marks from shrapnel and with enemy bullets still embedded in the armor, indicated just how many close calls Meyer had faced from his exposed position as the turret gunner. Meyer jumped off the HMMWV and ran behind the terrace wall that two Marines were using for cover. Meyer tried to gather information from the Marines concerning the whereabouts of the four advisers that had been at the head of the column, who were still unaccounted for. Meanwhile, Capt. William D. Swenson (CPT U.S. Army) and 1st Lt Ademola D. Fabayo returned to the CCP, offloaded ANA casualties, and then went with Rodriguez-Chavez back to the ORP to pick up an HMMWV with a functional crew-served weapon and to persuade more Afghan soldiers to move forward and assist.

Meyer, a combat lifesaver, remained at the CCP, providing security and assessing the casualties. He carefully examined Maj Kevin Williams' wounded arm, which was bleeding and turning very painful as the major's natural adrenaline level tapered off. Next Meyer turned his attention to 1st Sgt Christopher Garza, and in the process displayed his ability to take charge when those senior to him were partially incapacitated. Recognizing that Garza was uncharacteristically argumentative and behaving abnormally, Meyer correctly surmised that Garza had sustained a severe concussion from an RPG burst. Brushing aside Garza's vehement insistence that he intended to stay in the fight, Meyer persuaded Williams that Garza must be evacuated immediately. Garza was soon evacuated; follow-on treatment confirmed Meyer's judgment.

Meyer remained at the CCP until his comrades returned from the ORP for another attempt to find the four Americans. When they arrived, Meyer remounted the HMMWV, this time as a passenger. First Lieutenant Fabayo manned the MK-19, Rodriguez-Chavez drove, and Swenson sat in the front passenger seat. Three ANA HMMWVs and an ABP pickup truck followed them. The convoy pressed deep into the kill zone for what would be Meyer's and Rodriguez-Chavez's final time that day. Captain Swenson contacted the scout weapons team (SWT) OH-58D pilots and U.S. Air Force pararescuemen who were now orbiting in a UH-60 helicopter to assist in looking for the missing Marines and sailor as the small convoy continued into the valley toward the village of Ganjgal.

After a few low passes, the SWT was able to spot some personnel lying motionless in a ditch near the town. The pararescuemen also spotted motionless personnel whose location they marked with a purple smoke grenade thrown from above.

The helicopters continued to circle while taking fire from the town. Rodriguez-Chavez drove toward the smoke and got as close as the terrain would permit. Meyer immediately jumped out and began searching for his lost comrades amid continued small-arms fire, followed by Swenson and an ANA interpreter. The personnel the SWT had first located turned out to be dead ABP. Meyer continued searching for the missing Marines and corpsman, maintaining radio contact with helicopter pilots who assisted his search.

Even with the helicopter keeping an eye on him from above, Meyer was in a riskier position now than he would have been in had he stayed close to the vehicles with other members of his group. He was out in front of the group, moving near buildings and terrain that he could not see around, and drawing a high volume of enemy fire. The pilots deemed the area too hot to land. One pilot, who reported taking fire from windows and doorways in the village, informed Meyer that he had found what appeared to be four Americans in a ditch. Meyer, disregarding continuing small-arms, RPG, mortar, and machine-gun fire, ran in the direction of the helicopter until he came upon the bodies of all four missing advisers. He retrieved the lifeless body of one of his four fallen brothers and moved him out of the ditch, across the danger zone to the back of the ABP pickup truck. Swenson and the ABP commander assisted him in recovering the other three fallen advisers as enemy fire continued. Once the bodies were recovered, the five vehicles turned around and drove back to the ORP under fire. Swenson and Fabayo got full accountability of the coalition forces and then returned with the remainder of the combined force to Camp Joyce. In the course of the day, three U.S. Marines, one Navy corpsman, and ten Afghan national security agents would lose their lives, while five U.S. personnel and seventeen Afghan national security agents would be wounded. One of the wounded U.S. personnel would later succumb to his wounds.

During the course of this action, Meyer personally saved the lives of nine wounded ANA soldiers by ground medevac and, indirectly, fourteen to sixteen others as well as five Americans by covering their withdrawal or evacuation. His tenacious courage, technical and tactical proficiency, and cool presence of mind prevented further American and Afghan losses that day and ensured the recovery of the four fallen team members. His deliberate decision to risk his life by repeatedly entering the kill zone to assist wounded comrades or recover fallen ones was in keeping with the highest traditions of the Marine Corps and the United States Naval Services.

MEDAL OF HONOR CITATION

For conspicuous gallantry and intrepidity at the risk of his life above and beyond the call of duty while serving with Marine Embedded Training Team 2-8, Regional Corps Advisory Command 3-7, in Kunar Province, Afghanistan, on 8 September 2009. CORPORAL MEYER maintained security at a patrol rally point while other members of his team moved on foot with two platoons of Afghan National Army and border police into the village of Ganjgal for a predawn meeting with village elders. Moving into the village, the patrol was ambushed by more than 50 enemy fighters firing rocket propelled grenades, mortars, and machine guns from houses and fortified positions on the slopes above. Hearing over the radio that four U.S. team members were cut off, Corporal Meyer seized the initiative. With a fellow Marine driving, Corporal Meyer took the exposed gunners position in a gun-truck as they drove down the steeply terraced terrain in a daring attempt to disrupt the enemy attack and locate the trapped U.S. team. Disregarding intense enemy fire now concentrated on their lone vehicle, Corporal Meyer killed a number of enemy fighters with the mounted machine guns and his rifle, some at near point blank range, as he and his driver made three solo trips into the ambush area. During the first two trips, he and his driver evacuated two dozen Afghan soldiers, many of whom were wounded. When one machine gun became inoperable, he directed a return to the rally point to switch to another gun-truck for a third trip into the ambush area where his accurate fire directly supported the remaining U.S. personnel and Afghan soldiers fighting their way out of the ambush. Despite a shrapnel wound to his arm, Corporal Meyer made two more trips into the ambush area in a third gun-truck accompanied by four other Afghan vehicles to recover more wounded Afghan soldiers and search for the missing U.S. team members. Still under heavy enemy fire, he dismounted the vehicle on the fifth trip and moved on foot to locate and recover the bodies of his team members. Corporal Meyer's daring initiative and bold fighting spirit throughout the 6-hour battle significantly disrupted the enemy's attack and inspired the members of the Combined Force to fight on. His unwavering courage and steadfast devotion to his U.S. and Afghan comrades in the face of almost certain death reflected great credit upon himself and upheld the highest traditions of the Marine Corps and the United States Naval Service.

Information for this account is drawn from the U.S. Marine Corps "Award Summary of Action" (2009) and the Medal of Honor Citation for Dakota L. Meyer (2011), from a personal interview with Meyer at Quantico, VA, 9 November 2010, and from a personal interview with J. J. Rodriguez-Chavez at Arlington, VA, 15 September 2011.

SSGT JOHN S. MOSSER

COMPANY H, 2ND MARINE SPECIAL OPERATIONS BATTALION,
MARINE SPECIAL OPERATIONS COMMAND

BORN: DRIPPING SPRINGS, TEXAS

AWARDED THE NAVY CROSS FOR HEROIC ACTIONS ON 26 JUNE 2008,
FARAH PROVINCE, AFGHANISTAN

On 26 June 2008 Combined Joint Special Operations Task Force Afghanistan directed that Marine Special Operations Team (MSOT) 1 and MSOT 2 respond to a time-sensitive target in the Farah Province, Afghanistan. They combined forces and executed a combat reconnaissance patrol to action a high-value target located in the mountains. Attached to the combined patrol was an element of twenty-four Afghan National Army soldiers. The combination of forces was led by a captain as the team leader and by SSgt John S. Mosser as the team sergeant. The patrol moved under cover of darkness to a draw in the mountain range where the high-value target and his security element were known to be in hiding. The patrol was tasked to enter and, if necessary, clear the draw of any enemy personnel. Upon conclusion of the clearing operation, the unit was to exploit the site for tactical information and anything of value. The terrain in and around the target area was restrictive and mountainous. Large rocks and boulders lined the path along the entire route into the target area. The path traveled along the draw and had multiple curves behind rock outcroppings, making it impossible to view from the mouth of the draw. MSOT 1 was tasked with clearing the area while MSOT 2 was tasked with providing security at the entry to the draw.

As elements entered the draw heading north, their two lead ground mobility vehicles (GMV) turned a corner and came upon two vehicles, a white Toyota Land Cruiser and a red pickup truck. The Toyota was thirty meters off the road to the east and the pickup was in the middle of the road blocking all forward movement. There were no indications or signs of enemy personnel at that time. When element members dismounted and began clearing the area, enemy machine guns fired on the dismounted force from high on the mountainside to the west. Rounds began impacting both on the forward element and the rear element of the dismounts, effectively blocking escape in either direction. Due to a bend in the road, the two GMVs and all twenty-four dismounted personnel were trapped in the open kill zone.

Mosser immediately began firing on enemy fighting positions with his M4 while receiving direct fire. As he returned fire, he and the team leader directed personnel deeper into the draw and in the open in order to peel back to covered positions behind the GMVs. His accurate covering fire allowed six personnel trapped in the kill zone to break contact and maneuver to cover. Once his team members had reached cover, he broke contact and maneuvered to a small rock outcropping, simultaneously giving detailed situation reports to his team and the security element at the opening of the draw. As he reached cover, he realized the GMV crew-served weapons gunners were having difficulty identifying the enemy fighting positions. With complete disregard for his own safety, he moved from his covered position into the kill zone and directed the gunners onto enemy targets positioned in the dominating terrain. At this point two team members were wounded by direct fire from the enemy positions on the mountain. Both Marines were shot in their legs and fell wounded in the kill zone. Despite accurate enemy sniper fire, Mosser heroically exposed himself to enemy fire and ran ten meters into the kill zone to render first aid to one of the casualties. As he ran into the kill zone, he immediately engaged targets with his M4 and despite absolute chaos calmly assessed the casualty's medical condition and reassured him that he was going to be taken care of. While still under fire, he grabbed the casualty and dragged him to the covered position ten meters away while continuing to suppress the enemy with his M4, firing with one hand. Upon reaching cover he continued to evaluate the casualty's condition and applied desperately needed medical attention.

Meanwhile, seven others became trapped behind the lead GMV. Due to the orientation of the vehicles and the high angle of the enemy's firing positions, there was minimal cover provided by the vehicle. As Mosser applied medical aid to his first casualty, one of his team corpsmen received a gunshot wound to the chest. When the enemy observed their own accuracy, they increased their rate of fire in and around the GMV while members of the team attempted to provide medical attention to their wounded comrade. As Mosser witnessed the increased rate of fire on the GMV, he made the decision to move from his covered position, directly exposing himself to enemy fire, to suppress the enemy. His selfless actions drew fire away from the GMV, allowing medical attention to continue. He remained in the line of fire, returning fire, until his men behind the GMV could move the doc (as Marines call their hospital corpsmen) to a better position of cover and continue medical attention. After finding a covered position, Mosser began directing security element vehicles and personnel to position themselves in such a way that they could suppress enemy fighting positions. Concurrently, he continued to assess, monitor, and apply critical aid to his wounded teammate. Mosser continued to calmly assess the situation and command and control the men trapped behind the GMV. Still under accurate enemy fire, Mosser's composure allowed the members of the team to maintain stability and minimize any chaos that could have ensued based on the situation at that time.

Over an hour had elapsed and close-air support (CAS) arrived on station. The team leader, while pinned down, directed Mosser to have the primary joint terminal air controller (JTAC), located with MSOT 2, employ CAS assets to drop a series of bombs on the enemy's location. Unknown to the team leader, the JTAC was approximately five hundred meters away and, due to the distance and terrain, could not observe the ambush area. With accurate fire still pinning him down, Mosser, a qualified JTAC, moved from cover into the kill zone to identify enemy positions and generate accurate ten-digit coordinates for the aircraft to engage. After exposing himself yet again to generate target coordinates, he returned to cover and relayed all information to the primary controller. As the aircraft engaged the enemy in the mountains to the west, Mosser again exposed himself to enemy fire to identify the impacts, mentally noted the corrections needed to adjust them onto target, and returned fire. As he relayed these corrections to the primary controller, he continued to command and control his troops on the ground, who remained pinned down. As the aircraft continued to engage enemy positions, a Marine was shot in the head and another was shot in the shoulder. Assessing the situation and acting immediately, Mosser directed one of the GMVs to back up and move the casualties to a patient transfer point closer to the opening of the draw. He coordinated the transfer of patients from the GMV to one of the security element vehicles while taking accurate fire on his position. He again exposed himself to accurate enemy machine-gun and sniper fire to provide covering fire for the movement of the casualties. As he was providing cover fire, he also provided corrections to the aircraft as they continued to engage targets closer and closer to friendly positions.

Despite the CAS, all elements in the draw remained pinned down with heavy and accurate enemy fire. While seeking cover behind a GMV and providing aide to his fallen comrades, another corpsman received a gunshot wound to the leg, and the situation continued to get more and more desperate. The medevac helicopter that had been called in remained in orbit outside of the draw and was now nearing critical fuel status. The medevac crew informed the ground forces that they had only five minutes of time left on station if they were going to be able to make it back to Farah. Mosser knew that at least one patient would certainly die if he did not get to a medical facility very soon. Understanding the gravity of the situation, he immediately and without hesitation developed a plan to break out of the current position. He again exposed himself to enemy fire, returned fire at enemy positions, and made a last attempt to accurately identify the enemy positions. He coordinated with the controller to have the aircraft drop a five-hundred-pound bomb on the enemy position while dismounted personnel prepared to move. Next the aircraft would drop a two-thousand-pound bomb inside "danger close" safety parameters, and the members would move with the casualties to a large rock outcropping where Afghan National Army soldiers were currently behind cover. After the two-thousand-pound bomb impact, he ordered everyone to hold their position and ran into the kill zone to ensure that the munitions had the desired effect on the enemy targets. He then gave the order to move, and all members began crossing the kill zone to the rock outcropping. During this time he returned to his position and dragged his casualty, with assistance from another Marine, the twenty meters across the kill zone to the hastily established casualty collection point (CCP). As the enemy recovered from the air engagement, they began firing as Mosser and another Marine dragged the casualty to the CCP; Mosser continued to return fire while dragging the casualty.

With all members finally consolidated, Mosser instructed the team on the next portion of the plan. He told the drivers that they were to drive forward to an area where they could turn around and reposition their vehicles to serve as a shield for the dismounts, with one vehicle pulling up to the CCP in order to transfer casualties. As the vehicles reached their position, he led the team out into the kill zone to transfer the patients into the GMV for movement out of the draw and to the medevac landing zone. Once the casualties had been transferred and the GMVs had departed for the landing zone, he instructed the remaining members to establish a defensive position at the CCP and prepare to repel any enemy attacks that might occur.

As the defensive perimeter was established, Mosser coordinated with his team leader for another GMV to come down to his position in the draw in order to extract all remaining personnel, including the last two casualties. He wisely instructed that this vehicle back down the road in reverse in order to allow for a faster extract (turning the vehicle around would have been too time consuming, if not impossible). The driver of the GMV could not see behind him and had extreme difficulty backing his vehicle down the winding road, almost flipping it at one point. Mosser realized the problem and immediately broke cover and ran through the kill zone to the vehicle and remained outside of it, verbally guiding the driver back into position. At this point he began organizing the remaining personnel and prepared them for movement into the vehicles for extract. Once everyone was in position, he gave the order to move and established a firing position, firing on the enemy positions and covering the movement of his fellow teammates.

Mosser's heroic actions were directly responsible for saving the lives of all twenty-three members trapped in the draw that day. Additionally, doctors confirmed that if Mosser had not provided medical attention to the first casualty, who had a gunshot wound to the leg, he would have, at a minimum, lost his leg if not died due to femoral bleeding. Mosser's overwhelmingly calm and decisive leadership in the most chaotic of situations allowed each member of the team to remain calm and confident that he would get them out of the ambush. At the conclusion of the engagement, there were seven confirmed enemy killed in action and estimates of forty enemy killed in action. There were also numerous midlevel targets killed during the engagement, causing a severe blow to and greatly disrupting the growing insurgent network in western Afghanistan.

Navy Cross Citation

The President of the United States of America takes pleasure in presenting the Navy Cross to STAFF SERGEANT JOHN S. MOSSER, United States Marine Corps, for extraordinary heroism in connection with combat operations against the enemy while serving as Team Sergeant, Marine Special Operations Company H, Second Marine Special Operations Battalion, U.S. Marine Corps Forces, Special Operations Command, in support of Operation Enduring Freedom on 26 June 2008. While maneuvering through restrictive terrain to prosecute a time-sensitive high value target, dismounted patrol members were engaged with heavy volumes of high-angle automatic and sniper fire. Within seconds, two Marines lay wounded in the kill zone unable to seek cover. With disregard for his own safety, Staff Sergeant Mosser maintained keen situational awareness and calm under fire as he rushed to the aid of the nearest Marines. He single-handedly dragged the wounded Marine over 35 feet to a covered position and administered first aid. With the entire patrol desperately pinned down, one Marine killed, and five more severely wounded, Staff Sergeant Mosser devised a plan to break contact and extract his team. While adjusting close air support, he personally shielded and moved the wounded Marine through the kill zone a second time to safety. He then ordered the extraction of the remaining 22 members trapped in the ambush. As he instructed the team to move, Staff Sergeant Mosser exposed himself repeatedly to enemy fire and engaged the enemy until all members were safe. By his courageous actions, bold initiative, and total devotion to duty, Staff Sergeant Mosser reflected great credit upon himself and upheld the highest traditions of the Marine Corps and of the United States Naval Service.

Information for this account is drawn from the U.S. Marine Corps "Award Summary of Action" (2008) and the Navy Cross Medal Citation for John S. Mosser (2009).

CPL MICHAEL W. OUELLETTE

Company L, 3rd Battalion, 8th Marines, Special Purpose
Marine Air Ground Task Force, Afghanistan

home of record: Manchester, New Hampshire

Awarded the Navy Cross, posthumously,
for heroic actions on 22 March 2009, Now Zad District,
Helmand Province, Afghanistan

On 22 March 2009 Cpl Michael Ouellette led his rifle squad on a combat patrol near known enemy positions in Now Zad District, Afghanistan. A Marine in the patrol triggered an improvised explosive device (IED) that detonated next to Ouellette, severing his left leg at the knee and inflicting multiple shrapnel wounds to his arms and right thigh. The Marines around him were blown off their feet by the blast and stunned but not seriously injured. Ouellette immediately took charge of the situation. He called for one Marine to help him apply tourniquets to both his legs and drag him free of the blast crater while directing the remainder of the squad to establish security in the area, ensuring that his M249 squad automatic weapons (SAW) were positioned to counter a possible attack. As he gave his orders, enemy forces began firing on the squad from multiple directions, including within hand-grenade range of his position.

Unable to maneuver because of his injuries and the substantial pressure-plate IED threat, Ouellette immediately controlled the fire of his squad while simultaneously passing his own medevac request and directing his radio operator to request reinforcements and close-air support. Over the next thirty minutes Ouellette continued to give directions to his squad by voice and intrasquad radio, orchestrating the defense of their position while waiting for the mounted quick-reaction force (QRF) to reach the nearest link-up point accessible by vehicle. Once the QRF reached that position several hundred meters away, he dispatched one fire team and a combat engineer to clear a path through the pressure-plate minefield to link up with the QRF and guide them to his position.

Although his squad members' fire halted several enemy attempts to overrun their position, they could not suppress the enemy enough to maneuver themselves. Ouellette calmly directed his radio operator in the employment of a section of AH-1W Cobra attack helicopters. With Ouellette's guidance, the radio operator brought gun and rocket runs against the enemy fighters within fifteen meters of the squad's position. Although the air support was effective, the enemy resumed firing shortly thereafter, including indirect fire against both his squad and the dismounted element of the QRF that was moving forward to assist. Ouelette ordered the aircraft to continue its runs as he continued to direct the fire of his squad members and prepared them to bound back. After the reaction force arrived on scene, Ouelette directed his radio operator to call a mortar obscuration mission. Still under fire, he continued to give direction and encouragement to his squad from the litter that carried him to the medevac vehicles. He turned over control of the squad only as he was being loaded into the ambulance. While in the mobile trauma bay awaiting the medevac helicopter's arrival, Ouellette finally succumbed to his wounds and experienced severe respiratory failure. Oullette's ultimate disregard for his personal safety in order to protect his fellow Marines exemplified the core values of honor, courage, and commitment that define the United States Marine Corps. His sacrifice was for the personal safety of the Marines in his charge.

NAVY CROSS CITATION

The President of the United States of America takes pride in presenting the Navy Cross (posthumously) to CORPORAL MICHAEL W. OUELLETTE, United States Marine Corps, for conspicuous gallantry and intrepidity in action against the enemy while serving as the 2nd Squad Leader, 1st Platoon, Company L, 3rd Battalion 8th Marines (Reinforced), Special Purpose Marine Air Ground Task Force, Afghanistan in support of Operation Enduring Freedom. On 22 March 2009, Corporal Ouellette was leading his squad on a combat patrol in Nowzad District, Afghanistan, when an improvised explosive device exploded beneath his feet, severing his left leg and spraying him with shrapnel. Following the explosion, he directed his squad to prepare a hasty defense while helping to treat his own injuries. Moments later, enemy fighters opened fire on his squad with assault rifles and machine guns from point blank range. Even as a corpsman worked to stem his massive bleeding, Corporal Ouellette continued to direct the fire of his squad. When attack helicopters arrived, he coolly talked his radio operator through the employment of the aircraft as they made repeated strafing runs within 20 meters of the squad's position. These expertly-applied fires suppressed the enemy long enough for a fire team to link up with reinforcements and bring them forward to Corporal Ouellette's position. He held that position and continued to give orders to his squad as they fought, allowing himself to be evacuated only when the entire squad was ready to move out of the area. He continued to give directions to his team leader up until he was loaded into an ambulance, where he soon lost consciousness. He later succumbed to his wounds. By his bold leadership, wise judgment, and complete dedication to duty, Corporal Ouellette reflected great credit upon himself and upheld the highest traditions of the Marine Corps and the United States Naval Service.

Information for this account is drawn from the U.S. Marine Corps "Award Summary of Action" (2009) and the Navy Cross Medal Citation for Michael W. Ouellette (2010).

SGT JOSEPH M. PEREZ

COMPANY F, 2ND BATTALION, 2ND MARINES,
MARINE EXPEDITIONARY BRIGADE–AFGHANISTAN

AWARDED THE SILVER STAR MEDAL FOR HEROIC ACTIONS ON
27 DECEMBER 2009, GARMSIR DISTRICT OF
HELMAND PROVINCE, AFGHANISTAN

O n 27 December 2009 Sgt Joseph Perez's squad, part-nered with a fire team of Afghan National Army (ANA) soldiers, conducted an area reconnaissance patrol to the south and west of Luguryan village, where his and other squads had had numerous contacts with the enemy in the past. He openly welcomed the mission and requested to proceed to the west side of the Helmand River. International security assistance force (ISAF) units had never patrolled in this partic-ular area, and based on multiple intelligence reports, Taliban fighters used this location as a staging area for future attacks. Perez's squad departed Patrol Base Lakari at 1000 and was in place east of the river shortly after 1100. At this time, his squad received sensitive reporting that indicated enemy fighters were moving up five medium machine guns to ambush the squad of Marines as they patrolled farther west. Sensitive reporting also indicated that the Taliban had completely surrounded the squad with the plan to ambush the Marines with machine-gun fire from three sides. According to the official summary of action, when Perez was asked by his higher headquarters' combat operations center (COC) what his patrol's next actions would be, Perez calmly responded, "We'll attack."

Perez and his partnered squads' next actions can be under-stood only in the context of what he and his unit had experi-enced over the previous two months of often daily contact with the enemy. Perez's decision to attack fundamentally changed the enemy and friendly situation throughout the entire com-pany battle space from that day forward. Lessons learned from Perez's experiences prior to 27 December indicated that in 95 percent of the circumstances, if an ISAF unit wanted to successfully close with and destroy the enemy when in contact, it had to rapidly (in seconds) assess the enemy situation and then violently attack using only the unit's organic weapons. Perez wanted neither to allow the enemy to escape nor to be responsible for hurting any Afghan civilians because of calling in external fire support assets.

Immediately after telling the COC that they would attack, Perez sent his fire teams in three different directions approximately seventy to one hundred meters apart to areas that would allow the most sufficient mutual support while taking the fight to the enemy. Seconds later, the enemy fighters massed medium machine-gun fire on Perez's first fire team, with whom he had positioned himself, as the base unit of the squad. The first fire team was initially pinned down by a heavy volume of enemy machine-gun and small-arms fire.

The call came back from a Marine that the squad's point man had been hit and lay yelling in a ditch with his hands to his face. Perez ordered the squad to increase the rate of fire to the rapid rate to gain fire superiority over the enemy. At this time, Perez was informed by the COC that sensitive reporting indicated that the enemy fighters would try to take the injured Marine alive and to push their attack toward the pinned-down fire team. Perez immediately exposed himself to the onslaught of incoming machine-gun fire in an attempt to reach the pinned-down and injured Marine. However, due to the massive amount of incoming enemy machine-gun fire, he was unable to reach the Marine. Perez then ordered his second fire team to attack the enemy's position from the north and to destroy the attacking Taliban fighters. As a result of his tactically sound positioning of the fire teams before assaulting the enemy, Perez's team was able to observe two enemy fighters moving from south to north in an attempt to reinforce the enemy ambush force. These fighters were immediately engaged; one was killed instantly and the other fell to the ground after being shot, as indicated by sensitive reporting. As the second fire team closed on the enemy's position, fire on Perez and the first fire team's position decreased. Then Perez sprinted through fifty meters of open field while still under heavy enemy machine-gun fire from multiple positions to render aid to the isolated Marine. Upon arriving and assessing the injured Marine, he determined that the sustained injuries were only superficial wounds to his face. Perez's leadership and courageous actions inspired the Marine to regain his composure and continue the attack.

Then Perez led his base unit to rapidly close with the enemy positions. At multiple times throughout the attack, Perez's fire teams briefly slowed their movement as a result of enemy fire. Each time, Perez, exemplifying the qualities of a true fighter and leader, exposed himself to the enemy fire while showing his fire team leaders what he expected of them to keep up the pace of the attack, regardless of the enemy's fire. As a result of his actions, his squad aggressively counterattacked, fighting its way through a well-planned and coordinated ambush from at least eight and potentially as many as fifteen enemy fighters. By the end of the fight Perez's squad had outmaneuvered the enemy with its rapid and violent actions, combined with a textbook employment of placing the enemy in a combined arms dilemma, using only those weapons assigned at the rifle squad level.

Ultimately, Perez's squad aggressively closed over four hundred meters of open terrain under intense enemy fire and confirmed two enemy fighters dead and one wounded. Sensitive reporting after the battle indicated that multiple enemy fighters had also been evacuated due to wounds. While searching the enemy's firing positions, Perez's squad also retrieved two enemy PKM machine guns, one enemy RPK light machine gun, one chest rig, and several hundred 7.62-mm rounds. Upon consolidation, Perez ensured that his corpsman properly treated the wounded enemy fighter while he called in a medevac for him.

The impact of Perez's partnered squads' actions on this day has been felt throughout Mian Poshteh and Lakari ever since. Both areas had long been Taliban strongholds because the innocent people in the region were afraid of the Taliban, some even believing the Taliban were invincible to attack and all-knowing. Multiple Afghan nationals had observed, from a distance, Perez leading his unit as it closed on the enemy. Upon consolidation, Perez and the ANA soldiers spoke to these people in an attempt to find out the names of the killed and wounded enemy fighters. The Afghan nationals refused to share this information, saying that the enemy fighters were not from the area. In the days, weeks, and months after the fight, multiple partnered patrols were told that they heard and knew about what the Marines and ANA soldiers did to the Taliban southwest of Luguryan. Additionally, multiple elders, some of whom had recently returned to the area after refusing to leave Lashkar Gah for three years due to fear of the Taliban, told a company commander about Perez's partnered squads' actions and about how Perez, forcing his will on the enemy and crushing them on the moral, mental, and physical levels, gained Afghani confidence to return to their homes and to support ISAF efforts in Mian Poshteh and Lakari.

SILVER STAR MEDAL CITATION

The President of the United States of America takes pleasure in presenting the Silver Star to SERGEANT JOSEPH M. PEREZ, United States Marine Corps, for conspicuous gallantry and intrepidity in action against the enemy while serving as Squad Leader, 1st Squad, 3d Platoon, Company F, Second Battalion, Second Marine Regiment, Regimental Combat Team-7, Marine Expeditionary Brigade-Afghanistan, on 27 December 2009 in support of Operation Enduring Freedom. On this day, while on patrol in the vicinity of Luguryan Village, Helmand Province, Sergeant Perez received sensitive reporting that Taliban fighters had completely surrounded his squad and were ready to ambush from five mutually-supporting machinegun positions. Unhesitatingly, he split his squad into three maneuver elements in anticipation of the enemy's actions. Seconds later, the enemy fighters opened fire, pinning down Sergeant Perez and his base unit, and injuring and isolating the squad's pointman. Knowing the enemy's intention to capture the isolated Marine, Sergeant Perez attempted multiple times to reach him, but was denied by heavy enemy fire. He then ordered his 2d Fire Team to attack from the north, a move which effectively reduced the enemy's fires. While still under direct heavy enemy fire, Sergeant Perez sprinted through 50 meters of open field to the isolated Marine and rendered aid to him. Repeatedly exposing himself to enemy fire, Sergeant Perez directed the internal fire support of his squad and violently led his base unit toward the enemy positions. After closing on the enemy positions, Sergeant Perez found two enemy fighters that had been killed and captured one that was wounded along with his machineguns and ammunition. By his bold leadership, wise judgment, and complete dedication to duty, Sergeant Perez reflected great credit upon himself and upheld the highest traditions of the Marine Corps and the United States Naval Service.

Information for this account is drawn from the U.S. Marine Corps "Award Summary of Action" (2009) and the Silver Star Medal Citation for Joseph M. Perez (2010).

SSGT MARK ROBINSON

Marine Special Operations Team 5, Marine Special
Operations Advisor Group, U.S. Marine Corps Forces,
Special Operations Command

home of record: Great Bend, Kansas

Awarded the Silver Star Medal for heroic actions on
28 October 2008, Badghis Province, Afghanistan

On 28 October 2008 SSgt Mark Robinson was part of a combined Afghanistan National Security Force and U.S. Special Operations Force combat reconnaissance patrol that was tasked with confirming the presence of insurgent sanctuaries in the vicinity of Bala Murghab. The patrol was divided into two sections, Alpha and Bravo. Robinson was assigned to the Alpha section, and he carried an M249 squad automatic weapon throughout the patrol. His patrol moved south along a road and would periodically stop and speak with Afghans along the way to determine the atmosphere of the area. Robinson maintained flank security for the patrol and covered the exposed eastern riverbank. As the patrol approached its limit of advance, it came under a barrage of rocket-propelled grenade (RPG) and machine-gun fire.

Robinson immediately identified insurgents on rooftops to the south and engaged them with his automatic weapon, allowing the remainder of the Alpha section to move to a covered position. One insurgent was wounded and knocked off the rooftop, and the other was wounded but managed to seek cover. The Alpha section leader then decided to close on the insurgent-held compound. Robinson and three other Marines pushed into the next compound and cleared the outside. The section rejoined in the compound and cleared the house. Once inside the house, defensive positions were established and the team began taking accurate small-arms fire from insurgents who had positioned themselves on rooftops surrounding the compound. Robinson took another Marine to the entrance of the compound in an attempt to draw enemy fire, thereby enabling the Alpha section to identify the insurgents' exact locations. He then moved to the north side of the compound and unsuccessfully attempted to locate the Afghan National Army soldiers who had been separated from the Alpha section during the early part of the engagement.

Shortly after he returned to the house, an RPG struck the top of the entrance, sending Robinson and three other section members to the ground. The section was forced to move deeper into the building and establish new defensive positions. Almost immediately insurgents were seen maneuvering on the eastern side of the compound toward the building from the riverbank. Robinson positioned himself in the northeastern room and engaged the insurgents. A number of insurgents were wounded by his fire; however, they continued to mass and move toward the compound. At the same time, insurgents tried to breach the openings in the walls of the compound to the south and the west. The other section members repelled the insurgents from their sectors. It became apparent that the section was outnumbered and surrounded.

Robinson reported that he had five or six insurgents within fifty meters of his position. He single-handedly held them off with accurate fire as rounds entered the room's windows, barely missing him. The RPGs left holes in the wall and completely filled the room with smoke and debris. He was temporarily forced away from the window after his position was repeatedly hit with RPG fire. The insurgents exploited this opportunity and were able to move up to the outside of the building. Robinson reported that insurgents were outside his room, and a fight began, with insurgents attempting to thrust their muzzles inside the windows of the building, firing directly into the room. Robinson repelled numerous attempts by throwing hand grenades out of the windows, forcing the insurgents to move away from the walls. He continued this one-man battle until an RPG struck the eastern wall, leaving a large hole and throwing him into the hallway. He regained his composure and continued to hold his position from the corridor. The insurgents breached the single entrance point of the building from the south, and he was forced to join other members of the section in the northwest room. Insurgents shot through the windows into the room and struck the section leader in the forearm. Robinson fired back through the window at the insurgents, allowing the section's corpsman to commence treatment of the injured Marine.

As dusk began to settle, the section members attempted to break out of the house. As they moved to the corridor, an insurgent stepped into the entranceway and fired, hitting the section leader in the arm a second time and forcing them back. Robinson moved to the doorway and fired down the corridor, allowing the exposed members to prepare grenades and throw them out the entrance. As the section members exited, Robinson encountered two insurgents approximately ten meters away and engaged them while on the move. The section turned right toward the northern part of the building, and a group of insurgents fired light machine guns, hitting the section's corpsman. Robinson stepped around the corner and engaged the insurgents, allowing the wounded corpsman to get to his feet and seek cover. At that moment, three members of the section who had moved halfway across the compound began receiving heavy fire.

Robinson rushed down the length of the building, engaging three insurgents as he went, thus allowing the separated section members to make it safely to the far side of the compound wall. From this position, Robinson killed two additional insurgents, enabling the remaining members to rejoin the section around the wall. Robinson took up rear security and moved north with his section. Shortly after this, close-air support began "danger close" gun runs, allowing the section to move to the north. Robinson again assumed rear security for the entire movement, allowing the section members to evacuate their wounded comrades. As the Alpha section continued to fight its way to the north, Robinson assisted in relaying corrections for the close-air support and marked the position of friendly forces. He continued to engage the insurgents who were pursuing his section as it moved back more than eight hundred meters. Once the section had linked up with the medevac platform, he ensured that the wounded members were loaded and only then mounted the vehicle for movement back to the firebase.

Throughout the firefight, Robinson distinguished himself with repeated acts of courage. He placed the welfare of the other members of his section before his own. He showed incredible courage in the face of the enemy. He was personally responsible for killing more than eight insurgents and wounding numerous others. He single-handedly held off an overwhelming enemy force until the room that he occupied alone was all but destroyed. Robinson maintained a warrior spirit that rallied all those around him. His tactical decisions and weapons employment were flawless. Robinson's actions that day undoubtedly saved lives and minimized the casualties suffered by his unit.

SILVER STAR MEDAL CITATION

The President of the United States of America takes pleasure in presenting the Silver Star to STAFF SERGEANT MARK ROBINSON, United States Marine Corps, for conspicuous gallantry and intrepidity in action against the enemy as Element Leader, Marine Special Operations Team 5, Marine Special Operations Advisor Group, U.S. Marine Corps Forces, Special Operations Command, in support of Operation Enduring Freedom. On 28 October 2008, Sergeant Robinson's patrol came under attack from insurgent forces fighting from elevated and concealed positions. After the initial contact, his section assaulted and cleared a nearby enemy held compound. The insurgents immediately counter-attacked this compound with superior numbers. As the insurgents assailed the position he was defending, he single-handedly held them off with accurate fire with his M249 squad automatic weapon. He held his position until a rocket propelled grenade blast threw him into the building's interior corridor. After the impact of the rocket propelled grenade, he quickly regained his composure and, with a high volume of accurate fire, prevented the insurgents from overwhelming his element. When the assistant team leader was wounded, he exposed himself to enemy fire so that the team corpsman could treat the wound. When the decision was made to withdraw, Sergeant Robinson fought a rear guard action against approximately 50 insurgents while moving over 800 meters, allowing his fellow team members to reach safety. His actions saved the lives of those Marines by allowing his isolated section to safely link up with the rest of the patrol. Sergeant Robinson's tremendous fighting spirit defeated the enemy's assault and inspired his fellow Marines. By his bold initiative, undaunted courage, and complete dedication to duty, Sergeant Robinson reflected great credit upon himself and upheld the highest traditions of the Marine Corps and the United States Naval Service.

Information for this account is drawn from the U.S. Marine Corps "Award Summary of Action" (2008) and the Silver Star Medal Citation for Mark Robinson (2009).

SSGT JUAN J. RODRIGUEZ-CHAVEZ

Embedded Training Team 2-8,
Regional Corps Advisory Command 3-7.

born: Mexico

Awarded the Navy Cross for heroic actions on 8 September
2009, Ganjgal village, Kunar Province, Afghanistan,
Operation Buri Booza II (Dancing Goat II).

On 8 September 2009 Embedded Training Team (ETT) 2-8 moved into the Ganjgal Valley, Kunar Province, Afghanistan, with elements of 1st Kandak, 2nd Brigade, 201st Corps of the Afghan National Army (ANA) and 2nd Kandak of the Afghan Border Police (ABP). The mission of this operation was to conduct a key leader engagement with the village elders of Ganjgal village and to document photographically any military-age males found in the village.

Although coalition forces entered Ganjgal Valley to discuss security and development plans with the elders, they had prepared to respond to enemy contact based on past operations in the area. According to the plan developed during the preceding days, the unit was organized into four elements: an observation post, a quick-reaction force (QRF), a dismounted patrol, and a security element at the objective rally point (ORP). The U.S. Army's Task Force Chosin provided a squad of scouts that manned the observation post overlooking the village of Dam Darye and a platoon that was mounted in highly mobile multiwheeled vehicles (HMMWV), mine-resistant ambush-protected (MRAP) vehicles, and armored security vehicles on Route Beaverton at the mouth of the Ganjgal Valley. The rest of the force was made up of an ABP platoon with two U.S. soldiers and an ANA company with Marine ETT advisers. The combined ANA/ABP unit traveled in HMMWVs and unarmored pickup trucks crossing the line of departure at 0300. They arrived at the ORP about an hour later and dismounted, leaving behind the vehicles with a security element of the ANA, SSgt Juan

Rodriguez-Chavez, and Cpl Dakota Meyer. The remaining ANA and ABP units, together with their Marine and Army advisers, continued to the village on foot.

As the combined unit climbed the valley floor toward Ganjgal, all of the lights in the village went out at about 0520, casting an ominous portent of things to come. At about 0530, while conducting the dismounted movement into the valley, the lead element was caught in a deliberate, complex ambush near the village of Ganjgal. The ambush was initiated with a furious volley of rocket-propelled grenades (RPGs), mortars, and machine-gun fire and at least one recoilless rifle and various small arms. The first fusillade erupted from the vicinity of the village using RPGs, mortars, and machine guns from concealed positions in the high ground surrounding the village and from the homes in the village itself, as well as from the village school. The enemy positions formed a U-shaped kill zone measuring approximately one kilometer in length. Under the assault of this murderous fire, the ANA soldiers and Marine ETT members took cover in the terraced landscape, returned fire, and attempted to call for fire with artillery and close-air support (CAS). CAS was denied. With no CAS available, indirect fire was called on the hills surrounding the village, and initial suppression of enemy positions was successful. However, the enemy continued to maneuver against the combined force as well as fire from buildings within Ganjgal. Subsequent fire missions were called to support these new positions, but the combined force was questioned because of the proximity to the village. While casualties mounted, the patrol remained pinned down without support for more than two hours. At about 0730, with CAS finally on station, the headquarters element of the patrol lost contact with the three Marines and one corpsman who were in the forward element of the patrol. During the next two hours the actions of Rodriguez-Chavez altered the course of the day for his fellow Marines and sailors.

Initially Rodriguez-Chavez remained in the ORP and monitored the radio as he maintained security with his gunner, Meyer. Frustrated by the reports of wounded and killed, he asked permission to move into the valley to provide support; however, permission was denied in an effort to prevent more people from becoming trapped in the ambush. After hearing that CAS had been denied and that indirect fire had ceased, Rodriguez-Chavez and Meyer agreed to disregard their own safety and move into the ambush area; the ANA soldiers and Afghan national police in the ORP refused to go with them. The two of them, alone, drove toward the sound of the guns. Rodriguez-Chavez skillfully negotiated the rugged, cross-compartmentalized terrain and established a trail that he would use many more times that day.

As Rodriguez-Chavez drove his HMMWV to the ambush site, the enemy to his front and flanks began to engage the vehicle with mortars, RPGs, machine guns, and other small-arms weapons. The lone HMMWV became a glaring target for the enemy gunners, making the fire so intense that Rodriguez-Chavez turned around to seek cover and try to determine another route to the village. Finding no other route available, Meyer and Rodriguez-Chavez steeled themselves to risk the gauntlet of fire again. As they pressed through the enemy fire, Meyer returned fire with the MK-19 40-mm machine gun and spotted several ANA wounded along the way. After five ANA soldiers were crammed into the HMMWV, Rodriguez-Chavez evacuated them to an area that provided better cover and concealment.

Rodriguez-Chavez drove into the kill zone a second time. Along the way elements of a coalition QRF from Camp Joyce were now in the vicinity. Only one U.S. Army HMMWV from the QRF left the ORP but had stopped short of entering the main part of the kill zone. Rodriguez-Chavez stopped to allow Meyer to ask them to follow. The crew of the lone vehicle refused on the grounds that they had no authorization to go any farther. As they advanced into the kill zone, the QRF HMMWV remained on the side of the road, leaving Rodriguez-Chavez and Meyer to fend for themselves. As Rodriguez-Chavez went forward in search of their comrades at the head of the column, he encountered four more wounded ANA soldiers, including a first sergeant. By this time the MK-19 had a malfunction that could not be cleared, and Meyer switched to using the vehicle's M240 machine gun. The wounded ANA soldiers climbed into the HMMWV, and Rodriguez-Chavez turned around to drop them with the wounded from the previous trip. The ANA first sergeant was stricken with fear and refused to get out of the vehicle. Rodriguez-Chavez forced the first sergeant to get out of the HMMWV and then headed back to the ORP to get another vehicle.

After picking up a new HMMWV with a functional .50-caliber machine gun, Rodriguez-Chavez and Meyer once again drove into the valley toward Ganjgal. This third advance into the ambush culminated with their spotting a yellow smoke grenade signaling friendly casualties. Rodriguez-Chavez gunned the engine and parked the HMMWV between their beleaguered comrades and where the bulk of enemy fire was coming from, thereby shielding them until they could get to cover. Meyer kept up a steady stream of fire from his .50-caliber and M240 machine guns. Once the advisers, carrying a casualty, had reached good cover, Rodriguez-Chavez drove his HMMWV out of the line of fire and into a draw in search of other Marines. At this point the .50-caliber gun had a malfunction that could not be cleared, and at the same time they encountered more wounded ANA soldiers and began to take more enemy fire. Meyer dismounted the HMMWV and found all the ANA soldiers to be dead. He mounted up again, and Rodriguez-Chavez turned his vehicle around to return to a hastily arranged casualty collection point (CCP) halfway back to the ORP.

At the CCP Meyer dismounted to render first aid to the wounded ANA soldiers, and Rodriguez-Chavez drove with no gunner back to the ORP to get another HMMWV with a functioning weapon. At the ORP he linked up with Capt. William D. Swenson (U.S. Army) and 1st Lt Ademola D. Fabayo (USMC); Both mounted the new HMMWV with a functional MK-19 machine gun, manned by Fabayo. They returned to the CCP and picked up Meyer, who rode as a passenger. They led the way into the kill zone for the fourth time to find the missing Marine advisers. Army helicopters circling overhead noted the position of what was believed to be the missing Marines and corpsman and marked it with smoke grenades. Rodriguez-Chavez relentlessly drove his HMMWV toward the smoke in an effort to link up with them and extract them under fire. The

enemy poured fire onto the HMMWV as they neared the village and the marked position. As he approached the smoke, his
gunner's MK-19 machine gun seized up and failed to function.
Rodriguez-Chavez stopped the HMMWV near the sputtering
smoke grenades and allowed Meyer to dismount in order to
continue the search. At this point three ANA HMMWVs and an
ABP pickup truck pulled in behind the lone adviser HMMWV.

Meyer found the isolated Marines and corpsman, all killed
by close-range rifle fire. Rodriguez-Chavez pulled his vehicle
in a position to shield Meyer and the others, allowing them to
carefully load the fallen into the bed of the ABP pickup truck
while under fire. After Meyer remounted the vehicle, Rodriguez-
Chavez managed to evade the remaining enemy fire, shielding
the unarmored pickup with his own vehicle, and return the
fallen advisers to the CCP, and eventually on to Camp Joyce. In
the course of the day, three U.S. Marines, one Navy corpsman,
and ten Afghan national security agents would lose their lives,
while five U.S. personnel and seventeen Afghan national security agents would be wounded.

NAVY CROSS CITATION

The President of the United States of America takes pleasure in presenting the Navy Cross to STAFF SERGEANT JUAN J. RODRIGUEZ-CHAVEZ, United States Marine Corps, for extraordinary heroism in action against the enemy as a member of Marine Embedded Training Team 2-8, Regional Corps Advisory Command 3-7, in Kunar Province, Afghanistan, on 8 September 2009 in support of Operation Enduring Freedom. Assigned to the security element while other members of his team led two platoons of Afghan National Security Forces into Ganjgal Village for a pre-dawn meeting with village elders, Staff Sergeant Rodriguez-Chavez heard over the radio that the dismounted patrol was ambushed by roughly fifty enemy fighters in fortified positions. With four members of his team in immediate danger of being surrounded, he drove a gun-truck, with one other Marine as his gunner, forward into the kill zone of a well prepared ambush. With only the machine gun fires of his gunner to suppress the enemy, he ignored heavy enemy fires and drove the vehicle into the kill zone three times to cover the withdrawal of the combined force and evacuate two dozen members of the Afghan National Security Forces. With complete disregard for his own personal safety, he made a fourth trip into the deepest point of the kill zone in another gun-truck with three other U.S. personnel to recover the bodies of the fallen team members. He positioned his vehicle to shield the U.S. members from the intense enemy fire as they dismounted to recover their bodies. By his decisive actions, bold initiative, and selfless dedication to duty, Staff Sergeant Rodriguez-Chavez reflected great credit upon himself and the Marine Corps and upheld the highest traditions of the United States Naval Service.

Information for this account is drawn from the U.S. Marine Corps "Award Summary of Action" (2009) and the Navy Cross Medal Citation for Juan J. Rodriguez-Chavez (2011), and from a personal interview with Rodriguez-Chavez at Arlington, VA, 15 September 2011.

HN JOSHUA E. SIMSON

Embedded Training Team 6-2,
II Marine Expeditionary Force

home of record: Overland Park, Kansas

Awarded the Silver Star Medal for heroic actions on
27 July 2007, Village of Saret Kholet, Afghanistan

During an extended period of contact on 27 July 2007, HN
Joshua Simson single-handedly provided aid to seventeen separate casualties, both Afghan National Army
(ANA) and U.S. Army soldiers, often willingly exposing himself
to both enemy observation and fire. After meeting with village
elders in Saret Kholet on the morning of 27 July 2007, Simson's
patrol moved east along the south side of the Landay River to
establish an observation post, allowing observation of the
Pitigal Bridge crossing.

While sending a small reconnaissance element to clear a
route for the unit to use, the remainder of the patrol received
both small-arms and rocket-propelled grenade (RPG) fire from
across the river, several hundred meters to the northeast. As
all elements of the patrol returned fire, another enemy element
fired from the northwest, again from effective range just across
the river. With Simson's patrol caught in the interlocking fire
of these two elements, the enemy was able to render multiple casualties in a short period of time using disciplined and
continuing volleys of fire from AK-47s, PKM machine guns,
and RPGs.

In an atmosphere of chaos, Simson left his covered position to provide medical attention to several wounded soldiers,
both ANA and U.S. Army, calling for aid in his immediate vicinity. Simson's first casualty was an ANA soldier who received
shrapnel to his leg. With the help of another adviser, Simson
pulled the ailing ANA soldier into a bunker to provide cover
while he administered medical aid. Shortly after entering the
bunker, they were rocked by a direct hit to the bunker from

an RPG. Though dazed and momentarily blinded by dust and debris, Simson regained his composure and completed care of the soldier. He next tended to a U.S. soldier who had been cleanly shot through his upper hamstring. Low crawling to the injured soldier as enemy fire continued, Simson was unable to find suitable cover and concealment. Remaining visible to the enemy occupying the higher ground across the river, Simson continued to provide care to the wounded soldier as small-arms rounds impacted within two feet. Exhibiting a composure that defined his actions throughout the day, Simson quickly stopped the bleeding and succeeded in aiding the soldier to a position where he could return fire while awaiting medical evacuation.

As the engagement continued, multiple enemy elements from both north and south of the river opened fired on the combined American and Afghan patrol, effectively creating a kill zone around their position. In the afternoon, and with the U.S. troop commander among those killed in action, the decision was made to move west out of the kill zone, where helicopters could evacuate the wounded. This movement used the up-armored highly mobile multiwheeled vehicles (HMMWV) for cover, but the enemy brought fire to bear on both sides of the vehicles, causing further casualties to the withdrawing column. Moving less than one hundred meters under steady small-arms and RPG fire, the column's wounded increased.

Simson worked with U.S Army medics from 1-91 Cavalry, but he chose to walk alongside the vehicles while the medics cared for the more gravely wounded inside the vehicles. As the movement continued, a U.S. soldier was shot in the face just to the front of Simson. He bandaged the soldier's face, applied pressure, and continued to move with his hand maintaining pressure on the wound. When a second U.S. soldier was injured and began losing blood rapidly, Simson immediately pulled the soldier to the side of the road and provided care for him. Unable to get the soldier into a vehicle where care could be provided with cover, Simson, for the third time, found himself administering aid to a fellow serviceman under fire. Clearly in sight of the enemy, fifteen to twenty small-arms rounds impacted within feet of the two warriors. This time Simson shouldered his rifle and returned fire as he moved the patient to a covered area. Simson was subsequently able to stop the bleeding and possibly save the life of the soldier.

As the withdrawal continued, an ANA soldier sustained a gunshot wound to the upper back, creating a sucking chest wound. The soldier fell in the center of the road, and Simson did not hesitate to go to his aid. Again he received small-arms fire, this time within a few inches, followed by an incoming RPG round impacting fifty meters from his position. He returned fire to the northwest in an effort to gain a few more seconds to save the life of this wounded solider. Falling back on his training and maintaining the composure that characterized his actions throughout this day, Simson attempted to seal the wound. Due to the amount of blood and sweat, he was unsuccessful. He then attempted to administer chest decompressions. After three attempts, Simson realized that there was nothing else that he could do to save the soldier's life. With assistance, he placed the body onto the hood of the HMMWV and continued to move.

Arriving at the helicopter landing zone, Simson found himself the only uninjured medical personnel. He quickly set about establishing the casualty collection point and continued to assess, care for, and monitor the injured, whose wounds included third-degree burns, partial loss of limbs, and multiple fragmentation injuries. Throughout the day, Simson called upon the training he had received as a corpsman to react to a mass casualty event under fire. His selflessness, willingness to expose himself to potential injury or death, and composure under fire were exemplary and inspiring to his fellow servicemen and the ANA.

Silver Star Medal Citation

The President of the United States of America takes pleasure in presenting the Silver Star to Hospitalman Joshua E. Simson, United States Marine Corps, for heroic achievement in connection with combat operations against the enemy as Hospitalman, Embedded Training Team 6-2, in support of Operation Enduring Freedom on 27 July 2007. While serving as an advisor to the 3d Kandak, 1st Brigade, 201st Corps of the Afghan National Army in Nuristan Province, Hospitalman Simson's patrol was ambushed as it neared the village of Saret Kholet. With enemy small-arms and rocket propelled grenade fire raining down on their position, casualties from elements of both the U.S. and the Afghan National Army mounted rapidly. Hospitalman Simson instinctively moved throughout the position, exposing himself repeatedly to enemy fire, enduring a direct hit on one triage position by a rocket propelled grenade, and often caring for the injured in plain view of the enemy. Supporting the withdrawal from the enemy fire sac, another Afghan soldier was shot down in the middle of a road. Again, Hospitalman Simson left cover and exposed himself to the incoming fire. With small arms impacting all about him, he feverishly worked to save the life of the fatally wounded soldier. Arriving at the landing zone, Hospitalman Simson found himself the only medical personnel uninjured and quickly set about establishing the casualty collection point, while continually re-assessing wounded. Hospitalman Simson's actions were seen across the battlefield, and his selfless willingness to expose himself repeatedly to potential injury or death coupled with his composure under fire was exemplary and inspiring to his fellow servicemen and the Afghan soldiers. By his zealous initiative, courageous actions, and exceptional dedication to duty, Hospitalman Simson reflected great credit upon himself and upheld the highest traditions of the United States Navy.

Information for this account is drawn from the U.S. Marine Corps "Award Summary of Action" (2007) and the Silver Star Medal Citation for Joshua E. Simson (2008).

CPL JOHN R. STALVEY

COMPANY I, 3RD BATTALION, 6TH MARINES, TASK FORCE 76

HOME OF RECORD: BRUNSWICK, GEORGIA

AWARDED THE NAVY AND MARINE CORPS ACHIEVEMENT MEDAL
FOR ACTIONS FROM MAY THROUGH OCTOBER 2004,
WAZIR VALLEY, AFGHANISTAN

During Cpl John R. Stalvey's first deployment as a Marine, he demonstrated superior leadership and dependable judgment during combat missions in and around Surobi, Ghazni, and Jalalabad, Afghanistan. During operations in Surobi from May 2004 through June 2004, Stalvey instructed Marines on the proper techniques and procedures for operating an effective vehicle checkpoint. Stalvey performed as the platoon's senior Humvee driver and trained other Marines in driving military vehicles. In Ghazni from late June 2004 through July 2004, Stalvey took charge of vehicle maintenance for six vehicles, hardback and high-back Humvees.

In Jalalabad from 28 to 31 August 2004, Stalvey participated in an improvised explosive device (IED) awareness training course. Upon completing the course with 100 percent scores on all tests, Stalvey gave a PowerPoint class to the Marines in his company on IED awareness and fundamental steps to identify an IED. This training gave Marines the knowledge necessary to operate in an area of high threat for IEDs, particularly during the unit's many mounted convoy patrols and missions. Stalvey's teachings prepared Marines by giving them signs to look for and safety measures to take.

On 23 October 2004, during Operation Wazir, Stalvey was driving an Army LMTV (5-ton vehicle) when an IED exploded underneath the front of the vehicle. Needing to get out of the kill zone immediately, Stalvey promptly moved to a safe distance from the blast. Once away from the IED site, Marines were able to quickly dismount, secure the perimeter, assess the situation, and search for the culprit of the remote-detonated IED.

As a very young noncommissioned officer, Stalvey continuously set the example for his Marines. He ensured that his Marines were prepared for patrols and continually taught them tactics and gave them the knowledge needed to operate effectively. Stalvey constantly sought self-improvement and continuously led from the front.

During this deployment, Stalvey continuously observed Marine scout snipers in positions intended to protect him and his Marines; he was told by a fellow Marine, "They are our guardian angels." After completion of this deployment, Stalvey volunteered to try out for the 3/6 scout sniper platoon and was accepted. He attended scout sniper school at the home of Marine Corps Scout Snipers, Quantico, Virginia.

NAVY AND MARINE CORPS ACHIEVEMENT MEDAL CITATION

Professional achievement in the superior performance of duty while serving as Fire Team Leader, 2nd Platoon, India Company, 3d Battalion, 6th Marines, Combined Joint Task Force 76 from 7 May 2004 to 31 October 2004 in support of Operation Enduring Freedom. As a company improvised explosive device trainer, CORPORAL STALVEY taught other Marines in improvised explosive device awareness and enemy tactics. During an operation in the Wazir Valley, a remote controlled improvised explosive device exploded under the front of his light mobile troop vehicle 5-ton. He immediately sped through the explosion, in an attempt to remove the 15 Marines in his vehicle out of a potential ambush kill zone. Due to his quick thinking and decisive action, Corporal Stalvey ultimately saved the lives of the Marines in his vehicle. Corporal Stalvey's professionalism and loyal dedication to duty reflected great credit upon himself and were in keeping with the highest traditions of the Marine Corps and the United States Naval Service.

Information for this account is drawn from the U.S. Marine Corps "Award Summary of Action" (2004) and the Navy and Marine Corps Achievement Medal Citation for John R. Stalvey (2005).

HM1 JEREMY K. TORRISI

COMPANY H, 2ND MARINE SPECIAL OPERATIONS BATTALION,
MARINE SPECIAL OPERATIONS COMMAND

BORN: CAMILLUS, NEW YORK

AWARDED THE SILVER STAR MEDAL FOR HEROIC ACTIONS ON
26 JUNE 2008, FARAH PROVINCE, AFGHANISTAN

—————————————— ——————————————

O n 26 June 2008 Combined Joint Special Operations
Task Force Afghanistan directed that Marine Special
Operations Team (MSOT) 1 and MSOT 2 respond to a
time-sensitive target in Farah Province, Afghanistan. They
combined forces and executed a combat reconnaissance patrol
to action a high-value target located in the mountains. Attached
to the combined patrol was an element of twenty-four Afghan
National Army (ANA) soldiers. The patrol moved under cover of
darkness to a draw in the mountain range where the high-value
target and his security element were known to be in hiding. The
patrol was tasked with entering and, if necessary, clearing the
draw of any enemy personnel. Upon conclusion of the clearing operation, the unit was to exploit the site for tactical information and anything of value. The terrain in and around the
target area was restrictive and mountainous. Large rocks and
boulders lined the path along the entire route into the target
area. The path traveled along the draw and had multiple curves
behind rock outcroppings, making it impossible to view from
the mouth of the draw. MSOT 1 was tasked with clearing the
area while MSOT 2 was tasked with providing security at the
entry to the draw.

As the team entered the draw heading north, the two lead
ground mobility vehicles (GMV) turned a corner and came
upon two vehicles, a white Toyota Land Cruiser and a red pickup
truck. The Toyota was thirty meters off the road to the east and
the pickup was in the middle of the road blocking all forward
movement. There were no indications or signs of enemy personnel at this time. When team members dismounted and began

clearing the area, enemy machine guns opened fire on them from high on the mountainside to the west, approximately two hundred meters away. Rounds impacted both the forward and rear elements of the dismounts, effectively blocking any escape in either direction. Due to a bend in the road, two GMVs and all twenty-four dismounted personnel were trapped in the open kill zone.

HM1 Jeremy K. Torrisi was in the GMV located at the rear of the convoy. The vehicle moved up beyond the remaining vehicles outside the kill zone and took up a position behind the last vehicle of MSOT 1. Torrisi began suppressing the enemy from the back of the GMV with his M240G machine gun. The enemy's extremely accurate sniper and machine-gun fire effectively trapped all individuals in the kill zone. The suppressive fire virtually pinned the dismounts within feet of the GMV. High-angle fire rained down with deadly precision and militated against any vertical cover provided by the vehicle. Two Marines in the forward element were shot and fell roughly fifteen meters east of and behind the lead GMV. Then a chief corpsman was shot in the chest and immediately fell into the kill zone. When he fell, the enemy fire increased and accurately impacted all around the GMV. Due to the severity of the situation, radio traffic was passed that no further personnel should enter the kill zone because of the angle and accuracy of the sniper fire. Close-air support (CAS) and a medevac had been called in; however, no wounded could be moved until the CAS arrived.

During this time, Torrisi continued suppressing the enemy with the M240G machine gun, as well as his M4. Shortly thereafter the medevac helicopters arrived, but CAS was still inbound. Upon hearing about two casualties in the kill zone, Torrisi realized he was the only corpsman/medic left unharmed. Knowing that several other Marines were wounded, and with total disregard for his own safety, he ran into the kill zone, against the advisement of his team leader, to render aid. Upon arriving at the site, Torrisi immediately began treating a casualty with a gunshot wound to the head. Once treatment had been administered and Torrisi felt that the casualty was stable, he moved him out of the kill zone and turned him over to the care of a Marine. He then immediately assessed the situation and, with total disregard for his own safety, ran deeper into the kill zone to another casualty's location. Upon reaching the casualty, Torrisi immediately began assessing the wounds. One of the casualties informed Torrisi that his position was exposed to enemy fire and that he had been struck by enemy fire in the same spot that Torrisi now occupied. Torrisi acknowledged the exposure and risk but stated that the current casualty's injuries were his only priority. Almost immediately Torrisi was struck in the upper leg by an enemy sniper's bullet. Undaunted by his injury, he announced that he had been shot, shifted his body position in order to allow a Marine to dress his leg wound, and continued to treat his casualty's catastrophic injuries.

Upon hearing that the medevac helicopters would depart within moments due to fuel shortages, Torrisi was instrumental in ensuring that his casualty was stable enough to move. Using the cover of danger-close air strikes, he moved his casualty from their currently exposed position to the relative safety of a large boulder and then again into one of the GMVs. Torrisi continued to treat two casualties until both were loaded into the medevac helicopter. Torrisi continued to refuse medical evaluation until he had treated an ANA soldier with a gunshot wound to the thigh. Only then would he allow an Army medic to further evaluate and treat the gunshot wound he had suffered hours earlier. Torrisi is directly responsible for saving the lives of four of his teammates. He risked his life on numerous occasions by moving through the kill zone to treat and extract the wounded.

SILVER STAR MEDAL CITATION

The President of the United States of America takes pleasure in presenting the Silver Star to HOSPITAL CORPSMAN FIRST CLASS JEREMY K. TORRISI, United States Navy, for conspicuous gallantry and intrepidity in action against the enemy as Team Corpsman, Marine Special Operations Company H, Second Marine Special Operations Battalion, U.S. Marine Corps Forces, Special Operations Command, in support of Operation Enduring Freedom on 26 June 2008. Petty Officer Torrisi courageously exposed himself to accurate fire numerous times when his company was pinned down in a mountainous draw by withering fire from a concealed enemy position. After several Marines and other medical providers were hit by enemy fire, he ran into the kill zone with total disregard for his own safety to provide desperately needed aid. After stabilizing one Marine and dragging him to cover, he ran back through a hail of bullets to the side of a fellow corpsman and began to administer life-saving medical care. Petty Officer Torrisi was subsequently shot in the leg, but continued treating casualties for several hours while refusing medical treatment for his own injuries. Under intense fire, while simultaneously directing the evacuation of the wounded Marines and sailors, he laid down suppressive fire until every team member had evacuated the kill zone. His actions ultimately saved the lives of four of his teammates, and his courage and quick thinking prevented further loss of life. By his relentless resolve, courageous fighting spirit, and unwavering dedication to duty, Petty Officer Torrisi reflected great credit upon himself and upheld the highest traditions of the United States Naval Service.

Information for this account is drawn from the U.S. Marine Corps "Award Summary of Action" (2008) and the Silver Star Medal Citation for Jeremy K. Torrisi (2008).

SGT ANTHONY L. VIGGIANI

COMPANY C, 1ST BATTALION, 6TH MARINES, 2ND MARINE DIVISION

BORN: STRONGSVILLE, OHIO

AWARDED THE NAVY CROSS FOR HEROIC ACTIONS ON 3 JUNE 2004,
VILLAGE OF KHABARGHO, ZABOL PROVINCE, AFGHANISTAN

O n 3 June 2004 Sgt Anthony Viggiani was serving as a squad leader near the village of Khabargho in Zabol Province. His squad had just passed through the village when they were told that fifteen to twenty people who appeared to be armed insurgents were pushing through the valley. At this point an Afghani was stopped and questioned and confirmed that they were indeed enemy fighters carrying AK-47s, rocket-propelled grenades (RPGs), and other weapons.

Viggiani and his Marines gave pursuit as they heard what appeared to be heavy weapons fire in the distance. Viggiani believed this meant the enemy was engaging friendly forces. Due to the terrain, radio communications were very difficult or spotty at best. As the squad approached a well-fortified ridge-line, heavy machine-gun fire rained down on them from inside a cave. The squad was pinned down and had two wounded Marines.

Maneuvering to a better position, Viggiani found himself peering into the cave through a small break in the rocks. When he saw a piece of cloth move, he fired off three or four rounds. He heard no sounds that would lead him to believe the enemies had been hit, so he grabbed a grenade and dropped it into the hole, killing three enemy combatants and destroying the cave. At this point Viggiani and 1st Sgt Ernest K. Hoopii climbed back up the ridge, again under heavy machine-gun fire. They called for air support, and Apache helicopters arrived, coming in hot to neutralize some of the enemy firing positions. As they continued to maneuver, the Marines killed fourteen enemy fighters. During this maneuver, a ricochet from a machine-gun round wounded Viggiani in the leg.

Hoopii ordered Viggiani to get help from a corpsman, but Viggiani refused until he knew his men were safe. Once his men had been treated, Viggiani agreed to be treated. After his corpsman bandaged his wound, he kept pushing through the valley with his fellow Marines.

NAVY CROSS CITATION

The President of the United States of America takes pleasure in presenting the Navy Cross to SERGEANT ANTHONY LESTER VIGGIANI, United States Marine Corps, for extraordinary heroism in action against anti-coalition force militia in Zabol Province, Afghanistan, serving as a Squad Leader for Charlie Company, Battalion Landing Team, First Battalion, Sixth Marines, Twenty-Second Marine Expeditionary Unit, Deployed with Commander, United States Fifth Fleet during Operation Enduring Freedom 3 June 2004. While leading a company assault against an enemy held ridgeline north of the village of Khabargho, Sergeant Viggiani and his squad came under heavy and accurate fire from an enemy force well entrenched inside a cave, pinning down one of his teams and wounding two of his Marines. Moving across exposed ground, under observation and fire from an adjacent enemy position, Sergeant Viggiani maneuvered to the cave opening, but achieving no effect on the enemy. Braving enemy fire from the adjacent enemy position, he went back to retrieve a fragmentation grenade. Again, under a hail of fire, he moved to within feet of the cave opening and employed the grenade to eliminate the enemy position, which was actively firing upon friendly forces. Killing three enemy fighters, Sergeant Viggiani destroyed the enemy strongpoint and allowed his company to continue their advance up to the ridgeline, solidly defeating the enemy by killing a total of fourteen anti-coalition fighters. In the process, he was wounded by rifle fire from the adjacent enemy position, yet he continued to lead his Marines in the attack. By his outstanding display of decisive leadership, unlimited courage in the face of enemy fire and utmost dedication to duty, Sergeant Viggiani reflected great credit upon himself and upheld the highest traditions of the Marine Corps and the United States Naval Service.

Information for this account is drawn from the U.S. Marine Corps "Award Summary of Action" (2004) and the Navy Cross Medal Citation for Anthony L. Viggiani (2005), and from personal interviews with Ernest K. Hoopii at Al Asad Air Base, Al Asad, Iraq, 2008, and Anthony L. Viggiani at Quantico, VA, 7 May 2011.

GYSGT ANTHONY L. VIGGIANI

Weapons Company, 2nd Battalion, 2nd Marines,
1st Marine Division

born: Strongsville, Ohio

Awarded the Navy and Marine Corps Commendation Medal
with Combat Distinguishing Device "V" for
heroic actions from October 2009 to May 2010,
Helmand Province, Afghanistan

O n 2 to 3 January 2010 Weapons Company conducted a twelve-kilometer dismounted nighttime infiltration of a known Taliban stronghold in Laki Village, achieving complete and total tactical surprise. GySgt Anthony L. Viggiani acted as the joint terminal aircraft controller—calling in close-air support (CAS) for this operation along with maneuvering the mounted element of the infiltration force. After the four-day clearing operation, Combined Anti-Armor Team (CAAT) 1 was then tasked with remaining and establishing a patrol base that would effectively expand the battalion's influence another ten kilometers into the enemy-controlled area in the southern Helmand River valley, effectively disrupting the enemy lines of communication and staging areas. CAAT-1 was selected to develop and shape the southern end of the battalion's area of operation (AO). CAAT-1, with Viggiani as its platoon sergeant, spent the remaining four months of the deployment in intense combat with the enemy. Additionally, Viggiani played a vital role in establishing a platoon-size patrol base to the south of the forward line of troops and four additional squad-sized checkpoints that projected influence and disrupted the enemy's ability to attack coalition forces to the north.

On 4 March 2010 Viggiani was leading an assault on a known enemy stronghold with two squads and a sniper team in support. As his squad approached the Taliban stronghold, they came under heavy enemy machine-gun and small-arms fire. Viggiani gained radio communications and coordinated

CAS with a section of AV-8B Harriers as his squads maneuvered and closed on the closest enemy machine-gun position. As they maneuvered, the sniper team acquired targets from another enemy position directly to the squads' east. Once the snipers reported that two enemy fighters had been engaged and hit, the enemy machine-gun team began displacing from the firing position that had been engaging the Marines. Viggiani reoriented and attempted to gain a battle damage assessment and recover the bodies of the enemy fighters. The Marines reached an obstacle created by a road and a large canal that they would have to cross. As they approached the road, a machine-gun-armed enemy engaged them with a principal direction of fire directly down the road. Viggiani ordered the squad leaders to set in security and, exposing himself to the enemy machine-gun fire, moved out onto the road, attempting to identify a crossing point. Unable to find one, he directed the squads to close with and destroy the enemy machine-gun position. As the two squads bounded toward the enemy positions, the enemy broke contact and retreated, ceasing fire on the two squads. When Viggiani's Marines returned to the place where snipers had reported two enemy fighters hit, it was evident the remaining fighters had taken the bodies away. He ordered tactical site exploitation to be conducted and collected before returning to base. Viggiani continued to track enemy movements with the air assets, identifying enemy rally points and setting conditions for future coalition ambush operations.

On 7 March 2010 Viggiani and his Marines were conducting a dismounted security patrol to prevent the enemy from interfering with a *shura* (a consultation or meeting) in the center of the company's AO. This same area had been attacked on two previous occasions. As he was positioning the Marines into a screen line, the men came under accurate and intense medium machine-gun and small-arms fire from at least three separate firing positions. With rounds impacting between the Marines and within feet of Viggiani's position, he directed the unit to return fire and assault the enemy. As he led his men through a tree line in the middle of two open fields, one of the corpsmen was hit by machine-gun rounds, which went through both of his legs. Viggiani was the closest Marine to the injured corpsman, and with incredibly mature tactical control and resolve, he directed his Marines' covering fire while calling in the casualty report. Applying a tourniquet and pressure dressing and administering morphine under the direction of the corpsman, he maintained control of the men while coordinating the pickup from the medevac helicopter. Viggiani then directed the sniper team into position to cover his movement while he personally escorted the wounded corpsman to the helicopter. Once the casualty had been safely evacuated, Viggiani continued to maneuver his Marines on the enemy positions. Feeling the pressure of the closing Marines, the enemy broke contact and escaped from the area. After pursuing the enemy, the three-hour firefight ended, and Viggiani patrolled his unit back to the forward operating base to set conditions for future operations.

On 4 May 2010 CAAT-1 was conducting a relief in place with a CAAT platoon from 3rd Battalion, 1st Marines. Viggiani was controlling CAS while on a leader's recon with both 2/2 and 3/1 Weapons Company commanders. The patrol was moving to a disputed intersection that had seen many firefights in previous weeks and was the site of a proposed squad-size checkpoint. As the patrol neared the intersection, Viggiani moved up with the battalion's explosive ordnance disposal (EOD) detachment to clear the path leading into the intersection. Weapons Company 2/2 had found more than seventy improvised explosive devices (IEDs) in the previous three months, and local reports indicated that there were multiple IEDs in this area. As contact was imminent, Viggiani risked his own safety to stay close and provide security for the EOD team as it moved through a side street up to the intersection. When one of the sweepers received a hard metallic hit with his metal detector, all other Marines were moved into cover, and Viggiani remained to provide security as the EOD Marine investigated the metallic hit. The team succeeded in removing a nonmetallic pressure plate from the ground that had been placed directly in their path on top of a high-fragmentation-producing metal cylinder IED.

Viggiani took up an overwatch position and ensured that the other Marines made it to cover safely. As the patrol finished up and the Marines retrograded to friendly lines, the

EOD team expressed the need to destroy the IED that had been found earlier. Viggiani and five of his Marines remained with the EOD team as the rest of the patrol moved back out of the area and toward friendly lines. As the EOD team members were prepping their explosive materials to dispose of the IED, the security element with them came under fire from enemy small-arms and machine-gun fire. The security element set up a base of fire and attempted to gain positive identification while Viggiani and the EOD team moved back to the IED and placed their charge. The fuse set on the charge failed to detonate, and after several minutes the enemy fire increased in volume and accuracy. It was necessary to ensure a detonation, so the EOD team prepared a second charge and Viggiani again exposed himself to enemy fire and led them back to the IED. He provided security for the EOD team members as they placed the second charge by engaging enemy targets and ensuring that the team was covered when it could not provide its own security. With the second charge the IED detonated and all explosive material was destroyed, rendering it harmless to the Afghan population. Viggiani then moved to a position of advantage so that he could observe enemy movement, and after being talked onto the enemy positions, he directed and observed impacts from an MK-19 grenade launcher to neutralize the enemy machine-gun positions. As the 40-mm high-explosive, dual-purpose rounds impacted, the enemy fire immediately ceased and all remaining enemy were seen fleeing from the area.

As the company moved into a hostile region of southern Helmand Province, Afghanistan, Viggiani regularly gained contact with the enemy forces and never failed to show courage and determination as he aggressively closed with the enemy. Viggiani was physically involved in fifteen engagements with enemy forces, and whenever he was not maneuvering on the enemy, he was coordinating CAS in the aid of the maneuver forces or attempting to strike the enemy with air assets. He was relentless in hunting down the enemy. He also aggressively countered the high IED threat by connecting with the Afghan population and employing adaptive tactics, techniques, and procedures, personally finding two IEDs. With an always-present IED threat, he helped develop standard operating procedures for the company to closely track friendly and enemy movements along with previous placement and tactics, techniques, and procedures used by the enemy.

Navy and Marine Corps Commendation Medal with Combat Distinguishing Device "V" Citation

Heroic achievement while serving as Platoon Sergeant, Combined Anti-Armor Team 1, Weapons Company, 2d Battalion, 2d Marines, Regimental Combat Team 7, 1st Marine Division Forward from October 2009 to May 2010 in support of Operation Enduring Freedom. GUNNERY SERGEANT VIGGIANI led his section on more than 90 combat patrols and was involved in 15 engagements with enemy forces. On 7 March 2010, while providing security for a *shura*, his unit came under heavy fire from multiple enemy positions. While maneuvering towards the enemy, a corpsman was seriously wounded in both legs by enemy fire. Without hesitation, Gunnery Sergeant Viggiana exposed himself to enemy fire and assisted the wounded corpsman while directing his unit towards the enemy. While maintaining command and control, he treated the casualty and coordinated his evacuation, undoubtedly saving his life. His energy, aggressive actions, and total understanding of operations created a dramatic and lasting positive change within the battalion's area of operations. Gunnery Sergeant Viggiani's initiative, perseverance, and total dedication to duty reflected credit upon him and upheld the highest traditions of the Marine Corps and the United States Naval Service.

Information for this account is drawn from the U.S. Marine Corps "Award Summary of Action" (2010) and the Navy and Marine Corps Commendation Medal Citation for Anthony L. Viggiani (2010), from a personal interview with Viggiani at Quantico, VA, 7 May 2011, and from interviews with Ernest K. Hoopii at Al Asad Air Base, Al Asad, Iraq, 2008.

ACRONYMS AND ABBREVIATIONS

AAF   anti-Afghan force
AAV   amphibious assault vehicle
ABP   Afghan Border Police
AK-47   Kalashnikov 7.62 × 39–mm assault rifle
ANA   Afghan National Army
AO   area of operation
BAS   battalion aid station
CAAT   combined anti-armor team
CACO   casualty assistance calls officer
CAS   close-air support
CCP   casualty collection point
Cpl   corporal
COC   command/combat operations center
Col   colonel
COP   combat outpost
CWIED   command-wire-initiated IED
DA   direct action
doc   affectionate term for a corpsman used by Marines
ECP   entry control point
EKIA   enemy killed in action
EOD   explosive ordnance disposal
ETT   embedded training team
EWIA   enemy wounded in action
F/A-18   fighter/attack aircraft
FLET   forward line of enemy troops
FOB   forward operating base
GMV   ground mobility vehicle
GySgt   gunnery sergeant
HA   hospitalman apprentice
HM1   hospital corpsman first class
HM2   hospital corpsman second class
HM3   hospital corpsman third class
HMMWV   highly mobile multiwheeled vehicle (aka Humvee or Hummer)

HQMC	Headquarters Marine Corps
I&I	inspector/instructor
IED	improvised explosive device
IP	Iraqi police
IRR	Individual Ready Reserve
ISAF	international security assistance force
JSS	joint security station
JTAC	joint terminal air controller
KIA	killed in action
LAR	light armored reconnaissance
LAV	light armored vehicle
LAV-25	LAV 25-mm gun variant
LAV-C2	LAV command and control variant
LAV-L	LAV logistical variant
LCpl	lance corporal
LMTV	5-ton vehicle
M1A1	U.S. main battle tank
M2	.50-caliber heavy machine gun
M9	9-mm handgun
M4	5.56-mm standard U.S.-issue assault rifle (retractable stock)
M14	7.62-mm assault rifle (sometimes used as a sniper rifle)
M16	5.56-mm standard U.S.-issue assault rifle
M40	7.62×51–mm USMC scout sniper rifle (built by Marines at Quantico)
M45	.45-caliber close-quarters battle weapon, handgun
M88	tank recovery vehicle, attached
M-113	armored vehicle
M240	7.62-mm medium machine gun
M249	5.56-mm light machine gun
Maj	major
MAP	mobile assault platoon
MEF	Marine Expeditionary Force
MEU	Marine Expeditionary Unit
MK-19	40-mm automatic grenade launcher
MRAP	mine-resistant ambush-protected vehicle
MSgt	master sergeant
MSOT	Marine Special Operations Team
MSPF	Maritime Special Purpose Force
OP	observation post

ORP	objective rally point
PB	patrol base
PFC	private first class
PKM	Kalashnikov 7.62 × 54R–mm medium machine gun
PPIED	pressure-plate IED
PSD	personal security detachment
QRF	quick-reaction force
R&S	reconnaissance and surveillance
RCIED	remote-controlled IED
RCT	Regimental Combat Team
ROE	rules of engagement
RPG	rocket-propelled grenade
RPG-7	rocket-propelled grenade launcher
RW/CAS	rotary wing close-air support
SAF	small-arms fire
SASR	special-application scoped rifle (.50 caliber sniper weapon system)
SAW	M249 squad automatic weapon
SFC	sergeant first class
Sgt	sergeant
SgtMaj	sergeant major
SOTG	Special Operations Training Group
SSE	sensitive site exploitation
SSgt	staff sergeant
STBIED	suicide-truck-borne IED
SVBIED	suicide-vehicle-borne IED
SWT	scout weapons team
TIC	troops in contact
TL	team leader
TTP	tactics, techniques, and procedures
UAS	unmanned aerial system
UXO	unexploded ordnance
VOIED	victim-operated IED

---- ★ ----

ABOUT THE AUTHOR

DAVID DEVANEY worked as a cook from 1980 to 1983 after graduating high school. In 1983 he joined the Marine Corps as an infantry rifleman. After two deployments overseas he was selected to the Surveillance and Target Acquisition (STA) platoon for duty as a scout sniper. SgtMaj Devaney has deployed ten times with Marine Corps units, was stationed overseas for six years in Okinawa, and has deployed five times with Army Special Forces elements, serving as a sniper for their ODAs (Operational Detachment Alpha). David retired from the Marine Corps in December 2013.

The Naval Institute Press is the book-publishing arm of the U.S. Naval Institute, a private, nonprofit, membership society for sea service professionals and others who share an interest in naval and maritime affairs. Established in 1873 at the U.S. Naval Academy in Annapolis, Maryland, where its offices remain today, the Naval Institute has members worldwide.

Members of the Naval Institute support the education programs of the society and receive the influential monthly magazine *Proceedings* or the colorful bimonthly magazine *Naval History* and discounts on fine nautical prints and on ship and aircraft photos. They also have access to the transcripts of the Institute's Oral History Program and get discounted admission to any of the Institute-sponsored seminars offered around the country.

The Naval Institute's book-publishing program, begun in 1898 with basic guides to naval practices, has broadened its scope to include books of more general interest. Now the Naval Institute Press publishes about seventy titles each year, ranging from how-to books on boating and navigation to battle histories, biographies, ship and aircraft guides, and novels. Institute members receive significant discounts on the Press's more than eight hundred books in print.

Full-time students are eligible for special half-price membership rates. Life memberships are also available.

For a free catalog describing Naval Institute Press books currently available, and for further information about joining the U.S. Naval Institute, please write to:

Member Services
U.S. Naval Institute
291 Wood Road
Annapolis, MD 21402-5034
Telephone: (800) 233-8764
Fax: (410) 571-1703
Web address: www.usni.org